'The eagle-bearer of the Tenth Legion, after a prayer
to heaven to bless his legion by his act, cried:
"Leap down, soldiers, unless you wish to betray your
eagle to the enemy; it shall be told that I at any rate
did my duty to my country and general."'

Caesar, Gallic Wars *4. 25*

The Complete Roman Army

Adrian Goldsworthy

With 245 illustrations, 107 in colour

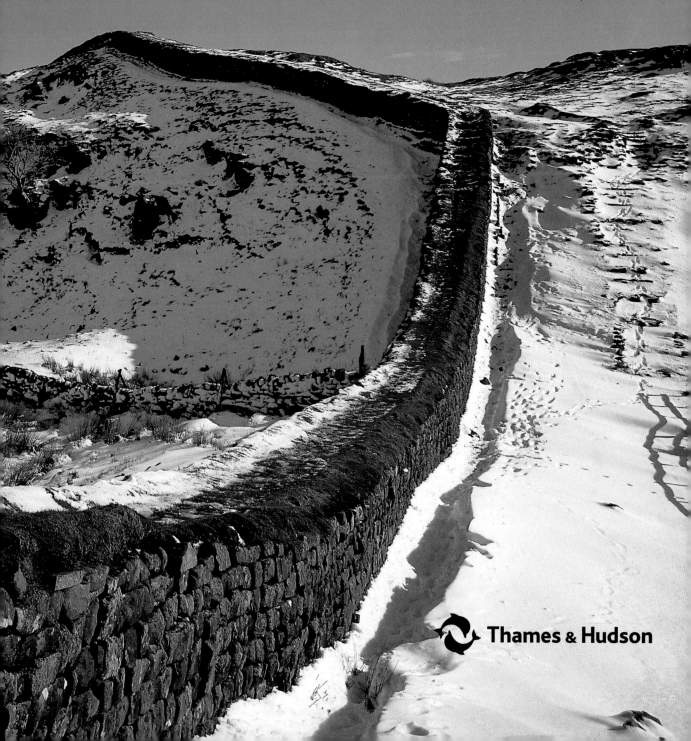

Thames & Hudson

Contents

Half-title: *A small bronze statuette showing a Roman soldier carrying an eagle (aquila). From the 1st century BC the eagle was the most important standard of a legion.*

Title-page: *Hadrian's Wall is the largest and most impressive of the monuments left by the Roman army. This view shows one of the best-preserved stretches to the west of Housesteads fort.*

Contents pages: *The 4th-century AD Arch of Constantine in Rome made extensive use of sculptures taken from earlier Roman monuments. It is unusual in that it openly celebrated Constantine's victory over another Roman army at the battle of the Milvian Bridge in AD 312.*

First published in the United Kingdom in 2003 by Thames & Hudson Ltd, 181A High Holborn, London WC1V 7QX

www.thamesandhudson.com

© 2003 Thames & Hudson Ltd, London

British Library Cataloguing-in-Publication Data
A catalogue record for this book is available from the British Library

ISBN 0-500-05124-0

Printed and bound in Hong Kong by Toppan

Introduction: A Brief Survey of Roman History

Rome grew gradually in size and splendour – most of the monumental structures visible in the Forum today, shown below, were built under the rule of the emperors. Warfare played a prominent part in Roman history, and as the city changed, so did the army that fought to protect it.

Roman tradition held that their city was founded by Romulus in 753 BC. At first a monarchy, the kings were expelled and a Republic created near the end of the 6th century BC. Rome gradually expanded, absorbing the other Latin-speaking communities and in time other Italian peoples, so that by the early 3rd century BC, she controlled all of the Peninsula south of the Po. A long and arduous struggle with Carthage brought Rome her first overseas provinces and, by the mid-2nd century BC, undisputed domi-

nance of the Mediterranean world. Expansion continued, but the vast profits of foreign conquest placed a great strain on the Republican system of government, causing politics to become increasingly violent. The 1st century BC witnessed a cycle of civil war and upheaval, ending only in 31 BC when Caesar's adopted son Octavian defeated his last rival.

Octavian, who later took the name Augustus, replaced the Republican system of government with a peculiarly Roman form of monarchy, known today as the Principate. Openly he presented himself as the senior magistrate and servant of the state, but in reality he had taken over the power of all the other political institutions, including the Senate and the People's Assemblies, and from early on in his reign he began to mark out a successor. Augustus continued the expansion of the Empire and by his death in AD 14 it had in many places reached the frontiers that it would hold for several centuries. There were a few exceptions – Britain was invaded by Claudius in AD 43 and Trajan annexed Dacia in AD 101–06 – but the great con-

quests were never repeated. The Principate gave Rome stability for over 200 years, and only twice, when emperors died without a clear successor, did civil war return.

In the 3rd century AD this changed, civil wars becoming as frequent as they had been in the last decades of the Republic. On average emperors lasted for no more than a few years, and the majority died violently as the army spent its strength in fighting itself. The Empire began to break up, some rulers controlling only small sections of it. At the same time its weakness encouraged foreign enemies and led to many defeats. In time the Empire split, the western and eastern halves each having their own emperor or emperors. Long-term stability never returned, though some strong rulers created decades of relative peace, yet Rome's strength was still far greater than that of any of her opponents. The western Empire eventually collapsed in the 5th century AD, but the eastern Empire with its capital at Constantinople endured, preserving many of Rome's military institutions until well into the Middle Ages.

The changing face of the Roman army

The Roman army played a central role in the city's history, creating and maintaining an Empire which came to encompass Europe, North Africa and the Near East. The popular image of the army is of a highly organized, rigorously professional and savagely disciplined force run on remarkably modern lines. At least some of this picture is true for at least some periods of the army's existence, but it conceals the massive changes that occurred in Rome's military institutions over the long centuries of its existence. In this book we will examine the three central phases in the history of the Roman army.

We shall begin with the militia army of the Mid Republic (3rd to 2nd centuries BC), for this is the period when our sources are sufficiently good to give us a clear impression of the Roman army. It was recruited from citizens who submitted to military discipline for the duration of a war and then returned to civilian life. Soldiers were propertied men, usually farmers owning enough land to allow them to afford their own weapons and equipment. For such soldiers service in the army was not a career, but a duty they owed to the state. It was the militia army that conquered Italy, defeated Carthage, and made Rome dominant throughout the Mediterranean.

The second phase (1st century BC to early 3rd century AD) began with the creation of the professional Roman army. Continuing expansion meant that wars were being fought further and further from Italy and created a requirement for large garrisons in conquered territory. The militia system was not capable of coping with these new conditions. Instead of a prosperous farmer serving for

Roman soldiers have often been depicted in epic films, although the accuracy of such reconstructions has varied enormously. This scene from Gladiator *shows a senior officer riding between lines of legionaries and eastern auxiliary archers. From a distance at least, the equipment of these men appears to be reasonably accurate and the scene certainly gives a good impression of the grubby appearance of soldiers on campaign.*

short periods of time out of a sense of duty to the Republic, the legionary was from now on usually a poor man, viewing the army as a career. The result was a fundamental shift in the relationship between the army and state, making possible the civil wars which destroyed the Republic. Eventually Augustus took care to make the army loyal solely to himself and his family, a practice followed by his successors. Under the Principate the Roman army reached the peak of its efficiency, completing the conquest of the Empire and then preserving Roman rule. It is during this period that the Roman army came closest to its popular image.

The final phase (3rd to 5th centuries AD) covers Late Antiquity, when the professional army faced increasing external threats whilst being continually ground down in civil wars. New types of units appeared, different equipment was adopted, and the structure of the army changed as it struggled to cope. Yet in spite of all this, much remained the same and there were greater differences between the Mid Republican army and the army of the Principate than between the latter and the forces of the Late Empire.

Sources of evidence

Although the Roman army existed for an immensely long period of time, it disappeared many centuries ago and left only traces of its passing in the remains of its bases and forts, the fragments of equipment and the descriptions of its deeds in the accounts of Roman and Greek writers. Taken together, we do have a considerable body of evidence with which to reconstruct the institutions and daily life of the Roman military, but each type of source presents its own problems of interpretation. It is worth pausing briefly to consider the nature of our sources.

1 *Literature:* Politics and war were the two main concerns of Roman historians. History was first and foremost a branch of literature and was expected to display high levels of stylistic and rhetorical skill, sometimes at the expense of accuracy. Accounts of the army on campaign tend as a result to focus most of all on the dramatic incidents, such as battles and sieges. There were also literary themes or set-pieces (known as *topoi*) that educated readers expected to find in an historian's narrative.

A gateway that is part of the extensive 19th-century reconstruction of the Roman fort at Saalburg in Germany. Such projects inevitably represent a combination of known facts recovered through excavation and a good deal of conjecture. It is probable that the towers on either side of the gate ought to be higher.

At best this led the writer to select appropriate subjects for inclusion, but at worst it could lead to outright invention. Although the historians provide many accounts of the army at war, they are far less likely to describe the more mundane day-to-day aspects of frontier patrolling, policing and the many activities of peacetime.

Another result of the importance of style and readability to ancient historians manifests itself in a reluctance to include too much technical information. Topographical description, even of features of importance to a specific campaign, is often brief and vague. Detailed information about the army's equipment, organization, tactics and logistical system are exceptionally rare, and often consist of fragments mentioned incidentally by an author. Some writers may have omitted such information simply because they assumed that it would all be immediately familiar to their audience. Julius Caesar, who left an invaluable account of the campaigns of his own army, tells us very little about the structure of the legions or their arms, never once mentioning that his men wore body armour, though we know from other sources that they did.

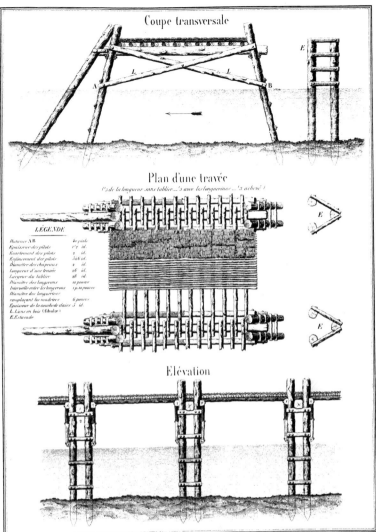

A 19th-century diagram of the bridge constructed by the legions to span the River Rhine in 55 BC, based on Julius Caesar's description of this structure in his Gallic Wars *rather than on direct archaeological information. Our literary sources provide a good deal of information about the army, although they do not always supply us with as much technical detail as we might wish.*

It is worth listing the main sources for each of our three periods and discussing their relative usefulness. For the Mid Republican army, our most important account is provided by the Greek historian Polybius who wrote his work around the 140s BC. A soldier himself, Polybius was originally sent to Rome as a hostage, where he became an intimate of the Roman general Scipio Aemilianus, accompanying him to the siege of Carthage in 147–146 BC. Polybius includes a detailed description of the Roman legions in this period, describing their organization, equipment and the layout of their temporary camps. The other major source for this period, the Roman historian Livy, wrote at the end of the 1st century BC and is far less reliable for military detail. Other sources for this period include the Greek historian Appian and the biographer Plutarch, both of whom wrote in the early 2nd century AD and sometimes preserve information from earlier sources which have not survived.

For the professional army, Julius Caesar's *Gallic Wars* of his campaigns in Gaul and the civil war are invaluable for understanding the army at war. Tacitus, who wrote in the early 2nd century AD, provides us with much detail for the army of the Early Principate. The Jewish historian Josephus, who had fought against Rome during the Jewish Rebellion of AD 66 before changing sides, provides a more detailed account of a single conflict, as well as a description of the army mirroring the one provided by Polybius for the Republic.

The literary sources for the army in the 2nd and 3rd centuries AD are few and rarely reliable. For part of the 4th century, Ammianus Marcellinus provides

Chronology of Rome's Wars

BC

753	Traditional date for foundation of Rome by Romulus.
509	Traditional date for expulsion of Rome's last King, Tarquinius Superbus.
396	The Romans introduce pay for their army.
390	Rome sacked by Gauls.
280–275	War against King Pyrrhus of Epirus.
264–241	First Punic War.
225	Invading Gallic army defeated at Telamon.
218–201	Second Punic War.
214–205	First Macedonian War.
200–196	Second Macedonian War.
192–189	The Syrian War against the Seleucid King Antiochus III.
172–167	Third Macedonian War.
149–146	Third Punic War.
112–106	War against King Jugurtha of Numidia.
105	Cimbri and Teutones destroy a large Roman army at Arausio.
102	Marius defeats Teutones at Aquae Sextiae.
101	Marius and Catulus defeat Cimbri at Vercellae.
91–88	The Social War, the last great rebellion by Rome's Italian allies.
88	Sulla marches his legions on Rome.
88–85	First Mithridatic War.
83–82	Civil War won by Sulla.
83–82	Second Mithridatic War.
74–66	Third Mithridatic War.
73–70	Spartacus' rebellion.
58–50	Caesar's Gallic campaigns.
55	Caesar's first expedition to Britain.
54	Caesar's second expedition to Britain.
53	Crassus defeated and killed by Parthians under Surenas at Carrhae.
52	Major Gallic rebellion led by Vercingetorix.
49–45	Civil War between Caesar and Pompey.
44	Caesar assassinated by conspiracy led by Brutus and Cassius.
44–31	Repeated civil wars, first between Caesar's supporters and the conspirators, and then between Antony and Octavian.
31	Antony defeated by Octavian in naval battle at Actium. Octavian (soon to be given the name Augustus) becomes effectively the sole ruler of the Roman Principate of Augustus (27 BC–AD 14)
16–15	Conquest of the Alpine tribes.
12–7	Conquest of Pannonia and Germany.

AD

6–9	Major revolt in Pannonia.
9	Major revolt in Germany. Varus and Legiones XVII, XVIII and XIX ambushed and massacred in the Teutoburg Wald.

The Julio-Claudians: Tiberius, Caligula, Claudius and Nero

14–37	Principate of Tiberius.
14–16	War against Arminius.
37–41	Principate of Gaius (Caligula).
41–54	Principate of Claudius.
43	Invasion of Britain.
54–68	Principate of Nero.
55–64	War with Parthia over control of Armenia.
60–61	Rebellion of Boudicca in Britain.
66–74	The Jewish Rebellion.
68–69	Civil War – 'The Year of Four Emperors'. Galba, Otho and Vitellius seize the throne in rapid succession, but war eventually won by Vespasian.

The Flavians: Vespasian, Titus and Domitian

70–79	Principate of Vespasian.
70	Jerusalem captured after a long siege.
73–74	Masada besieged.
79–81	Principate of Titus.
81–96	Principate of Domitian.
85–89	War with King Decebalus of Dacia.
96–98	Principate of Nerva.
98–117	Principate of Trajan.
101–02	Trajan's First Dacian War.

Following his conquest of Dacia (modern-day Romania) in AD 106 the Emperor Trajan ordered the construction of a new forum complex in Rome, at the centre of which was Trajan's Column, decorated with scenes from the wars. Although stylized, the column provides a detailed view of the Roman army of the early 2nd century AD on campaign. In this scene Roman legionaries, wearing the famous segmented armour, cross a pontoon bridge, watched on the left by the spirit or god of the river. At the head of the column are the massed standards.

105–06	Trajan's Second Dacian War.
113–17	Trajan's Parthian War.
117–38	Principate of Hadrian.
122	Construction of Hadrian's Wall begun.
131–35	Bar Kochba Revolt in Judaea.
138–61	Principate of Antoninus Pius.
140–43	Construction of Antonine Wall begun.
161–80	Reign of Marcus Aurelius.
162–66	War with Parthia conducted and won by Marcus' co-ruler, Lucius Verus.
167–80	Almost constant warfare against German tribes on the Danube.
180–92	Reign of Commodus.
193–97	Civil War, eventually won by Severus.
197–208	Reign of Septimius Severus
211–17	Caracalla's reign ends with his murder. This is followed by another period of civil war.
222–35	Reign of Severus Alexander.
235–38	Reign of Maximinus ends with his murder.
238–44	Reign of Gordian III ends with his murder.
244–49	Reign of Philip the Arab killed by Decius in battle.
249–51	Reign of Decius ends when he is defeated and killed by Goths at Forum Trebonii. Renewal of civil war.
253–60	Reign of Valerian ends when he is captured by the Persians.
260–68	Reign of Gallienus ends with his murder.
268–70	Reign of Claudius II 'Gothicus' ends when he dies of disease.
270–75	Reign of Aurelian. He suppressed the revolt of Queen Zenobia of Palmyra, but is eventually murdered by his officers.
275–76	Reign of Tacitus.
276–82	Reign of Probus ends with his murder.

284–305	Reign of Diocletian and the creation of the Tetrarchic system. The Empire is formally divided into west and east, with a senior Augustus and junior Caesar ruling in each half. Diocletian eventually retired, but the system in its pure form did not endure for long.
306	Constantius, Augustus of the west, dies in York. The army proclaim his son Constantine Emperor.
312	Constantine defeats his rival Maxentius at the battle of the Milvian Bridge outside Rome, and becomes Emperor of the west.
324–37	Reign of Constantine as undisputed ruler of the entire Empire. He gives official recognition to Christianity.
337–60	War with Persia.
357	Julian the Apostate (Caesar in the west) defeats the Alamanni in a pitched battle at Strasbourg.
363	Julian's Persian expedition.
394	Battle of Frigidus won by Theodosius.
410	Gothic auxiliaries led by Alaric sack Rome.
429	Vandals invade and overrun Africa.
451	Aetius turns back the offensive of Attila's Huns at Châlons (Campus Mauriacus).
469–78	Visigoths overrun Spain.
476	The last Emperor of the west, Romulus Augustus, deposed by Odovacer who creates the Ostrogothic Kingdom of Italy.
502–06	War with Persia.
526–32	War with Persia.
533–54	Emperor Justinian attempts to re-conquer North Africa and Italy.

A face mask from a Roman helmet excavated at Kalkriese in Germany, most probably the site of the Teutoburg Wald, where an entire army of three legions was wiped out in AD 9. The analysis of finds of military equipment has allowed the emergence of a much clearer picture of the appearance of Roman soldiers. However, this does not mean that it is always straightforward to interpret this evidence. It has normally been assumed that face masks were only worn on parade or for certain ceremonies, and yet this item was found on a battlefield.

It is rare to find much trace of the army on campaign, still less of the many battles it fought and very, very few battle sites can be positively identified, though the recent excavations of the disaster in AD 9 in the Teutoburg Wald in Germany are an exception. During sieges, which lasted longer than battles, the army often constructed substantial works in the form of surrounding ditches and ramparts, temporary forts, or assault ramps, and these have sometimes survived. Such siege lines have been found at Numantia (Spain), Alesia (Gaul), and Masada (Judaea) amongst other sites. A few places have also revealed evidence of the army's ferocity when it captured an enemy stronghold, most notably the gruesome skeletons found at Valencia in Spain and Maiden Castle in Britain. Taken together, the archaeological evidence for the Roman army at war is very slim.

Archaeology is far better at revealing cameos of

(Right) Aerial view of the Roman camp facing the Iron Age hillfort at Burnswark in Scotland. Shot from artillery and sling bullets were found around the gates of the hillfort. For a while a number of scholars argued that this camp was established after the hillfort had been abandoned and was used as a training area by the Roman army. However, most now believe that this was the site of a genuine siege and not simply routine training. Such controversies illustrate how difficult it can be to interpret archaeological evidence.

an exceptionally detailed account of large-scale invasions and sieges as well as relatively small-scale raiding. A staff officer himself, Ammianus had actually witnessed some of the events he described.

A genre distinct from history, though just as much considered primarily a form of literature, was the theoretical manual, several of which have survived. For the army of the Principate we have Frontinus' *Stratagems*, a collection of ploys used by generals in the past, Arrian's *Battle Order against the Alans* and *Tactics*, and Pseudo-Hyginus' *On the Construction of a Camp*. Near the end of the 4th century Vegetius produced his *Concerning Military Affairs* which drew upon many earlier sources and presents an often confusing patchwork of different periods and perhaps some pure invention. All of these sources are useful, but it is important to remember that theoretical works were inclined to depict the army as it should ideally have been, rather than necessarily as it actually was.

2 Archaeology: Our literary sources have been known and studied for centuries, and it is now extremely unlikely that any new text will ever be discovered. By contrast, archaeological excavation offers an ever-expanding resource and has contributed massively to our understanding of the Roman army. A huge number of military sites have been identified and many partially excavated, though few auxiliary forts and no legionary fortresses have undergone full excavation. Military equipment and traces of the presence of soldiers also occur on sites less immediately associated with the army.

life in a certain place at a certain period, and taken together the evidence from many sites allows us to discern longer-term trends. A solidly constructed base occupied for decades or even centuries by the army will inevitably produce far more evidence than a marching camp occupied for a single night. Excavation can reveal the size and layout of a base, hopefully the date of its foundation and of any significant subsequent re-buildings or changes in its structure. It will not explain why the site was chosen, whether the buildings were always fully occupied or what the garrison was doing.

3 *Sub-literary sources – papyri and writing tablets:* Some texts have survived directly from the ancient world to be discovered by archaeologists, unlike the works of the ancient authors which exist because they have been copied time and again over the centuries. In the eastern provinces, especially those with hot, dry climates such as Egypt, many military documents and private letters to or from soldiers

Fragments of a letter written on a wooden writing-tablet found at the site of the fort at Vindolanda and dating to the end of the 1st century AD. Such material will only survive in certain conditions, but already similar documents have been found at other sites in northern Europe. The Vindolanda tablets include official and unofficial correspondence of the fort's commanding officers, as well as many documents connected with the army's administration.

have been preserved on papyrus. In Europe similar documents are beginning to crop up on wooden writing tablets, most famously at the fort of Vindolanda in northern Britain. These texts are concerned primarily with day-to-day life and the routine of soldiering. Some are concerned with the administration of a unit, such as strength reports, inspections of equipment, or applications for leave, whilst others represent private correspondence. Neither these, nor the texts dealing with business transactions or legal disputes, deal with the great events described by the historians or the long-term trends revealed by archaeology. In most cases these were issues and actions only of significance to those immediately involved. Yet more than anything else these documents tell us what it was like in an army garrison.

4 *Epigraphy:* Another major source of evidence is provided by inscriptions in Greek or Latin erected by units or individual soldiers. Official inscriptions were often set up to commemorate the completion of building work, and where we are fortunate enough to have these they allow us to date precisely such projects. Religious inscriptions, very often on altars, can tell us a good deal, and not simply about the soldiers' beliefs. Individuals often mention their rank and unit and sometimes we also have altars dedicated by an entire unit led by its commander as part of the army's formal religion. The other most significant type of inscription is the tombstone or memorial, many of which list a soldier's unit and service record and occasionally the details of his career. Much of our understanding of the rank structure and system of promotion in the army comes from the epigraphic record.

Care needs to be taken when interpreting inscriptions as with any other source. They tell us

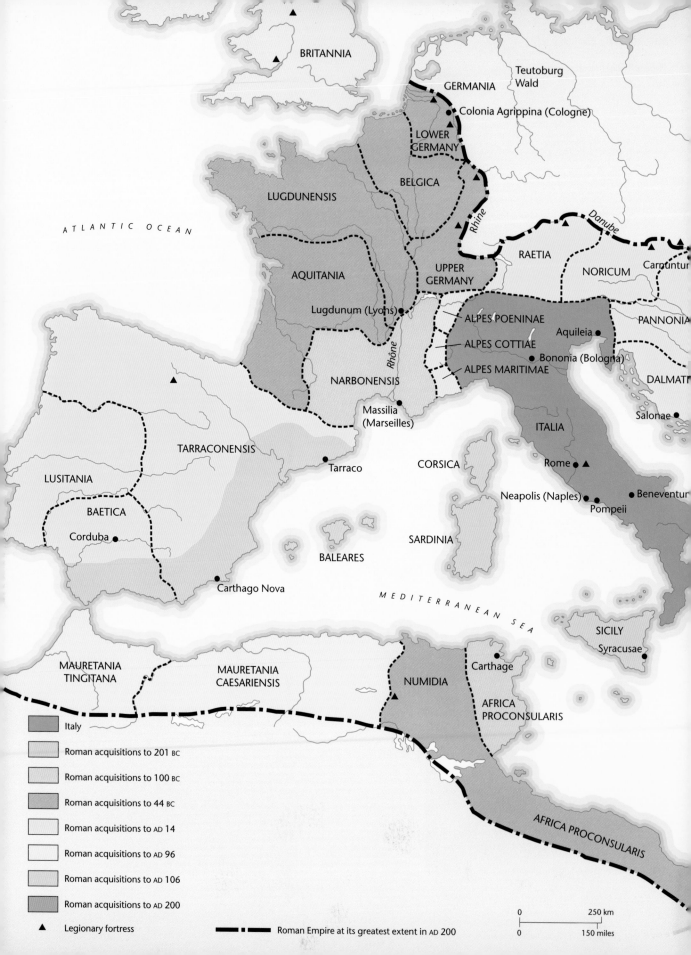

BRITANNIA

GERMANIA

Teutoburg
Wald

Colonia Agrippina (Cologne)

LOWER
GERMANY

BELGICA

LUGDUNENSIS

Rhine

Danube

ATLANTIC OCEAN

RAETIA

Carnuntur

NORICUM

AQUITANIA

UPPER
GERMANY

ALPES POENINAE

PANNONIA

Aquileia

Lugdunum (Lyons)

ALPES COTTIAE

Bononia (Bologna)

Rhône

ALPES MARITIMAE

DALMATI

NARBONENSIS

ITALIA

Salonae

Massilia
(Marseilles)

Rome

TARRACONENSIS

CORSICA

Neapolis (Naples)

Beneventur

Tarraco

Pompeii

LUSITANIA

BAETICA

Corduba

SARDINIA

BALEARES

Carthago Nova

MEDITERRANEAN SEA

SICILY

Syracusae

MAURETANIA
TINGITANA

MAURETANIA
CAESARIENSIS

NUMIDIA

Carthage

AFRICA
PROCONSULARIS

AFRICA PROCONSULARIS

▨	Italy
▨	Roman acquisitions to 201 BC
▨	Roman acquisitions to 100 BC
▨	Roman acquisitions to 44 BC
▨	Roman acquisitions to AD 14
▨	Roman acquisitions to AD 96
▨	Roman acquisitions to AD 106
▨	Roman acquisitions to AD 200

▲ Legionary fortress

Roman Empire at its greatest extent in AD 200

0   250 km

0   150 miles

The Rise of the Roman Empire

PARTHIAN
EMPIRE

BLACK SEA

DACIA

rmium

UPPER
MOESIA

LOWER
MOESIA

THRACE

CAPPADOCIA

BITHYNIA AND PONTUS

MESOPOTAMIA

Byzantium
(Istanbul)

Nicomedia

Ancyra (Ankara)

MACEDONIA

Philippi

Thessalonica

ASIA

GALATIA

• Carrhae

EPIRUS

Pergamum

Tarsus

Antioch

• Palmyra

Actium

ACHAEA

Ephesus

LYCIA AND
PAMPHYLIA

CILICIA

SYRIA

Athens

CYPRUS

CRETE

MEDITERRANEAN SEA

JUDAEA

• Cyrene

Alexandria

ARABIA

CYRENAICA

AEGYPTUS

RED SEA

A relief from the early 2nd-century AD Tropaeum Traiani at Adamklissi in Romania showing three standard-bearers. Each man wears mail armour, and two carry a square vexillum flag, while the man in the centre bears a signum. The signum was the standard of a century and was carried by an officer known as a signifer. This monument was constructed by the army itself and includes many details of the equipment actually in use rather than the more idealized portraits of soldiers on such official monuments as Trajan's Column.

(Right) Another useful source of information concerning military equipment comes from the depictions of soldiers on their tombstones. This stone commemorated Flavinus, a standard-bearer of the Ala Petriana, and is now in Hexham Abbey, Northumberland. He is shown wearing a crested helmet, and carrying a standard.

definitely no more and no less than their text, that such and such a unit built a new gateway, that an officer dedicated an altar to a local deity, or that a man died at the age of so many years after a period of military service and served in this unit and that rank. From evidence of this sort we try to infer many things, for instance the identity of the unit in garrison at a fort, or the ethnic background of its soldiers, based usually on their name and perhaps the god or goddess they chose to venerate. Yet much of this must remain conjectural, and all we really have is attestation that a unit carried out a task in that place when this is specified, or that an individual had an altar erected or died in that place.

5 *Art and sculpture:* Archaeology has provided us with many examples of some types of Roman equipment. Metal pieces – helmets, armour, weapons, belt buckles, harness decoration, etc. – are comparatively plentiful, but leather items, for instance boots or belts, are rarer, surviving only in certain conditions. Textiles, including clothing of all types from cloaks to tunics to socks, hardly ever survive and then only in the most fragmentary form. Therefore, in order to gain a clearer picture of what Roman soldiers actually looked like, we need to employ the images of soldiers depicted in various forms of art, from mosaics and wall-paintings to sculpted figures on coins and monuments.

Trajan's Column was erected in Rome to commemorate that Emperor's victory over the Dacians in AD 106 and is inscribed with scenes forming a narrative of the campaigns. It is a celebration of the army as much as of the Emperor who led it and depicts an ideal Roman army, the different troop types all in their regulation uniforms. The contemporary Tropaeum Traiani at Adamklissi in Romania was built by one of the provincial armies that had taken part in the same set of wars and depicts their part in it. This is very different in style from the more sophisticated column in Rome, showing local variations in weapons and equipment, and probably more closely depicts what the soldiers actually looked like. Other columns and arches depicting the army have survived, though none quite rival these for detail, accuracy and high state of preservation.

On a smaller scale, but no less important, are the many representations of soldiers such as those found on some tombstones. These present the image that the soldier or his commemorators wished to project, which is not always the same as the official view seen on the larger monuments. In some cases equipment is represented in great detail, though in others the men chose to be shown in undress uniform without armour or weapons.

Bringing the sources together

The different sources together provide us with a great body of information, from which we can attempt to build up a picture of the Roman army. However, we should never forget that our evidence represents a tiny fraction of what was once available. The majority of histories, biographies and military manuals written in the Roman period have not survived even in a fragmentary form. The sub-literary texts hint at massive amounts of written military records and thriving exchanges of correspondence, but preserve only a statistically insignificant sample of this. Though we have a good number of military tombstones, infinitely more men who served in the Roman army left no such memorial to themselves. Excavation of military bases has tended to deal with only a small proportion of each site and some wider projects have proved very surprising in what they revealed. The study of any aspect of life in the ancient world, including the Roman army, involves making the best of a limited amount of information.

Nor is this information evenly spread. Literature leaves almost blank the greater part of the 2nd and 3rd centuries AD. The archaeological evidence, along with the epigraphic record, tends overwhelmingly to come from the professional army of the Principate and, to a much lesser degree, Late Antiquity. The militia soldiers of the Mid Republic were still the Roman people under arms. At the end of the campaign they returned to normal life not to purpose-built barracks, and blended back into the wider population. Such a force left little distinct trace archaeologically.

Each type of source provides us with a slightly different perspective on the Roman army and contributes towards the creation of a broader picture. However, we should not expect the different types of information always to fit together neatly and seamlessly. It is certainly a mistake to interpret one type of source from the perspective of another. The different phases discerned in the layout and size of a fort should be dated and explained on their own merit and not forced to conform to some wider view of policy within that province. Where such correspondence does appear to emerge, it is best that the complementary interpretations grow up independently. It is salutary to recall that Hadrian's Wall, probably the most substantial and certainly the most intensively studied frontier monument of the Roman army, is mentioned only a handful of times in extant Greek and Latin literature, and its purpose never clearly explained. The Roman army was a large institution that remained in existence for many centuries. We should not be dismayed if different sources appear to suggest very different practices within it. It is doubtful that we can guess at the real complexity and at the great variations over time and in different parts of the Empire of the real thing.

'For who is so worthless or indolent as not to wish to know by what means ...
the Romans ... have succeeded in subjecting nearly the whole of the inhabited
world to their sole government.'

Polybius 1. 1. 5 (Loeb translation)

Polybius was writing in the late 2nd century BC, and had in his own lifetime witnessed Rome's rise to a position of unchallenged dominance in the Mediterranean world. In a little over 100 years the Romans had defeated and utterly destroyed the powerful trading empire of Carthage. This was followed by victories won with almost disdainful ease over the famous Hellenistic kingdoms of Macedonia and Seleucia. Polybius believed that one of the most important factors in Rome's success was the peculiar institutions of the Roman army, a subject which he described in detail. The legions of this period differed markedly from the popular stereotype of the Roman army as a professional and rigidly disciplined fighting force. They were not professional soldiers at all, but ordinary citizens for whom military service was an interruption to their normal life.

The Roman army described by Polybius had gradually evolved over several centuries, changes often reflecting trends in society and politics. Rome had begun sometime in the 8th or 7th centuries BC as one of many tiny Latin-speaking communities in central Italy. In those days its frequent wars with neighbouring peoples were waged by warrior aristocrats and their bands of followers. Over time Rome grew in size and population, and the obligation to serve as a soldier was extended to every adult male citizen able to provide himself with the necessary equipment. Such men fought when the Republic required them to do so and then at the end of a campaign returned home to their ordinary lives. Military service was a duty owed to the community of which they were a part, rather than a career. Many contemporary states had once recruited their armies in this way, but all those which expanded to any size abandoned the system, and came to rely instead on professional soldiers. Uniquely the Roman Republic persisted with this militia system, and, just as uniquely, its citizens willingly subjected themselves to the extremely harsh system of discipline enforced within the legions. When properly trained and competently led, the legions demonstrated a tactical flexibility which made them superior to all other contemporary military systems.

A tomb painting from Paestum in Italy dating to the 4th century BC showing several Samnite warriors. The Romans were engaged in a tough series of wars against the Samnites, but eventually absorbed them and converted them into allies, who supplied soldiers to fight in Rome's wars.

I   The Republican Army

The Origins of the Roman Army

The earliest armies

Rome grew in size slowly, and was for centuries a very small community whose wars were fought on a similarly small scale. Later memories of this period suggest frequent hostility with their close neighbours, as rival aristocrats led their warrior bands on plundering raids. There is little reliable literary evidence for the early periods of Rome's history, since it was not until the very end of the 3rd century BC that the Romans themselves began to write history and even they had comparatively few sources available. The stories of the kings and the creation of the Republic may contain elements of true events and real people, but it is impossible now to separate fact from myth. There is no way of knowing whether Romulus actually existed, and if he did, whether he

really had a bodyguard of 300 warriors known as *celeres*. Even apparently plausible incidents in the early narratives of Livy and Dionysius of Halicarnassus, both of whom wrote in the late 1st century BC, cannot simply be accepted as fact, or rationalized to produce a more 'plausible' version of events. We simply cannot know.

Archaeology at least helps to give us some idea of the weapons and equipment available at this time. Iron was at first comparatively rare, and only gradually were bronze spearheads, daggers and swords replaced. Helmets varied in pattern, but tended to provide most protection for the top of the head and did not yet possess significant neckguards or cheek-pieces. The Villanovan pattern is probably the most visually impressive, consisting of a bowl made from two halves, the join being decorated with a tall, arrow-shaped plate standing up from it. Of little or no practical value, this pattern did make the wearer look considerably taller and thus more frightening to an enemy. Other types of helmet, such as the 'bell' type, lacked the high metal crest but were otherwise similar in shape. Body armour remained fairly simple, usually consisting of metal pectoral plates. A good deal of our evidence is sup-

(Right) This Etruscan helmet of the Villanovan pattern was found at Tarquinia. Such helmets tend to occur in funerary contexts from the 9th to 7th centuries BC in northern and central Italy. The tall central plate does not appear to have served any practical purpose.

(Opposite left) A warrior depicted on a 4th-century BC ivory plaque found at Palestrina, shown wearing a typical hoplite panoply. He wears a metal – probably bronze – cuirass, bronze crested helmet and greaves, and has a round shield at his side. His main armament consists of a heavy thrusting spear.

plied by objects deposited as part of funerary rituals – both cremation and inhumation being known – although this is supplemented by some artistic representations of warriors. It is important to remember that the goods deposited in a grave may not necessarily represent those normally in use. At the very least they will tend to show the equipment of the wealthy, but it is also possible that certain objects were chosen or even specially made for these rites. For instance, the solid bronze shields discovered in Italy and elsewhere clearly cannot have been intended for actual use in war, since the thin metal of these would split so easily, and may have been used for ceremonies or as spectacular grave goods. It is logical to assume that they reflected the design of more practical wooden shields, but since these have not survived we cannot be sure precisely what they looked like. It is as problematic to estimate just how many warriors in a band may have carried swords or worn armour as it is to suggest how numerous such bands were.

Farmer and soldier: The 'hoplite revolution'

At some point the Romans adopted the hoplite phalanx, which had probably first been introduced to Italy by Greek colonists. Hoplites were heavily armed spearmen, whose name derived from the circular hoplon shield, some 90 cm (3 ft) in diameter and made of wood covered with a sheet of bronze. Such shields offered excellent protection at the cost of being very heavy, and had to be held not simply by a handgrip but also by a strap fastening to the elbow of the left arm. Additional protection came from a bronze helmet, some versions of which covered the face as well as the top of the head, greaves fitted to the lower legs and a cuirass either of bronze or stiffened linen. A few men were also

(Below) A bronze muscle cuirass found in Italy, but now in the British Museum, that could easily have been worn by a hoplite similar to the one shown in the previous photograph. Armour of this type offered good protection, but was heavy, uncomfortable and expensive. As the army expanded in size to include many less wealthy soldiers, solid armour of this sort became rare.

21

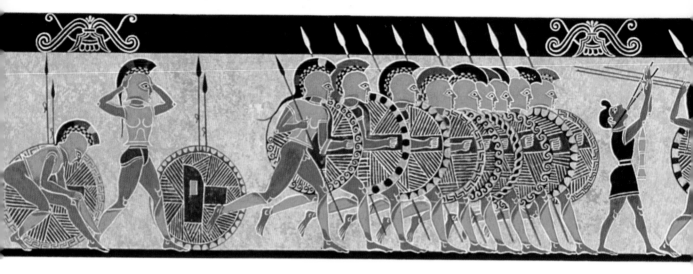

able to afford arm and shin guards. The main offensive weapon was a spear, 2.45 m (8 ft) or so in length, used for thrusting and not throwing, and provided with a butt spike both as a counterweight and as a weapon should the head break off. A sword, usually one of the short slashing or thrusting types, was carried as a secondary weapon.

Hoplites fought in close formation, the men standing close together so that their unguarded right side was offered at least a little protection by their neighbour's shield. Their aim was to close with the enemy and force the battle to a swiftly decisive conclusion, jabbing with their spears at opponents no more than a pace or so away to fight their way into the enemy formation. Although his shield, helmet and armour offered a hoplite very good protection, such determined, close-quarter fighting was inevitably very dangerous, especially when fighting another similarly equipped and aggressive enemy. The hoplite phalanx first appeared in

(Right) A detail from a 4th-century BC wall-painting found near Naples showing a man wearing an Italian version of the Attic helmet. In many respects – the face protected only by cheek-pieces and the ears left exposed – this design has much in common with later helmets. The use of feathers as a plume was common in the Roman army of Polybius' day.

Greece, perhaps in the 8th century BC though debate still rages about this, and it seems that even a victorious phalanx suffered on average five per cent casualties. Most of these losses came in the front ranks of the formation. So stressful was hoplite fighting that it was considered necessary to make phalanxes very deep, so that it was rare to deploy in fewer than eight ranks and there are cases of formations as many as 40 deep. Men in the second rank had some opportunity to stab their spears over the shoulders of the men in front, and also replaced any casualties, but the men in the ranks behind this could not join the fighting. Their role was primarily to provide moral support for the fighters. The mass of men packed behind an attacking line helped to intimidate the enemy, ideally persuading them to flee before the appalling clash of two phalanxes occurred. Even more importantly the physical presence of the rear ranks prevented the men in the front line from running away. Dense formations such as a phalanx inevitably collapsed from the back when the men in the rear, and thus furthest from actual danger, panicked and fled. Deeper phalanxes had more staying power in combat.

A phalanx was intended for massed fighting between large groups of densely packed men. There was far less scope in battles of this sort for displays of conspicuous bravery by individual aristocratic heroes. The adoption of this style of fighting at Rome, as in other cities, was not simply a matter of military evolution, but was part of major social and political change. Hoplites needed to provide themselves with expensive equipment and therefore were men of some property. In nearly every state the hoplite was a landowner, a farmer who fought well because he had a vested interest in the state. The development of the phalanx marked the growth of Rome's population and was also a sign that a significant part of that population owned land. In the past the leaders of warbands owed their power within the community to their

(Above) This painting is based upon the 7th-century BC Chigi vase, which provides one of the few depictions of hoplite phalanxes in battle. In a similar way to the Bayeux Tapestry, dense blocks of men are shown as soldiers overlapping each other. The spearheads appearing above the hoplites actually fighting may be an attempt to represent the ranks behind.

(Right) A man representing a Greek hoplite, heavily protected by a helmet which covers most of his face, a bronze cuirass and bronze greaves which clip onto his calves. Beside him is the 0.9-m (3-ft) wide bronze faced shield or hoplon.

prowess in war. The military role of farmers as hoplites was accompanied by greater political influence.

The phalanx was a formation for fighting pitched battles in open country. To a great extent hoplite equipment was tailored to this particular type of fighting, although it is clearly an exaggeration to state that helmets, armour and even the heavy shield were useless in more open fighting. Even after it is clear that the Romans possessed a hoplite phalanx, our sources continue to speak of raids and skirmishes as well as battles. Frequently this smaller scale of fighting seems to have involved aristocrats and their bands of warriors and kinsmen. The adoption of the phalanx did not mean a complete break with earlier patterns of warfare. Rome remained a comparatively small community engaged in local squabbles with other similarly small neighbours.

The Comitia Centuriata and the Servian reform

One tradition claims that the Romans adopted the phalanx after they had encountered Etruscan hoplites, and in this way were eventually able to defeat them. This is plausible enough, as is the common assumption that the Etruscans had in turn learnt these tactics through contact with the Greek colonies in Italy. When a hoplite army appeared at Rome is much harder to estimate, especially since it now seems likely that there was not an immediate switch from noble warbands to a citizen phalanx.

The Romans credited Servius Tullius, the sixth of their seven kings (578–534 BC) with a major reform of the Roman army. Whether or not Servius actually existed, traces of an early military organization were preserved down to the end of the Republic in the structure of the Comitia Centuriata, one of the most important voting assemblies of the Roman people.

Livy and Dionysius describe the Servian system in great detail, differing only on minor points. A census of all adult male citizens recorded the value

The Infantry in the Servian System

This chart shows the structure of the Servian system. All male Roman citizens were divided into groups according to their property rating, and the totals given here indicate numbers of centuries. The size of individual centuries varied considerably, and each class was divided into senior and junior centuries on the basis of age.

Class	Property (asses)	Equipment	Juniores	Seniores	Total
I	100,000	Helmet, round shield, greaves, cuirass, spear, sword	40	40	80
II	75,000	Helmet, oblong shield, greaves, spear, sword	10	10	20
III	50,000	Helmet, oblong shield, spear, sword	10	10	20
IV	25,000	(Oblong shield in Livy), spear, javelin	10	10	20
V	11,000	Sling, stones, (javelin)	15	15	30

Infantry Total: 170

Supernumeraries:
18 centuries of cavalry
2 of engineers
2 of musicians
1 *proletarii* (*capite censi* or head count. Citizens who lacked property sufficient to provide them with even the most rudimentary equipment. They were not obliged to serve and were listed only as a total number).

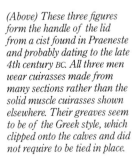

(Above) These three figures form the handle of the lid from a cist found in Praeneste and probably dating to the late 4th century BC. All three men wear cuirasses made from many sections rather than the solid muscle cuirasses shown elsewhere. Their greaves seem to be of the Greek style, which clipped onto the calves and did not require to be tied in place.

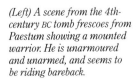

(Left) A scene from the 4th-century BC tomb frescoes from Paestum showing a mounted warrior. He is unarmoured and unarmed, and seems to be riding bareback.

of their property and divided them accordingly into classes. These classes were in turn divided into centuries, which may or may not have ever been intended to number 100 men. Each class was obliged to provide itself with a minimum panoply of equipment, so that the wealthiest (*equites* or equestrian order) served in the 18 centuries of cavalry. Class I appears to represent fully equipped hoplites, and some have speculated that these men formed the original phalanx, the other classes being added as population and prosperity continued to grow over the years.

The version of this system provided by our sources appears decidedly odd. The differences in equipment between Classes I–III (and possibly IV) are too minor to have had real significance, although the use of differently shaped shields in the same army appears to be confirmed by the figures on the Certosa situla. More importantly, it makes little sense for any society to have had the majority of its population in the highest property grouping, since Class I almost equals the total number of the rest of the infantry. It is more than probable that Livy and Dionysius, or perhaps their sources, were working from the known structure of the Comitia Centuriata and creating a military system from that. The Romans felt it to be proper for the wealthy to have a disproportionately strong say in state affairs, and therefore each century in Class I contained fewer members than the lower classes, so that the vote of each man counted for more.

The Servian reform certainly suggests the existence of a hoplite army, for the link between citizenship, property and military role are fundamental elements in such a system, but it would be rash to put too much weight on any of the details. It is not until the Mid Republic that we can finally describe the Roman army with confidence.

The 'Polybian' Legion

Polybius wrote his detailed description of the Roman army's organization in the mid-2nd century BC, although it is positioned within his work to accompany his account of the Second Punic War. The Greek historian seems to have believed, almost certainly correctly, that few significant changes had occurred in the army's basic structure since the early 3rd century BC.

The Roman army remained a temporary militia, and the census recorded those citizens with sufficient property to make them eligible to serve. To share the burden of military service, no man was obliged to serve for more than 16 campaigns or years. Each year the Senate – the senior council of the Republic – decided how many soldiers to raise

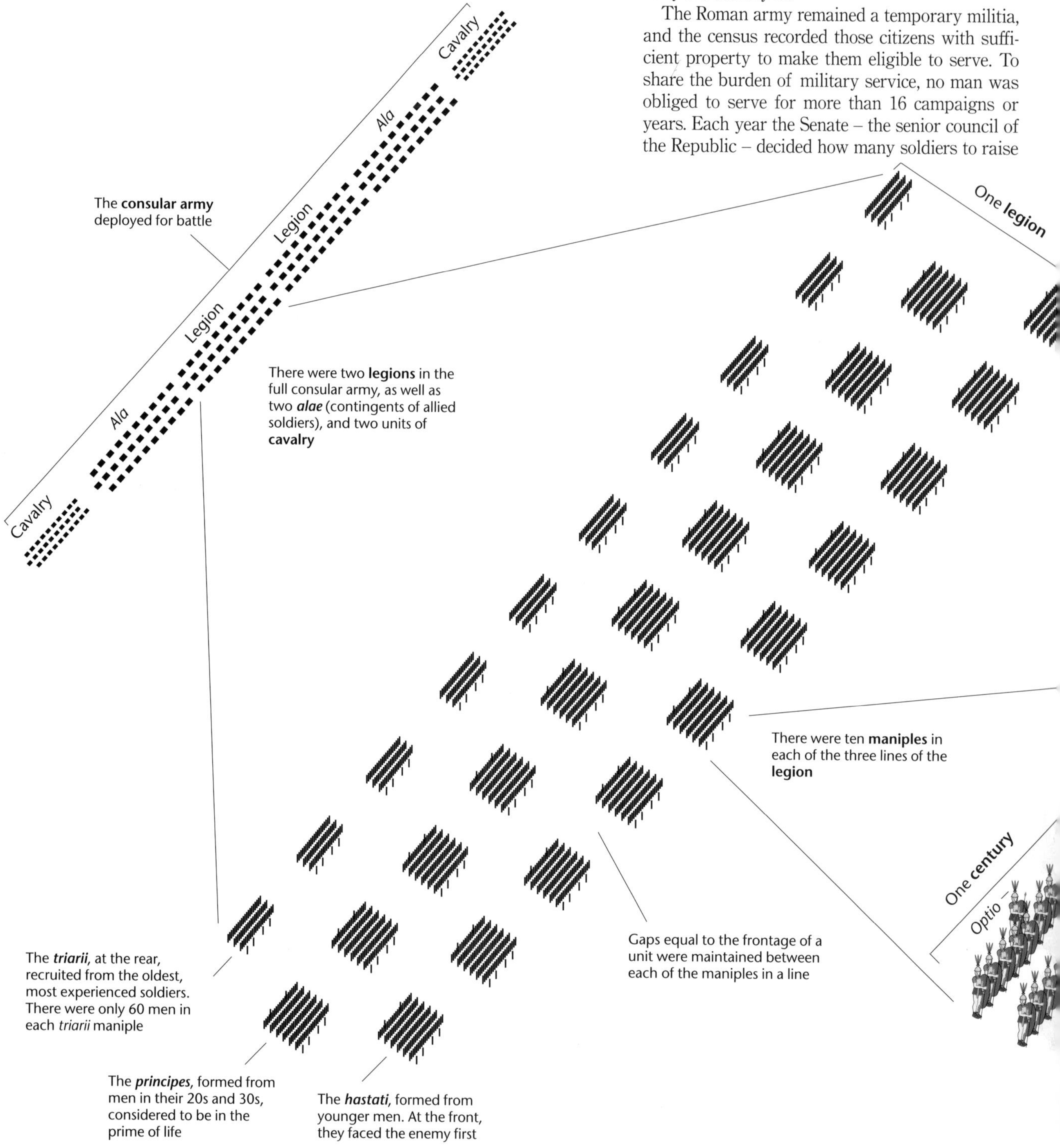

Cavalry

Ala

Legion

Legion

The **consular army** deployed for battle

Ala

Cavalry

There were two **legions** in the full consular army, as well as two *alae* (contingents of allied soldiers), and two units of **cavalry**

One legion

There were ten **maniples** in each of the three lines of the **legion**

One **century**

Optio

Gaps equal to the frontage of a unit were maintained between each of the maniples in a line

The *triarii*, at the rear, recruited from the oldest, most experienced soldiers. There were only 60 men in each *triarii* maniple

The *principes*, formed from men in their 20s and 30s, considered to be in the prime of life

The *hastati*, formed from younger men. At the front, they faced the enemy first

and where they would be sent. Armies were commanded by elected magistrates who held power (*imperium*) for 12 months, although the Senate could choose to extend this. The two consuls elected each year were the senior magistrates and given the most important military tasks. Smaller-scale operations could be entrusted to praetors, the next magisterial college in seniority to the consuls. The number of praetors rose from one per year to six during the course of the Punic Wars. When Rome was a small community it had usually sent all its men to fight a single conflict, but the growth of the state and the increasing number of military problems required the division of military effort. Legion (Latin *legio*) had originally meant 'levy' and referred to the entire Roman people under arms, but by at least the 4th century BC it had come to mean the most significant unit of the army. In Polybius' day it was normal for a consul to be given an army of two legions, whilst praetors more often led only one.

The standard legion consisted of 4,200 infantrymen and 300 cavalrymen. As before, the wealthiest men formed the cavalry (*equites*) and were divided into 10 troops (*turmae*) commanded by three decurions or 'leaders of 10'. The nucleus of the cavalry remained the 18 equestrian centuries – the centuries consisting of the wealthiest citizens – all of whom were entitled to have the cost of their horse refunded by the state should it be killed in battle, but by this period large numbers of other wealthy men voluntarily served in this way. Polybius tells us that the *equites* had long since adopted Hellenistic-style equipment, but, assuming that his audience was familiar with this, does not bother to describe it. However, we can deduce that Roman cavalrymen fought in close order, were armed with a spear and sword and protected by helmet, cuirass and circular shield.

The infantry of the legion were allocated to their roles according not just to their property, but also their age. The poorest citizens, who still owned enough to make them eligible for service, unlike the *capite censi*, acted as light infantry (*velites*), as did men too young to fight in the main battle line. The *velites* were equipped with a bundle of light javelins, a sword (at least from the early 2nd century BC and probably before) and a round shield. Some at least wore helmets, and all were supposed to wear pieces of animal skin, especially wolf skins, attached to these or their caps. Polybius tells us that this was intended to allow their officers to identify them in battle and reward or punish their behaviour accordingly, but it may originally have had some totemic significance. Usually there were 1,200 velites in each legion, but we do not know how they were organized or commanded in any detail.

The main strength of the legion lay in its close-order infantrymen, who were formed into three distinct lines. The first (*hastati*), nearest to the enemy, were formed from the younger men – probably in their late teens or early 20s. Behind them were the *principes*, men in their later 20s or early 30s, a time considered to be the prime of life. In the rear were the *triarii*, recruited from the oldest and most experienced soldiers. There were normally 1,200 each of the *hastati* and *principes*, but only 600 *triarii*. Each line was divided into 10 maniples and these were the basic tactical unit. However, for administrative purposes the maniple was divided into two centuries each commanded by a centurion, supported by a second-in-command (*optio*), standard-bearer (*signifer*), and guard commander (*tesserarius*). The centurion of the right-hand century was appointed to his command and was the senior of the two, taking charge when both were present. He then chose the man to serve as the centurion for the left-hand century. Polybius tells us that centurions were chosen to be especially steady and determined leaders, men who would stay with their troops and not charge off on their own. The legion

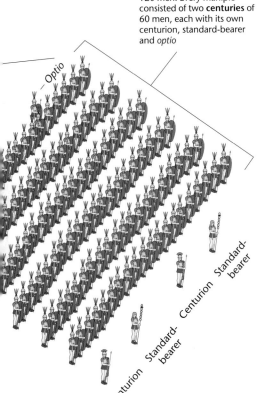

One **maniple**, the basic tactical unit of the army, containing 120 men. Every maniple consisted of two **centuries** of 60 men, each with its own centurion, standard-bearer and *optio*

Optio

Centurion   Standard-   Centurion   Standard-
bearer   bearer

Centurion   Standard-
bearer

(Left) The deployment of the manipular legion in battle. The formation of the maniples was very flexible, far more so than the solid phalanx favoured by Hellenistic armies. It allowed the Romans to move across uneven terrain without falling into serious disorder and also permitted readier reaction to a developing crisis during a battle.

27

itself did not have a single commanding officer. Instead there were six military tribunes, and command rotated between pairs of these officers.

The legion did not need to number precisely 4,200 foot and 300 horse to function properly. Sickness and casualties inevitably eroded a unit's strength on campaign. The Senate might also decide to form especially strong legions if they felt that the military situation demanded it, and we hear of legions with between 5,000 and 6,000 men being raised at times of particular crisis. Both the *equites* and the *triarii* were recruited from a limited pool, so when larger legions were formed the extra men were divided equally amongst the *hastati*, *principes* and *velites*. In the field each legion was also supported by a similarly sized contingent of allied soldiers, known as an *ala* or 'wing', recruited primarily from the Latin peoples. An *ala* normally had as many infantry as a legion but three times the number of cavalry. It was subdivided into cohorts, but it is unclear to what extent these were tactical units, how many there were to each *ala* and whether they were of a fixed size. This may simply have been a vague term meaning contingent which referred to all the troops provided by a single Latin colony. Allied cohorts are recorded numbering 400–600 men and their size may have varied with the size of the *ala*. The *ala* was commanded by three prefects (*praefecti sociorum*) who were invariably Roman citizens. In battle the legions formed the centre of the army whilst the *alae* were formed on their flanks. In a consular army of two legions and two *alae* the latter were known as 'Left' and 'Right' respectively. The pick of the allies were separated from the *alae* to form the *extraordinarii*, a force of cavalry and infantry at the immediate disposal of the consul.

In this period none of the army officers were professional soldiers. The magistrates commanding the armies and the tribunes were elected, and the other officers appointed, and neither experience nor ability were necessarily of primary importance in their selection.

Weapons

The pilum: Polybius tells us that each *hastatus* and *princeps* carried two heavy javelins, one heavier than the other. These were the famous *pila* which remained in the arsenal of the legions for over five centuries. A *pilum* consisted of a wooden shaft, some 4 ft (1.2 m) or so in length, joined to a thin iron shank, perhaps 2 ft (60 cm) long, and topped by a small pyramid-shaped point. A *pilum* was heavy, and all of its weight when thrown was concentrated behind its small head, giving it tremendous penetrative power. When it punched through an enemy's shield, the long, thin shank slid readily through the hole and had the reach to strike the man's body. Even when the man avoided a serious wound, the *pilum* was difficult to dislodge and weighed down his shield. Modern tests of reconstructed *pila* have suggested that they had a maximum range of about 100 ft (30 m), with an effective range of perhaps half that. These tests also confirmed its great penetrative power.

A scene from the 1st-century BC altar of Gnaeus Domitius Ahenobarbus showing two legionaries in the typical uniform of the last 200 years of the Republic. Each man wears a Montefortino-style helmet topped by a flowing, horse-hair crest. They wear mail armour fastening over the shoulders and reaching down to well below the hips. The shield is the oval scutum constructed from plywood covered with leather to give it both strength and flexibility.

The gladius: At some point in the 3rd or very early 2nd centuries BC, the Romans adopted the 'Spanish sword' (*gladius hispaniensis*) as their principal sidearm, replacing the various short, thrusting types in use before this. Copied from a Spanish design, the Romans may have first come across this weapon when facing Iberian mercenaries in Carthaginian employ during the First Punic War or when the first Roman armies campaigned in the Spanish peninsula during the Second War. It was a point of pride for the Romans to be willing to copy

and employ the effective tactics or equipment of their enemies, and this was not the only example of this practice. Mail armour, cavalry harnesses and saddles and some tactics were all to be copied from the Gauls. Debate continues to rage over when the Romans adopted the Spanish sword and precisely which type of native weapon was copied.

Only a very small number of Roman swords dating to the Mid Republic have been discovered. The sample is really too small to make it certain that this was normal, but all are somewhat longer than

Legionaries of the Late 3rd Century BC

This scene shows a group of legionaries on campaign at the beginning of the Second Punic War (218–201 BC). Like soldiers throughout history, Roman legionaries doubtless spent much of their time waiting, and this group are playing dice – a common passion amongst Romans of all classes for many centuries. On the left is a *hastatus* or *princeps*, standing beside him is a *veles*, while a veteran of the *triarii* kneels on the right.

These short-term citizen soldiers provided their own equipment and therefore show considerably more variation in clothing, armour and weapons than troops of the later professional legions. However, evidence for equipment and dress in this period is comparatively poor and much of this illustration remains conjectural.

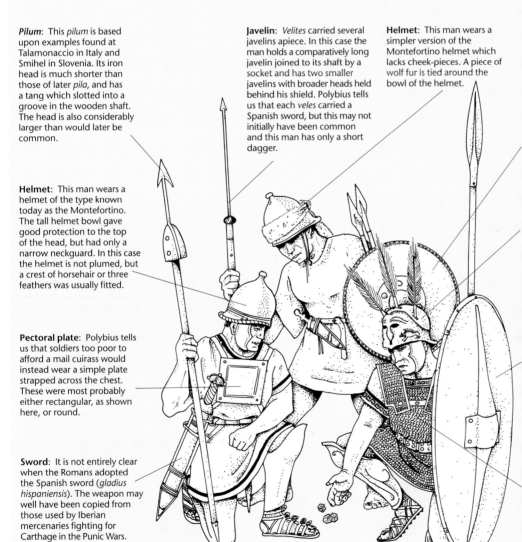

Pilum: This *pilum* is based upon examples found at Talamonaccio in Italy and Smihel in Slovenia. Its iron head is much shorter than those of later *pila*, and has a tang which slotted into a groove in the wooden shaft. The head is also considerably larger than would later be common.

Helmet: This man wears a helmet of the type known today as the Montefortino. The tall helmet bowl gave good protection to the top of the head, but had only a narrow neckguard. In this case the helmet is not plumed, but a crest of horsehair or three feathers was usually fitted.

Pectoral plate: Polybius tells us that soldiers too poor to afford a mail cuirass would instead wear a simple plate strapped across the chest. These were most probably either rectangular, as shown here, or round.

Sword: It is not entirely clear when the Romans adopted the Spanish sword (*gladius hispaniensis*). The weapon may well have been copied from those used by Iberian mercenaries fighting for Carthage in the Punic Wars.

Javelin: *Velites* carried several javelins apiece. In this case the man holds a comparatively long javelin joined to its shaft by a socket and has two smaller javelins with broader heads held behind his shield. Polybius tells us that each *veles* carried a Spanish sword, but this may not initially have been common and this man has only a short dagger.

Helmet: This man wears a simpler version of the Montefortino helmet which lacks cheek-pieces. A piece of wolf fur is tied around the bowl of the helmet.

Polybius tells us that the *velites* decorated their headgear in this way so that their officers could recognise each man as an individual.

Shield: The *velites* fought as skirmishers for whom the heavy *scutum* would have been far too cumbersome. Instead they carried a smaller and lighter round shield.

Helmet: This *triarius* wears an Etrusco-Corinthian helmet, a type which seems to have been almost as common as the Montefortino. It is crested with three feathers, which were either purple or black according to Polybius.

Shield: The shield is a fairly standard oval *scutum*, its rim protected at top and bottom by bronze binding. The central spine is reinforced by a metal shield boss. Reconstructions of shields of this type are very heavy, weighing in at some 10 kg (22 lb). Behind the shield this man has rested his 2.4-m (8-ft) thrusting-spear.

Mail cuirass: Wealthier soldiers wore mail armour, which may have been copied originally from the Gauls. The shoulder doubling fastened the cuirass into place and also gave added protection to this part of the body.

the types used by the later professional army. They are well-balanced blades, primarily designed for thrusting but also capable of delivering an effective slash. Livy claims that in 200 BC a Macedonian army was dismayed to see corpses of men killed with the Spanish sword, and describes horrific wounds, such as heads and limbs severed from the body, all of which were the result of cuts.

The *pugio*

Some Roman soldiers carried a dagger (*pugio*) as well as a sword. Although Polybius does not mention daggers, examples have been found in what is probably a 2nd-century BC context in Spain. The *pugio* provided an additional weapon, but was probably more often employed in the day-to-day tasks of living on campaign. The later practice was to wear the *pugio* on the left hip and the *gladius* on the right.

The spear

Although Polybius tells us that the first two lines of infantry were equipped with the *pilum*, the third line, the *triarii*, still employed the old hoplite spear. This was a heavy weapon, intended for thrusting and not throwing. On one occasion in 223 BC the *triarii*'s spears were taken from them and issued to the *hastati*, who then kept in close formation to weather the initial storm of a Gallic charge. Dionysius of Halicarnassus claims that in the war with Pyrrhus the *principes* had also used spears, which they wielded two-handed. This is somewhat strange, for it is difficult to see how a man equipped with such a weapon could also have used the normal Roman shield, but some scholars have taken this to mean that the adoption of the *pilum* was a gradual process and that all three lines had originally been spearmen. The evidence is too poor to resolve this question.

Defensive equipment

Body armour: Several types of body armour were in use at this period. The most expensive and best was mail, consisting of a cuirass made from linked iron rings. This offered good protection and was flexible enough to permit relatively easy movement. Its only disadvantage was that it was also heavy. Most of the weight fell on the wearer's shoulders, although a belt helped to spread this. Mail appears to have been copied from the Gallic tribes of northern Italy, and may have been a Celtic invention. Roman and some Celtic mail shirts were reinforced by a double layer on the shoulders to protect against downward cuts.

Some men may have worn scale armour consisting of small bronze plates. Less flexible than mail, such a cuirass could be polished to a high sheen to look more impressive. Many men wore a greave to protect their left leg, the one nearest the enemy. Senior officers and some cavalrymen appear to have

used various forms of muscled cuirass, probably usually of bronze. Some form of jerkin, probably padded, was worn beneath all types of metal armour.

Not all men could afford any of these alternatives, and Polybius tells us that instead these wore a pectoral plate. Usually round or rectangular, these bronze or iron plates were fastened with straps onto the front of the chest.

Helmets: A number of helmets survive from this period, although in most cases we cannot associate them with the Roman army with absolute certainty. Since each soldier provided his own equipment it was inevitable that there was no single standard pattern of body armour or helmets in use. The commonest type of helmet was the Montefortino helmet, a high domed pattern topped by a crest knob, with a stubby neckguard and hinged cheekpieces. Another type was the Etrusco-Corinthian, which appears to have developed from the Corinthian-type hoplite helmets. These had covered the face, obscuring hearing and allowing vision through small eye-holes, but could be pushed back and worn on top of the head more comfortably when not actually in combat. The Italian development of this was always worn in this way, though it preserved the eye holes for decoration. Some Attic types were certainly in use in southern Italy and were probably also employed by the Romans or their allies. All of these helmets were made from bronze beaten into shape.

The Montefortino was of Gallic origins, as were the similar though usually lower Coolus types

A statue of a young Gallic nobleman from Vachères in southern France, providing a good image of the Gauls who fought against and as auxiliaries with Roman armies. It is quite possible that the Romans copied the design of the mail cuirass from the Gauls, for the features shown clearly here – notably the shoulder doubling – are characteristic of the mail worn by the Roman army. The torque worn as decoration around the neck would later be adopted as an award for bravery by the Roman army.

which appear in the Late Republic. The Romans also began to copy some iron Celtic helmets, such as the Agen and Port types. These fitted better to the head and had broader cheek-pieces which offered superior protection to the face. The design of Roman helmets until Late Antiquity would owe much to all these patterns already in use in the Republic.

Cavalry seem to have worn most or all of these types. However, Boeotian helmets, a Greek design specifically intended for horsemen, seem also to have been in use.

The shield (scutum): Polybius describes the shield carried by the heavy infantry as semi-cylindrical and about 1.2 m (4 ft) in length and 76 cm (2 ft 6 in) in width. Sculptural evidence shows that it was normally oval in shape. It was made from two layers of plywood, the boards laid at right angles to each other, and the whole thing covered with calfskin. This combination gave both strength and flexibility. Iron binding protected the top and bottom to prevent the layers from splitting as a result of blows, and in the centre was an iron boss.

The only example of a shield of this pattern was found at Kasr el-Harit in Egypt. It is probably, though not certainly, Roman. It does not have a metal boss, but a wooden, barley-corn-shaped boss covering the horizontal hand-grip. A reconstruction modelled on this example weighed 10 kg (22 lb), heavier even than the bulky hoplon, and unlike the hoplite shield all of the weight was supported in the left hand as there was no shoulder strap for use in battle.

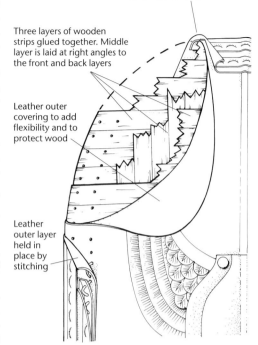

Leather sheet stitched to rear of shield board overlaps sheet covering the front

Three layers of wooden strips glued together. Middle layer is laid at right angles to the front and back layers

Leather outer covering to add flexibility and to protect wood

Leather outer layer held in place by stitching

A diagram showing the construction of a shield (scutum) based on the example found in Egypt and the description given in Polybius. Although heavy, the oval scutum offered very good protection. It could also be used offensively to knock down or unbalance an opponent.

(Below) A badly corroded relief from the Aemilius Paullus monument at Delphi commemorating the Romans' defeat of King Perseus of Macedon on 22 June 168 BC. On the left of the picture two Roman horsemen charge into contact with Macedonian cavalrymen, one of whose horses is collapsing. The Romans wear mail armour very similar in design to that of the Vachères warrior.

Roman cavalry employed significantly smaller and lighter shields, which appear to have been round. Rather unhelpfully, Polybius describes an obsolete pattern of cavalry shield, but not the type actually employed by the *equites* in his day.

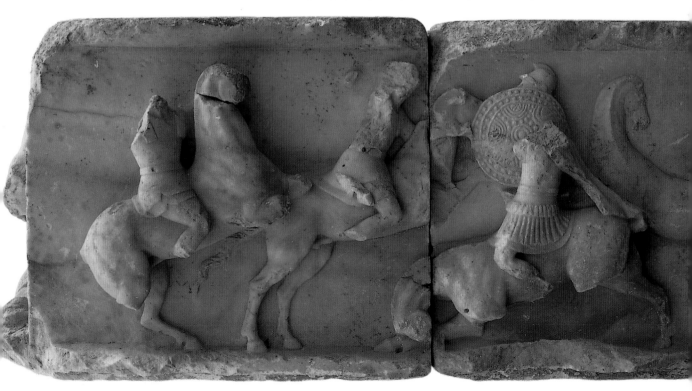

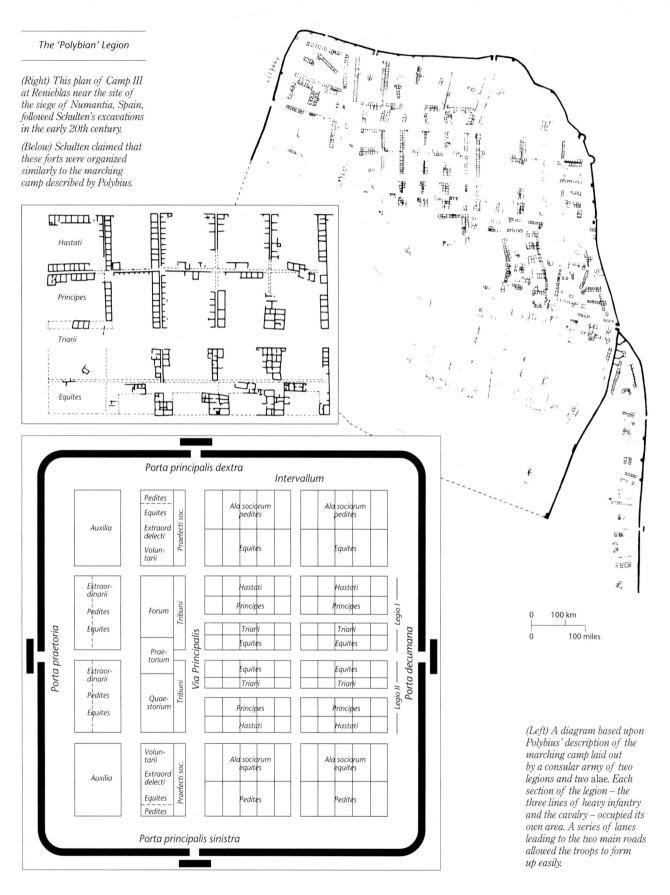

(Right) This plan of Camp III at Renieblas near the site of the siege of Numantia, Spain, followed Schulten's excavations in the early 20th century.

(Below) Schulten claimed that these forts were organized similarly to the marching camp described by Polybius.

Hastati

Principes

Triarii

Equites

Porta principalis dextra

Intervallum

Auxilia

Pedites
Equites
Extraord delecti
Volun- tarii

Praefecti soc.

Ala sociorum pedites

Equites

Ala sociorum pedites

Equites

Extraor- dinarii
Pedites
Equites

Forum

Praetorium

Triboni

Via Principalis

Hastati

Principes

Hastati

Principes

Legio I

Porta praetoria

Triani

Equites

Triani

Equites

Extraor- dinarii
Pedites
Equites

Quae- storium

Triboni

Equites

Triani

Equites

Triani

Legio II

Porta decumana

Principes

Hastati

Principes

Hastati

Auxilia

Volun- tarii
Extraord delecti
Equites
Pedites

Praefecti soc.

Ala sociorum equites

Pedites

Ala sociorum equites

Pedites

Porta principalis sinistra

0   100 km

0   100 miles

(Left) A diagram based upon Polybius' description of the marching camp laid out by a consular army of two legions and two alae. Each section of the legion – the three lines of heavy infantry and the cavalry – occupied its own area. A series of lanes leading to the two main roads allowed the troops to form up easily.

The camp and military life

The militia army was always essentially imperman-ent, and it seems that, even when legions remained in existence for some time, they were re-numbered at the beginning of each consular year. Men were enrolled, and served usually for no more than the duration of a campaign and returned to civilian life. The Romans had instituted pay for their soldiers in 396 BC, but this covered no more than basic living expenses and was not a significant source of income. The prospect of booty may have attracted some soldiers, especially when the enemy was per-ceived to be wealthy, for plunder was supposed to be fairly distributed throughout the army. However, most citizens served because they closely identified themselves with the state. For the duration of their military service, Roman citizens willingly submit-ted to an extremely harsh system of discipline, losing most of the legal rights which protected them in civilian life. Soldiers could be flogged or executed on the command of their officers. Cow-ardice brought the death penalty, as did sleeping on guard duty, and also such crimes as theft and sodomy within the camp. Both legally and ideologi-cally, a marked distinction was maintained between the status and appropriate behaviour of Romans at home (*domi*) and at war (*militiae*). Enrolment into the legions took place on the Campus Martius or 'Field of Mars', outside the formal boundary of the city to signify this change. The legions were only permitted into Rome itself on the day of a general's triumph, when he and they paraded through the streets to mark their victory over the enemy.

The temporary camps constructed by the Roman army symbolized the ordered existence of citizens whilst they served in the legions. Polybius describes in some detail the design and construction of the marching camps. At the end of each day's march a Roman force followed a standard plan as it laid down streets, tent-lines and horse-lines surrounded by a ditch and rampart. Each maniple knew where it would sleep and what duties it would perform, since fatigues were allocated according to a regular system. Pyrrhus is supposed to have realized that he was not dealing with mere barbarians when he saw the order of the Roman camp.

Archaeology has discovered very few temporary camps from this period. However, a series of camps around the Celtiberian stronghold of Numantia (near modern-day Burgos in Spain) appear to date to the 2nd century BC. Several camps were evidently occupied for more than just a night or two, for they show traces of simple internal buildings, corre-sponding to the tents of an ordinary marching camp. The best-preserved camp of a series at Renieblas can with the eye of faith be seen to reflect some features of the Polybian camp, with the legions divided into lines and maniples.

The marching camp offered protection against surprise attack. Day and night pickets were main-tained at a set distance beyond the ramparts to warn of any attack and slow the enemy down. Troops performing this duty were bound with a solemn oath not to abandon their position. Nor-mally the rampart and ditch surrounding the camp were sufficient only to delay attackers and not to stop them, although if the army remained in the same camp for some time then its defences could be made far more formidable. The Romans rarely, if ever, planned to fight from inside the walls of their camp, but to advance and meet the enemy in the open, relying on the resilience and tactical strength of the legions. Between the ramparts and tent-lines of a camp was a wide open area known as the *inter-vallum*, which ensured that the tents were out of range of missiles thrown or shot from outside the camp. More importantly, this space allowed the army to form itself up ready to deploy into battle order. Three columns would be formed, with some-times a fourth for the cavalry. Each column would become one of the three lines, and the maniples were positioned in the order they would take up in the fighting line, with the unit that would form on the right heading the column, and the one on the left at the rear. Each column would march from one of the four gates of the camp to the position where battle order was to be formed. The temporary camp played a vital role in allowing Roman armies to enter battle in an organized manner.

A section of the relief from the Domitius Ahenobarbus monument showing a figure – possibly intended to represent the war god Mars – dressed in the uniform of a senior officer of the Republican army. The six tribunes who commanded each manipular legion would probably have closely resembled this man.

The Roman Navy

Origins

For a long time the Romans felt little need for a navy, since enemies in Italy could all be fought and defeated by the legions on land. In 311 BC the Republic created a board of two officials (*duoviri*) with responsibility for constructing and maintaining warships. Each *duumvir* commanded a squadron of 10 ships, which were most probably triremes, or 'threes' (three banks of oarsmen: see below). We hear very little about the activities of these squadrons, apart from when the Romans suffered a humiliating defeat at the hands of the Tarantine navy in 282 BC. On the rare occasions that greater forces were required, the Republic called upon allied cities with strong maritime traditions, so that these, the naval allies (*socii navales*), were obliged to supply them with ships and crews rather than soldiers.

In 265 BC the Romans sent an expedition to Sicily where it swiftly came into conflict with the Carthaginians. Carthage possessed the largest and best-trained fleet in the western Mediterranean, making it difficult for the Romans to maintain and supply forces on the island. The Romans also soon realized that the enemy's main strength and martial pride was invested in the navy, and that the defeat of this would be a far greater blow than any successes achieved on land. In 261 the Republic ordered the construction of a fleet of 100 quinqueremes, or 'fives', and 20 triremes. It was the beginning of a massive programme of ship construction as, through determination in spite of appalling losses to bad weather, the Romans confronted and destroyed Punic naval power.

Battle at sea

The warships in ancient fleets were oared galleys, their narrow hulls carrying a very high number of crewmen in proportion to their size. Although some of the larger ships carried artillery, this was not of sufficient destructive force to sink or cripple an enemy ship. Instead there were two basic methods of naval combat, ramming and boarding.

Every warship was fitted with a metal ram attached to the front of its keel at or just below the waterline. This never formed an actual part of the keel since this would have transferred too much of the force onto the structure of the ramming ship. A ramming attack was best delivered against the side or stern of the target vessel, preferably at a shallow angle since otherwise there was a risk of driving the ram so deeply into the enemy's hull that it would be impossible to extricate it. Instead the aim was to rupture the timbers of the enemy ship. Another method of using the ram was to row at speed along the side of the target vessel, shearing off its oars,

A relief depicting a Roman warship with a line of soldiers on deck. It was common practice before a major battle to embark large numbers of troops on board each galley to strengthen its normal crew, the bulk of whom were rowers. Ships were rowed by men drawn from the poorest classes of citizens or from allies. Only on a handful of desperate occasions were slaves employed in this role.

A bronze ram dating to the 3rd century BC, found off the promontory of Athlit in Israel and now in the Maritime Museum in Haifa. Although from a Hellenistic warship, it is unlikely that the design of Roman rams differed in any significant way. The ram is relatively blunt, since the attacking ship did not wish it to become too firmly embedded into the hull of the target.

but this required an exceptionally high standard of skill from the attacking crew and captain if they were not to suffer damage to their own oars.

Boarding involved coming alongside the enemy ship and firmly grappling it. Then, marines could fight their way on board and seize control. Sheer numbers, aided by skill and aggression, were the decisive factors in this type of fighting. Ramming was best practised by fast, highly manoeuvrable ships and very well trained crews. Boarding favoured larger ships carrying more men.

The *corvus*

In 261 BC the crews of the newly constructed Roman vessels lacked the training of their Carthaginian counterparts, making them clearly slower and far less manoeuvrable. Trusting instead to the legionaries drafted on board to serve as marines, the Romans sought a way to force the enemy to fight on their terms. The result was the raven (*corvus*), an → *p.38*

The corvus *or boarding bridge in action. Having been dropped so that the spike on its end has speared into the deck of a Carthaginian ship, the Roman soldiers flood across the bridge and take the enemy galley by boarding. In spite of its greater skill at seamanship, the Carthaginian navy proved unable to devise a practical response to the* corvus *throughout the First Punic War.*

The Battle of Ecnomus

256 BC

In 264 BC the Roman Senate despatched an army to Sicily and came into direct conflict with the powerful mercantile Empire of Carthage. During the course of this long and costly First Punic War the Romans created a navy to counter the massive Punic fleet. In 256 the rival fleets clashed off the coast of Sicily near Mount Ecnomus as the Carthaginians tried to stop a Roman fleet intent on invading Africa.

The forces

1 The Romans: 330 galleys (mostly quinqueremes or 'fives', but with at least two 'sixes' and probably a number of smaller vessels). Each quinquereme was manned by 300 crew and 120 marines, giving a grand total of some 140,000 men. In command were the consuls Lucius Manlius Vulso and Marcus Atilius Regulus.

2 The Carthaginians: *c.* 350 galleys (again mostly 'fives') carrying some 150,000 men. The fleet was controlled by Hamilcar, the senior commander of all land and sea forces in Sicily.

The fighting

The Roman fleet divided into four squadrons, the first two deployed in a wedge shape, the third behind these, towing transport ships, and the fourth (nicknamed the *triarii*) covering the rear. The Carthaginians formed a wide line angling forward at the point nearest the

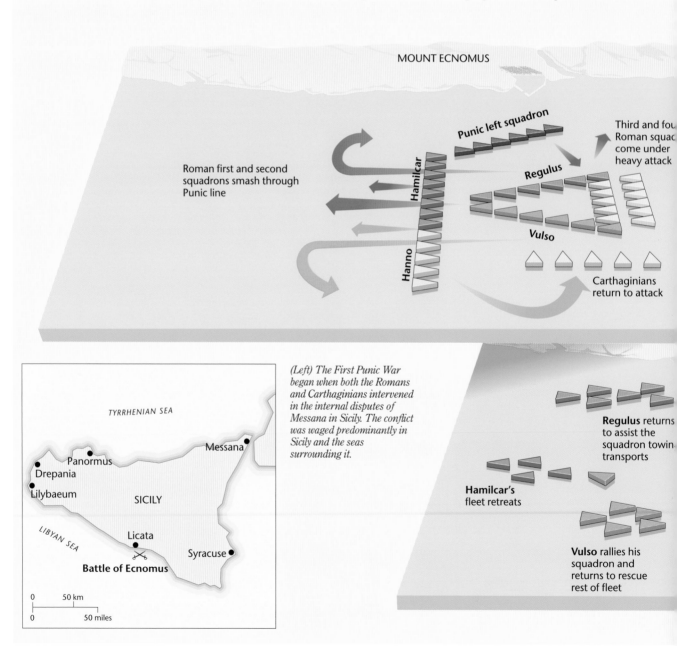

MOUNT ECNOMUS

Roman first and second squadrons smash through Punic line

Punic left squadron

Third and fou[...] Roman squa[...] come under heavy attack

Hamilcar

Regulus

Vulso

Hanno

Carthaginians return to attack

TYRRHENIAN SEA

Messana

Panormus

Drepania

Lilybaeum

SICILY

LIBYAN SEA

Licata

Syracuse

Battle of Ecnomus

0   50 km

0   50 miles

(Left) The First Punic War began when both the Romans and Carthaginians intervened in the internal disputes of Messana in Sicily. The conflict was waged predominantly in Sicily and the seas surrounding it.

Regulus returns to assist the squadron towin[...] transports

Hamilcar's fleet retreats

Vulso rallies his squadron and returns to rescue rest of fleet

coast. Hamilcar hoped to break the Roman fleet up into small groups and allow his faster and more manoeuvrable ships to destroy them separately. The battle opened when the consuls led the first and second Roman squadrons against the Punic line, whose ships at first backed away to draw the enemy on. By the time that the ships came into contact in this area other Carthaginian ships had surrounded the third and fourth Roman squadrons. However, in spite of the success of his plan, Hamilcar's men failed to find an answer to the *corvus* – the boarding bridge carried on the prow of every Roman ship. Whenever a Punic vessel attacked a Roman galley, the *corvus* was dropped to spear through the enemy deck and pin the

A relief from Praeneste, probably dating to the late 1st century BC, depicting a Roman warship crewed by legionaries. Near the prow of the ship is a fighting tower, from which men would be able to throw missiles down onto the enemy deck.

two ships together. In a series of confused actions that developed it was the Romans who had the better of almost every encounter. The consuls managed to keep more control over their ships and at the critical moment led the victorious first and second squadrons back to the aid of the rest of the fleet.

Casualties
1 Roman: 24 ships sunk, but none captured.
2 Carthaginian: 94 ships lost, 30 sunk and 64 captured.

Results
The Roman fleet had won a clear victory, but was for the moment tired and returned to Sicily. Shortly afterwards the invasion force sailed across to Africa unopposed.

◄ Marcus Atillus Regulus (Roman)

◄ Lucius Manilius Vulso (Roman)

◄ Squadron towing transports (Roman)

◄ Triaril or reserve squadron (Roman)

► Punic left squadron (Carthaginian)

► Hamilcar's fleet (Carthaginian)

► Hanno's fleet (Carthaginian)

MOUNT ECNOMUS

Fourth Roman squadron under attack

Hanno's fleet retreat after interception by Vulso's squadrons

innovative type of boarding bridge which was fitted to each Roman vessel. These consisted of a walkway, one end of which was hoisted to the top of a mast-like pole mounted on the deck. Beneath this raised end was an iron spike. When an enemy ship came close, or delivered a ramming attack, the corvus was dropped, the spike impaling the planks of the enemy deck. Firmly pinned and unable to escape, the enemy ship was then promptly boarded by Roman legionaries and captured. From its first appearance at the battle of Mylae in 260 BC the *corvus* proved spectacularly successful. Unable to find a means of dealing with this new tactic, the Carthaginian navy suffered defeat after defeat, managing to win only a single important battle in two decades of conflict. In the end the Romans abandoned the boarding bridge, and it has been plausibly conjectured that its weight made the Roman vessels unseaworthy and contributed to the appalling losses they suffered as a result of bad weather. By the time that this occurred the *corvus* had already served its purpose, for the Roman navy had gained valuable experience. In the final, decisive battle of the First Punic War, at the Aegates Islands in 241 BC, it was the Roman crews who displayed superior training and handled their ships far better than a weary Punic enemy.

Oared warships

There is still much that we do not understand about the oared warships of the Classical world. Remains of such vessels, as opposed to merchant ships, which were often primarily powered by sails, are exceptionally rare, only two examples found off the coast of Massala (ancient Lilybaeum) in Sicily being known from the entire period covered by this book. Classes of warship were named after the

(Below) A carved relief from a sarcophagus showing a heavily stylized version of a naval battle. In many ways battles at sea were even harder for a sculptor to depict accurately than land battles.

(Right) A photograph showing the reconstructed trireme or 'three' Olympias at sea. By the time of the First Punic War such vessels had been relegated to a supporting or scouting role, and the principal warship was the larger and heavier quinquereme or 'five'.

number in the basic team of rowers managing a set of oars on one side of the vessels. Therefore a trireme or 'three' had three banks of oars each rowed by a single oarsman, sitting on benches one above the other. Following the construction of a full-scale replica of a trireme and its extensive sea trials, we know more about this type of warship than any other. The reconstructed trireme proved exceptionally manoeuvrable as well as fast, capable of a speed of 8 knots in short bursts, such as would be suitable for delivering a ramming attack, or under sail.

Triremes were ramming vessels par excellence, but by the time of the Punic Wars these were too small to stand in the main line of battle and had been replaced by quinqueremes or 'fives'. The design of these vessels is still a subject of debate, but they were clearly higher, probably a little → *p.42*

The Battle of Cannae

2 August 216 BC

Part of a century long-struggle between Rome and Carthage, the Second Punic War (218–201 BC) began when the Carthaginian general Hannibal invaded Italy. He defeated a Roman army at Trebia in 218, and in the following year ambushed and destroyed another at Lake Trasimene. In 216 the Roman Republic mustered an unprecedentedly large number of soldiers to confront the enemy at Cannae.

The forces

1 The Romans: eight legions and eight allied *alae* totalling 80,000 infantry and 6,000 cavalry under the command of the two consuls, Lucius Aemilius Paullus and Marcus Terentius Varro.
2 The Carthaginians: 40,000 infantry – a mixture of Libyans, Spaniards and Gauls – and 10,000 Numidian, Spanish and Gallic cavalry under the command of Hannibal.

Phase one

The Romans were aware that Hannibal's cavalrymen were significantly superior to their own horsemen in both numbers and quality. Therefore, they chose a narrow battlefield between the River Aufidius and the high ground around the abandoned town of Cannae. This was intended to protect their flanks from envelopment by the enemy cavalry. The battle was to be won by the heavy infantry in the centre, and these were massed in a very dense and deep formation, abandoning the normal flexible manipular tactics.

Hannibal hoped to turn the Romans' own strength against them. His heavy cavalry was massed on the left, facing the Roman horse. On the right he stationed his Numidian light cavalry, with orders to keep the opposing allied horsemen occupied by skirmishing with them. The main line consisted of the Spanish and Gallic foot, with the centre advanced to draw the Roman infantry quickly into the attack. Behind each flank of this line was stationed a body of highly disciplined Libyan foot, who were equipped with captured Roman weapons.

Phase two

The fighting opened with indecisive skirmishing in front of the main lines. Then, the Punic heavy cavalry led by Hasdrubal charged and smashed through the Roman horsemen led by Paullus. In the meantime the Roman infantry had made contact with the Spanish and

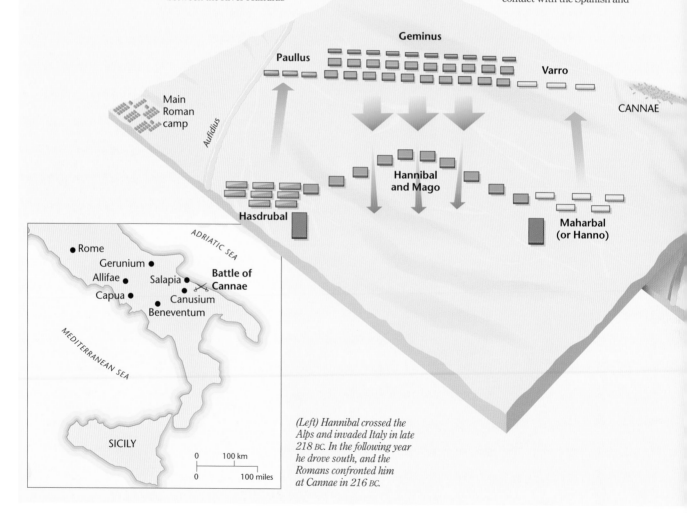

(Left) Hannibal crossed the Alps and invaded Italy in late 218 BC. In the following year he drove south, and the Romans confronted him at Cannae in 216 BC.

Gallic foot. After a struggle the Carthaginian foot in the advanced centre of the line gave way under the massive pressure. The legionaries streamed through the gap, all formation and order being lost as the troops degenerated into a huge crowd. Suddenly this mob was attacked on either flank by the Libyans, giving time for the Gauls and Spaniards to rally and rejoin the fight. The Romans were stopped in their tracks, unable to react to this new threat. Meanwhile, Hasdrubal had rallied his cavalry and moved round behind the Roman line to attack the allied horsemen in the rear, driving them from the field. He then turned his men against the rear of the Roman infantry. These were surrounded and, in a prolonged and bloody fight, massacred. The Roman army was virtually destroyed.

Casualties

1 Roman: 45,500 infantry and 2,700 cavalry killed, along with the consul Aemilius Paullus, and some 18,700 captured.
2 Carthaginian: c. 5,700–8,000 men killed.

Results

Cannae was an appalling disaster for the Romans, which led to the defection to the enemy of most of their allies in southern Italy. However, Hannibal was unable to turn his tactical victory into long-term strategic success, and the Romans continued to resist, eventually winning the war.

A bust that purports to show Hannibal in later life. At Cannae the Carthaginian general was still a young man, although disease had already robbed him of the use of one eye.

HANNIBAL (c. 247–188 BC)

The eldest son of Hamilcar Barca who had fought with some success against the Romans in the First Punic War (265–241 BC), Hannibal is said to have inherited his father's enmity towards Rome. When the Second Punic War began, Hannibal led an army from his base in Spain through Gaul and across the Alps into Italy. Once there he inflicted a series of devastating defeats on the Romans at Trebbia in 218 and Trasimene in 217 as well as Cannae in 216. These victories persuaded much of southern Italy to defect to Carthage, but in spite of this Hannibal was unable to force Rome to seek peace. For more than a decade his army remained in Italy and was never defeated in a serious action, but in 203 he was recalled to defend Carthage itself from a Roman invasion. In the following year he was beaten by Scipio Africanus at the battle of Zama and the Carthaginians were forced to make peace.

After the war, Hannibal's skilful administration contributed much to his city's rapid economic recovery, but eventually he was forced into exile by political rivals supported by the renewed antipathy of the Roman Senate. He became a mercenary commander at the court of the Seleucid King Antiochus III, but was given a subordinate role in the latter's unsuccessful war with Rome. Forced to flee, his steps dogged by Roman agents, one of the greatest generals of Antiquity was finally forced to take his own life.

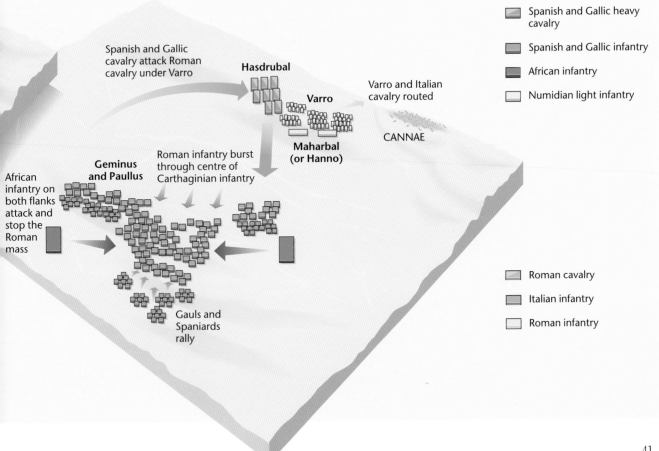

Spanish and Gallic heavy cavalry

Spanish and Gallic infantry

African infantry

Numidian light infantry

Spanish and Gallic cavalry attack Roman cavalry under Varro

Hasdrubal

Varro

Varro and Italian cavalry routed

CANNAE

Maharbal (or Hanno)

Roman infantry burst through centre of Carthaginian infantry

Geminus and Paullus

African infantry on both flanks attack and stop the Roman mass

Gauls and Spaniards rally

Roman cavalry

Italian infantry

Roman infantry

(Above) A wall-painting from Pompeii, giving one of the best views of warships manoeuvring at sea. Rams are visible at the waterline of each vessel, and the decks are packed with shielded infantrymen.

(Right) A coin minted in 49 BC depicting a warship. The vessel is shown with sail hoisted and oars extended, but it would normally have only used a single means of propulsion at one time. During the sea trials of Olympias, the trireme proved capable of making 8 knots under sail. Similar speeds could be achieved by the rowers in short bursts, but a steady cruise of 4 knots could be maintained for long periods of time.

broader and perhaps somewhat longer than triremes. The most probable distribution of the team of five rowers has them working three banks of oars, two men on each of the highest and middle bank and a single man wielding the lowest bank. Quinqueremes were less manoeuvrable than triremes, but their larger hulls were stronger and they were capable of carrying substantially larger complements of marines. At the battle of Ecnomus in 256 BC, Polybius tells us that the Roman quinqueremes were crewed by 300 men, probably about 20 deck crew and the remainder rowers, and carried 120 marines.

The Greek historian also claims that the first Roman quinqueremes were copied directly from a Carthaginian warship which had run aground and been captured, the first fleet being built in just 60 days. Although sometimes in the past dismissed as unlikely, this story has recently received strong support from the discovery of the remains of two small Punic warships on the seabed off Sicily. The timbers of the better-preserved ship revealed much about its construction. Numbers, and letters from the Punic alphabet, had been marked along the keel showing where the ribs were to be placed, and other instructions marked where joints or cuts should be made. This ship was clearly the product of a highly organized system of mass production to a standard design. It was probably this technique, as much as the particular sailing qualities of the vessel, that the Romans copied.

Naval strategy

With such a large crew in proportion to its size, the oared warship had a very limited strategic range.

There was very little space for carrying provisions, especially of fresh water which would be needed in great quantities by rowers labouring in the heat of a Mediterranean summer. Neither the rowers, nor any marines carried on board, could be allowed to move around much during a voyage without seriously upsetting the ship's trim, for the men's weight formed a significant proportion of the ballast. For these reasons it was rare for ancient fleets to remain at sea for much more than three days. Instead they would either put into port or beach their vessels, allowing the crews to rest and provisions to be taken on board. Control of good harbours, or at the very least of the coastline, was vital if naval power was to be projected over any distance.

The Militia Army: Triumphs and Decline

The militia system worked well until the middle of the 2nd century BC. It had two great advantages over rival military systems. The first was manpower. As the Romans had expanded throughout Italy their citizen population had grown. Some communities were eventually granted citizenship, whilst others received Latin or lesser status but still had an obligation to provide troops. Polybius claims that just before the war with Hannibal, the Roman Republic and its allies had over 700,000 men registered as of the age and with sufficient property to serve in the army. Only a proportion of these men was recruited at any one time, but these huge reserves of manpower allowed the Republic to absorb the appalling losses of the Second Punic War and still emerge victorious. No other contemporary state could have done this and time after time the Romans forced enemies to capitulate after inflicting far lower losses upon them. The second great advantage of the militia system was the willingness of Roman citizens and allies to submit to the army's discipline and formal command structure. When first recruited the legions and *alae* required extensive training. The longer that a Roman army remained in service, the more efficient it became. The armies of the last years of the Second Punic War and the next few decades were composed of very experienced and well-trained men, the match in battle for any professional soldiers.

Yet the militia system also had its weaknesses, chief amongst these being its essential impermanence. Veteran armies were discharged at the end of a conflict and each time a new army was raised it had to be trained and gain years of experience before it reached the peak of efficiency. There was no real way of preserving experience, since even if men were enrolled again they would not be serving with the same comrades, under the same officers and in the same units as before. Many of Rome's defeats were due to consuls giving battle with recently raised and insufficiently trained armies. At the same time the system had no real place for specialist troops or officers, such as those required for engineering or siege works. The army showed little aptitude for besieging cities in this period.

Expansion outside Italy brought problems of its own. Wars were now being fought further and further afield and might last for many years, whilst several overseas provinces required permanent garrisons. The farmers who formed the bulk of recruits for the main battle lines of the legions were taken from their land for years on end, causing great hardship and sometimes even ruin. Military service might now mean a decade of garrison duty and savage skirmishing in Spain with little glory or personal gain attached, instead of a swift and profitable campaign in Italy. Service was becoming less attractive and at the same time the Romans believed that the number of men eligible for service was declining. On several occasions the minimum

property qualification was reduced without significantly stopping this trend. A period of comparative peace between 180 and 155 BC reduced the collective experience of the pool of men available to lead and serve in the legions. The Romans remained confident, convinced that their victory was inevitable in any war and forgetting the hard preparation and careful training which had underlain earlier triumphs. From the middle of the 2nd century nearly every conflict began with Roman disasters, many of them humiliating. The Romans still won all of these conflicts, despatching more troops and more resources to the area until the enemy was overwhelmed, but the militia system was clearly coping badly with the new situation. Ultimately this was to lead to the abandonment of the militia system and the creation of the professional army.

Although carved sarcophagi frequently include scenes of a martial nature, artistic convention ensured that these were rarely accurate. This view of a cavalryman shows him wearing a muscled cuirass and ornate Attic helmet. It is extremely unlikely that such equipment was worn by more than a handful of senior officers.

The great struggles with Carthage and the Hellenistic powers were fought and won by Rome's militia army, but during the 2nd century BC this system of recruitment came under growing pressure. The acquisition of overseas provinces created a demand for large permanent garrisons and meant that many of the part-time legionaries were required to spend a decade or more in continuous military service. This interruption from normal life could easily spell ruin to one of the yeoman farmers who had traditionally made up the bulk of citizens eligible for military call-up. The Romans themselves began to worry that this class was in decline, and their fears for the future grew as a series of wars began with defeats and were only won after very hard struggles. Eventually the Republic was forced to abandon the militia system in favour of a professional army, recruited overwhelmingly from the poorest citizens. The change has sometimes been associated with the great commander Caius Marius, but may actually have happened far more gradually. Whether the change occurred as a result of long-term trends or sudden reform, it profoundly altered the character of the legions. Military service became a career which lasted for much of a man's adult life, so that soldiers were increasingly separated from civilians. Legionaries ceased to be men of property, which meant that they had no source of livelihood once the army no longer required their services, and many proved willing to fight for their commanders against other Roman armies. Prolonged periods of civil war in the 1st century BC resulted in the collapse of the Republic, which was replaced by a form of monarchy known as the Principate.

Under the Principate the process of creating a professional army was completed. All troops now served in permanent units, many of which existed for many centuries. The rank and file were professional soldiers who spent 25 years with the colours, but in many of the more senior ranks aspects of the old militia system survived. Officers from the senatorial and equestrian classes commanded legions and auxiliary units respectively. Most senators in particular spent only part of their public career with the army, interweaving this with civil posts in the traditional manner.

Detail from a relief found in Rome and probably dating to the early 2nd century BC showing a parade of Praetorian guardsmen. The men wear ornate classically styled helmets, muscled cuirasses, and carry heavily decorated shields.

II   The Professional Army

The Post-Marian Roman Army

Marius and the *capite censi*

The creation of a professional army has often been attributed to Caius Marius. In 107 BC he was elected consul and sent to replace the commander in the Numidian war in spite of strong opposition from the Senate. Denied the right to raise new legions to strengthen the army in Africa, Marius was only permitted to take volunteers with him. In an unprecedented move, he appealed to the poorest citizens, men who lacked sufficient possessions to qualify for military service. These, the 'head count' (*capite censi*), responded with enthusiasm and proved themselves to be fine soldiers. The link between property and military service was broken for ever, recruits now needed only to be citizens and came increasingly from the poor.

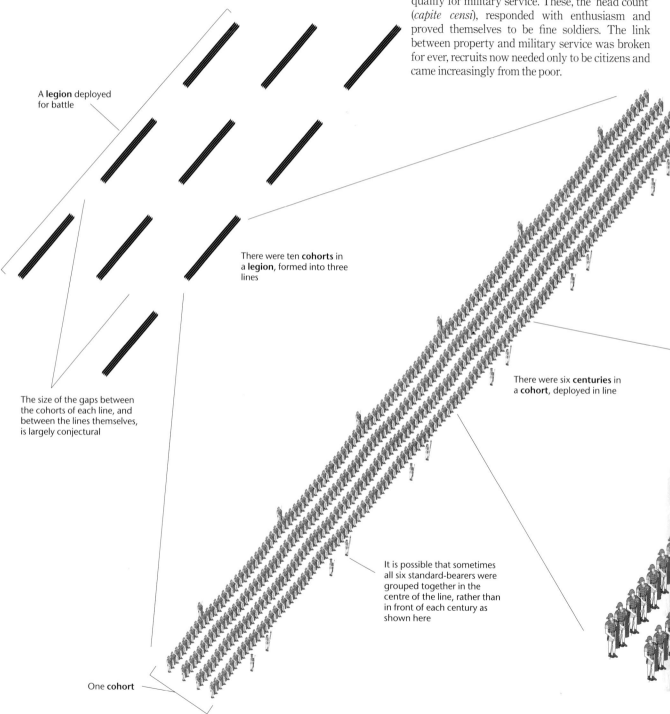

A **legion** deployed for battle

There were ten **cohorts** in a **legion**, formed into three lines

The size of the gaps between the cohorts of each line, and between the lines themselves, is largely conjectural

There were six **centuries** in a **cohort**, deployed in line

It is possible that sometimes all six standard-bearers were grouped together in the centre of the line, rather than in front of each century as shown here

One **cohort**

The change may not have been quite as sudden as this. Some scholars argue that Marius merely made open admission of a practice that was already common. Certainly the minimum qualification for service had been lowered, and there is a little evidence for poorer volunteers serving with the legions in many campaigns and effectively becoming career soldiers, although we do not know how many of these men there were. Even so, Marius' reform was certainly an important stage in the transition from militia to professional army. Soon afterwards the last great rebellion of Rome's Italian allies, an extremely brutal conflict known as the Social War, led to the granting of citizenship to virtually all of the communities south of the River Po. The *alae* disappeared, and now all troops were recruited into legions organized in the same way.

The new legions

Although many of the traditions of the militia legions were preserved, the new professional or semi-professional units were fundamentally differ-ent in their spirit and tactics. The new legions were much more permanent, keeping the same name and number throughout their existence. In the past each legion had carried five standards, an eagle, horse, bull, wolf and boar, but Marius gave each legion a single silver eagle as its standard. Legionaries who viewed the army as a career, not simply as an interruption to normal life, came to identify very strongly with their legion, and these units developed tremendous corporate spirit. Skilful leaders such as Caesar would play on soldiers' pride in their legions and rivalry with other units in the army.

Soldiers no longer provided their own equipment, instead being issued with weapons, armour and clothing by the state. The differences between the various classes in the legion vanished, the cavalry and light infantry disappearing with them. All legionaries were now heavy infantrymen, armed alike with *pilum* and *gladius*. The men were still organized into centuries, though these were now all 80-men strong, and a pair of centuries composed a maniple. However, the maniple was replaced as the basic tactical unit by the larger cohort. This consisted of three maniples, one from each of the old lines, whose names were preserved in the titles of the centurions, and mustered 480 men as 'paper strength'. Allied contingents had been organized into cohorts for some time, and Polybius twice mentions the formation in use with the legions in Spain during the Second Punic War. On one of these occasions he seems to say that a cohort consisted of three maniples, although the text is a little ambiguous. It may be that cohort was the term employed for any temporary unit larger than a maniple but smaller than a legion. It is also possible that conditions in Spain encouraged its use at certain times by the legions fighting there, but there is no good reason to believe that all legions at all times were organized into cohorts as well as maniples before Marius.

The cohort offered several advantages over the same number of men organized into maniples. In the first place it was a unit used to working together and must certainly have had its own commander, although none of our sources tell us this explicitly. He was most probably one of the six centurions commanding the centuries. One or several cohorts made up a coherent and effective detachment if a force was required for an operation not sufficiently large to warrant the use of an entire legion. In battle, the legion still most commonly deployed into the *triplex acies* formation, four cohorts in the front line and three in the middle and rear lines. However, each cohort was the same size and carried identical equipment. Such a legion could just as easily form in two or four lines if this suited the tactical situation. It was also far easier for a commander to control, since now he had only to convey his instruc-

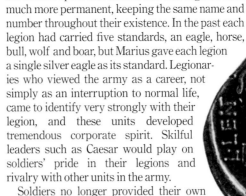

A silver denarius *minted in 49 BC showing a legionary eagle (*aquila*) flanked by two century standards (*signa*). Marius is credited with having given each legion a single eagle as its principal standard.*

One **century** of 80 men, deployed in four ranks. The greater size of individual centuries made them better suited to independent operations than the smaller maniples of the earlier period

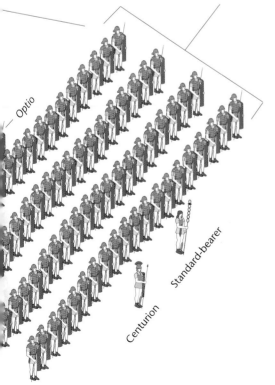

Optio

Centurion

Standard-bearer

(Left) A legion of 10 cohorts deployed for battle. All cohorts were equipped and trained to fight in the same way, which meant that they did not have to occupy a fixed position to be effective.

47

tions to 10 cohort commanders instead of the leaders of 30 maniples. Cohorts were not forced to move only with the rest of the line, but could be shifted as individual units. The legion of 10 cohorts was far more flexible tactically and strategically than its predecessor the manipular legion.

Professionalism and the new permanence of the legions brought other advantages. Experience and technical knowledge was more easily preserved and passed on to the next generation instead of being lost each time the army was disbanded. During the 1st century BC the Roman army first began to display a mastery of engineering works unrivalled by any of its opponents. Legions contained specialists and skilled craftsmen as well as soldiers who willingly provided a labour force. Julius Caesar's army included men capable of building a bridge across the Rhine, of constructing and repairing a fleet of ships, of building ramps and engines to storm Avaricum or lines of fortification to blockade Alesia into submission during his Gallic campaigns. These craftsmen were only formed into separate teams for the duration of a task, otherwise remaining dispersed throughout the cohorts and performing the same duties as the other soldiers.

The best legions produced by the militia system, hardened by long service and trained by experienced officers, had been very good indeed, perhaps as confident and tactically skilled as even the finest of the later professional legions. However, the new professional units were on average better trained and disciplined than their predecessors, simply because they were more permanent. The Romans believed that it took many years of successful fighting for a unit to reach the peak of its efficiency. One of Caesar's officers contrasted a legion in its eighth

campaign in Gaul and showing great promise, but still not quite as good as the veteran units of the army.

Under gifted and ambitious commanders the well-trained professional legions undertook the most intensive period of conquest in Rome's history. Lacking integral light infantry or cavalry, Roman armies now relied on allies, often locally raised to provide these supporting arms, but it was always on the legions that the brunt of any operation fell. Men such as Marius, Sulla, Pompey, Lucullus and Caesar demonstrated the flexibility of the cohort legions time and again. In Europe, North Africa and the Near East the Romans took on very different, and often far more numerous, enemies and destroyed them, often with contemptuous ease. Overconfidence contributed much to the disaster at Carrhae in 53 BC, when Crassus' army was virtually destroyed by the Parthians.

Professional officers

The legion of 10 cohorts still lacked a permanent commander. However, it became increasingly common for one of the governor's deputies (*legati*) to be placed in charge. When fighting the German King Ariovistus in 58 BC, Caesar placed his *quaestor* and five *legati* in command of his six legions. The *quaestor* was an elected magistrate, a senator at an early stage in his career who was supposed to administer the finances of the province and act as the governor's deputy. The *legati* were not elected but chosen by the governor from amongst his family, friends and political allies. Some of these might be former governors and army commanders, providing experienced, if still temporary, leadership at this level.

There were also still six tribunes in each legion. Some of these were still young, inexperienced aristocrats embarking on a political career, but an increasing proportion were from the equestrian order (the class was named after its original role as cavalrymen). Many of the latter were as professional as the men in the ranks, for it seems to have become common to serve over long periods of time. The frequency of foreign wars and the not-uncommon outbreak of civil conflict in the 1st century BC allowed many officers to see almost continual service.

Another important factor in preserving collected experience and skill in the army was the rise of the professional centurion. Although Polybius commented on the care taken to select determined fighters to fill the ranks of the centurionate, it is only in the Late Republic that these men become more prominent. In Caesar's narrative of his own campaigns, it is the centurions more than any other grade of officer who receive attention and praise, both collectively and as named individuals. Men like Sextus Baculus in Gaul and Crastinus at the battle of Pharsalus in Greece (48 BC, where Caesar defeated Pompey) are depicted as heroic figures, who inspired the soldiers under their command. On several occasions Caesar notes that he promoted gallant centurions from lower grades in veteran legions to higher positions in recently raised units. Only once in the entire Caesarian Corpus is a man specifically mentioned as having risen to the centurionate from the ranks of the legions, and the individual in question was serving with Pompey not Caesar. Otherwise we have no real clue to the selection of these officers and whether they entered the army as officers or were promoted from the ranks. What is clear is that once a man joined the centurionate, he became an individual of some status and in time often wealth.

Professional soldiers

The post-Marian army was in many ways a more flexible and effective force than its predecessor. Its relationship with the Republic was also very different. To a great extent the old militia army had been the entire state and people under arms. Men were granted varying degrees of political influence in relation to the capacity with which they served in the army. Military service was sometimes glorious and sometimes profitable, but generations of citizens were willing to serve out of a sense of duty to the Republic with which they strongly identified. In essence the old hoplite ideal was preserved, since the men fighting for the state were the ones who had a greatest stake in it.

The professional soldiers came overwhelmingly from the poorest classes, whose direct political influence was negligible. The army fed and clothed such men, giving them an income and a sense of purpose. All of this was lost as soon as they were discharged. The Senate refused to acknowledge that the army was no longer a militia of the propertied classes, instead of a force of soldiers dependent on the army for a livelihood. The soldiers therefore now looked to their commanders to provide them with some means of support, usually a grant of farmland, when they returned to civilian life. A good general, one who had campaigned long and successfully with an army, especially one who was a gifted leader, was now able to create an army whose loyalty was to himself far more than the state which ignored the soldiers' problems. It is a striking feature of the Late Republic that the times of greatest conquest were intermeshed with recurrent civil wars. Legion turned against legion with much the same ruthless efficiency that they had shown fighting foreign opponents. The great conquerors were the major leaders in these internal conflicts, as time and again legions were marched on Rome to seize political power by force. The professional army was a major factor in making possible the upheavals which in time destroyed the Republican system of government and led to the creation of the Principate, a monarchy in all but name.

A memorial commemorating Marcus Caelius Rufus, a senior centurion of Legio XIIX, and two of his freedmen. Caelius was killed at the age of 53 when his legion and two others under the command of Publius Quinctilius Varus were ambushed and destroyed in Germany in AD 9. The inscription concludes by granting permission for his remains to be deposited here if they were ever found.

The Army of the Principate

The legions

By the death of Rome's first Emperor, Augustus, in AD 14 the Roman army had become a fully professional and permanent institution. The heart of the army remained the legions, many of which would endure for centuries, vanishing only when destroyed in action or, more rarely, disbanded in disgrace. Augustus had inherited a force of over 60 legions by the end of the civil wars, but reduced this to 28. This total was only to fluctuate a little above or below 30 for the next 300 years. Each legion was given a number and most rapidly acquired names and titles as well. The system was never entirely logical, suggesting that there was strong resistance from some existing legions to give up their identity. As a result several numbers were duplicated and there were no fewer than three third legions. The situation became even more apparently confusing as later emperors raised new legions in sequences starting at 'one'. Under Augustus the highest-numbered legion was XXII Deiotariana. This had an unusual origin, since it was formed from the army of the Galatian King Deiotarus, who had equipped, organized and trained his soldiers on the Roman model. The original recruits appear to have been given Roman citizenship, but soon the legion was recruited from men who already possessed the franchise and treated in exactly the same way as all the other legions. Other unit titles preserved some trace of their origins. Three legions, X, XIII and XIV, were known as Gemina or 'Twin', suggesting that they were originally formed by the amalgamation of two units.

Some legions had developed a distinct identity and reputation in the post-Marian army, but the Augustan reforms institutionalized this trend. Their names sometimes expressed martial virtues, such as Ferrata (Ironsides) or Fulminata (Thunderer), or commemorated regions where the unit had presumably served with distinction. Traditions were now passed within a legion from one generation of soldiers to the next. Legionaries were proud of their unit and contemptuous of others. The standards and the symbols on men's shields, as well quite possibly as other peculiarities of dress and routine, made each legion unique. Even on short inscriptions, and especially on important ones such as epitaphs, legionaries usually mention their legion. Emperors carefully granted the right to titles to win the favour of their soldiers. Therefore after their prominent role in the defeat of Boudicca in AD 60, Nero added the names Martia Victrix (Mar's own, the Victorious) to the full title of Legio XIV Gemina. Trajan, whose full name was Marcus Ulpius Traianus, named Legion XXX Ulpia Victrix. Not all honours were won in war, Claudius granting the title Claudia pia fidelis (Claudius' own, pious and faithful) to Legio VII Macedonica and Legio XI when they refused to follow their commander in an attempted coup.

There had been no set term of service even after the Marian reforms, although the traditional maximum of 16 campaigns or years may have continued to apply. Legions sometimes served for the duration of a conflict, but many remained in garrison at a war's end. Augustus established the length of service in his new, permanent legions as 16 years with a further four as a veteran. Veterans remained with their legion, but were excused guard duty and fatigues and in theory only obliged to fight in defence of the legion's base or camp. However, a shortage of recruits resulted, later in Augustus' reign, in the extension of service to 20 years with an additional five as a veteran. Although the change was at first bitterly resented, it remained standard throughout the Principate.

Under Augustus the command structure of the legion was laid out more clearly and a permanent commander appointed. This was the *legatus legionis*, a senator, usually in his early 30s. The second-in-command was the only other senator in the unit, the *tribunus laticlavius*, a man usually in his late teens or early 20s and with little or no prior military experience. Third-in-command was the *praefectus castrorum*, or Camp Prefect, who was an experienced former chief centurion and had probably spent most of his adult life in the army. The Prefect seems to have been responsible for many aspects of administration which required some technical knowledge. There were also five tribunes recruited from the equestrian order, *tribuni angusticlavii*, who performed whatever tasks were allocated to them but commanded no specific section of the legion. Beneath these were the centurions, six to each cohort, whose titles preserved the

Roman soldiers had a sum annually deducted from their pay to provide for the costs of funeral ceremonies. However, this charge does not seem to have covered anything more than the most rudimentary of markers for the grave, and many individuals set additional money aside to pay for more substantial memorials. Even a simple, unadorned inscription like this would have represented a sizeable investment.

Legions of the Principate

Legion	Formed	Destroyed/disbanded	Notes
I Germanica	Late Republic	dis. AD 70	Disbanded after Civilis' revolt
I Adiatrix pia fidelis	Nero		Originally formed from men drafted from the fleet
I Italica	Nero		Raised in Italy. All the original recruits are supposed to have been 1.8 m (6 ft) tall
I Macriana	Nero	dis. AD 69–70	Short-lived, civil war legion
I Flavia Minervia pia fidelis	Domitian		Titles awarded for loyalty to Domitian
I Parthica	Severus		Raised for his Parthian expedition
II Augusta	Late Republic/ Augustus		Probably originally called Gallica
II Adiatrix pia fidelis	Nero		Originally formed from men drafted from the fleet
II Italica	M. Aurelius		Probably formed in AD 165
II Parthica	Severus		Raised for his Parthian expedition
II Traiana fortis	Trajan		'Strong', probably awarded for service in Dacia
III Augusta pia fidelis	Late Republic/ Augustus		
III Cyrenaica	Late Republic		
III Gallica	Caesar		
III Italica concors	M. Aurelius		'United', probably formed in AD 165
III Parthica	Severus		Raised for his Parthian expedition
IIII Macedonica	Caesar	dis. AD 70	Disbanded for defection to Civilis
IIII Flavia felix	Vespasian		'Lucky', formed from the legions disbanded in AD 70
IIII Scythica	M. Antony?		
V Alaudae	Caesar	dstr. under Domitian?	The 'Larks', originally raised in Transalpine Gaul
V Macedonica	Late Republic		
VI Ferrata fidelis constans	Caesar		The 'Ironsides', faithful and constant
VI Victrix	Late Republic		'Victorious'
VII Claudia pia fidelis	Caesar		Given titles for remaining loyal to Claudius in AD 42
VII Gemina	Galba		'Twin' – probably reformed from two legions c. AD 70
VIII Augusta	Late Republic		
IX (or VIIII) Hispana	Late Republic	dstr. under Hadrian?	Possibly destroyed during the Bar Kochba rebellion in Judaea
X Fretensis	Late Republic		Fretensis was the strait between Italy and Sicily
X Gemina	Caesar		'Twin', formed from amalgamation of two units
XI Claudia pia fidelis	Late Republic		Given titles for remaining loyal to Claudius in AD 42
XII Fulminata	Caesar		The 'lightening-thrower'
XIII Gemina pia fidelis	Late Republic		'Twin', formed from amalgamation of two units
XIV Gemina Martia Victrix	Late Republic		Another 'twin'. Other titles awarded for supressing Boudicca's revolt in AD 60–61
XV Apollinaris	Augustus		Augustus claimed a special relationship with the god Apollo
XV Primigenia	Caligula	dis. AD 70	Disbanded for defection to Civilis
XVI Gallica	Augustan	dis. AD 70	Disbanded for defection to Civilis
XVI Flavia Firma	Vespasian		Reformed as new unit from XVI Gallica
XVII	Augustus	dstr. AD 9	Destroyed in Germany
XVIII (or XIIX)	Augustus	dstr. AD 9	Destroyed in Germany
XIX	Augustus	dstr. AD 9	Destroyed in Germany
XX Valeria Victrix	Augustus		Probably awarded titles for suppressing the Boudiccan revolt in AD 60–61
XXI Rapax	Augustus	dstr. under Domitian?	'Grasping', i.e. greedy for victory
XXII Deiotariana	Augustus	dstr. under Hadrian?	Formed from the army of the Galatian King Deiotarus
XXII Primigenia pia fidelis	Caligula		
XXX Ulpia Victrix	Trajan		Raised for the Dacian Wars, during which it won the title 'victorious'

traditions of the old manipular legion. In ascending order of seniority these were called *hastatus posterior*, *hastatus prior*, *princeps posterior*, *princeps prior*, *pilus posterior* and *pilus prior*. *Pilus* was an alternative name for *triarius*.

A legion possessed a small cavalry force of some 120 men, but its main fighting strength remained the 10 cohorts. Each consisted on paper of 480 men, divided into six centuries each commanded by a centurion. There were 80 men in a century, divided into ten sections of *contubernia* of eight men. The *contubernium* shared a tent on campaign, and a pair of rooms in a barrack block, living and eating together. Such conditions tended to foster a very → *p.54*

The Defeat of Boudicca

AD 60

In AD 43 the Emperor Claudius invaded Britain. The most serious rebellion the Romans were ever to face in the island came almost a generation later in AD 60. It was led by Boudicca, widow of King Prasutagus of the Iceni tribe (who lived in the area of modern-day Norfolk) and was prompted by the brutal behaviour of certain Roman officials. The Queen rallied many supporters from her own and neighbouring tribes, sacked Camulodunum (Colchester), Verulamium (St Albans) and Londinium (London), and defeated a vexillation of Legio IX Hispana. When the revolt erupted the governor of the province, Caius Suetonius Paulinus, was campaigning in north Wales. He hastily returned and confronted the rebels at an unknown location.

The forces

1 The Romans: most of Legio XIV Gemina and part of Legio XX, supported by auxiliary infantry and cavalry. In total around 10,000 men commanded by the legate Suetonius Paulinus.
2 The Britons: there are no reliable statistics for the British army, but it was evidently several times larger than the Roman force.

Aware that he was heavily outnumbered, but that his men were far superior in training, equipment and discipline, Suetonius Paulinus deployed his army in a defile, with his flanks and rear protected by high ground and woodland. The legions were in the centre, the auxiliary cohorts on either side and the cavalry on

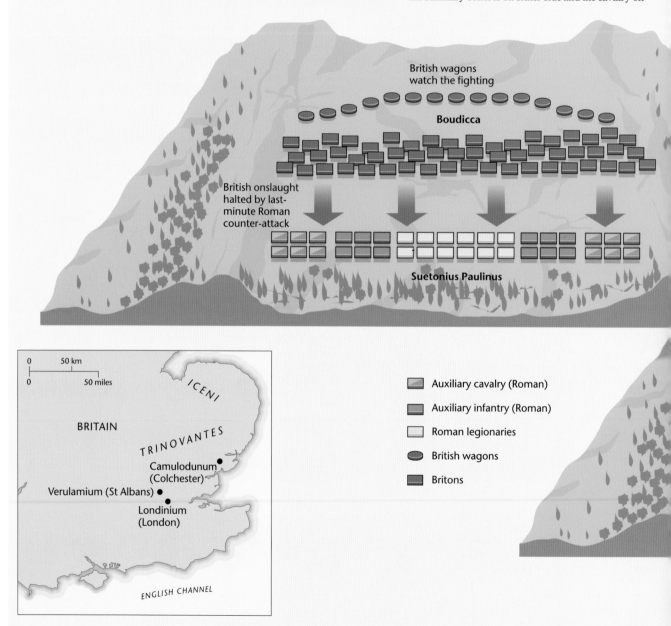

British wagons watch the fighting

Boudicca

British onslaught halted by last-minute Roman counter-attack

Suetonius Paulinus

0 50 km
0 50 miles

ICENI

BRITAIN

TRINOVANTES

Camulodunum (Colchester)

Verulamium (St Albans)

Londinium (London)

ENGLISH CHANNEL

Auxiliary cavalry (Roman)

Auxiliary infantry (Roman)

Roman legionaries

British wagons

Britons

the wings. Boudicca relied on her army's size rather than any subtle tactics to crush the enemy. Behind the massed warriors was a line of wagons, from which the men's wives watched the fighting. The Romans waited for the Britons to advance, but counter-attacked when they were very close. After heavy fighting the Britons were routed with great loss.

Casualties

1 Roman: around 400 killed and somewhat more wounded (*c*. 8–10 per cent).
2 Britons: one source claims as many as 80,000 were killed, and certainly their losses were very heavy.

Results

The rebellion was decisively defeated although further operations were required to stamp out its last embers. Boudicca is believed to have despaired and taken poison.

A heavily romanticized 19th-century statue of Boudicca riding in her scythed chariot.

BOUDICCA (died *c*. AD 60–61)

Boudicca was wife of King Prasutagus of the Iceni, who had made his peace with the Romans soon after the Emperor Claudius invaded Britain in AD 43. British tribes often had more than one king at a time and it is probable that Prasutagus ruled only one section or clan of the Iceni. Boudicca's name was probably derived from Bouda, a Celtic goddess of victory. When Prasutagus died in AD 60 bequeathing his possessions jointly to his daughters and the Emperor Nero, the Roman Procurator Decianus Catus (an official in charge of provincial finances) plundered his kingdom. His men flogged Boudicca and raped her daughters, outrages which immediately prompted rebellion.

The historian Dio Cassius, writing a century and a half later, described Boudicca as very tall, with long red hair, piercing eyes and a harsh voice – a picture which may owe more to the stereotype of the northern barbarian than the Queen's actual appearance. He also says that she habitually wore a many coloured dress (probably tartan or checked), a golden torque around her neck, and a long cloak pinned in place with a brooch.

Britons retreat
with huge losses

Roman flanks and
rear protected by
high ground

The Romans gradually
force their way into the
confused mass of Britons

close bond between its members, of the type observable in the small units of modern armies. *Contubernalis* developed as a word for close comrade and was used by officers and men alike. To assist the centurion in running the century he had the same group of subordinate officers (*principales*)

as the old Republican army, the *optio*, *signifer*, and *tesserarius*.

The first cohort appears to have been different. At the very least by the later 1st century AD, some, and perhaps all, legions had a first cohort broken into five instead of six centuries. Each century was

Legionaries in the Teutoburg Wald, AD 9

At the end of the 1st century BC the Emperor Augustus' commanders undertook the conquest of a new province of Germany, covering the area between the Rhine and the Elbe. However, in AD 9 a major rebellion was led by Arminius, a chieftain of the Cherusci tribe. Feigning loyalty to Rome until the last minute, he led the provincial legate, Publius Quinctilius Varus, into an ambush. The Roman army – consisting of Legiones XVII, XIIX and XIX, supported by three cavalry *alae* and six infantry cohorts of auxiliaries – was lured into the woods and

marshes of the Teutoburg Wald where it was destroyed in several days of bitter fighting. Varus committed suicide before the end and only a handful of his men managed to escape. The loss of a tenth of the entire Roman army proved a terrible blow to the ageing Augustus, who is said to have wandered around his palace banging his head against the walls and shouting out 'Quinctilius Varus, give me back my legions!' Although other Roman armies were sent against Arminius and inflicted some reverses upon him, they proved unable to recover the lost province.

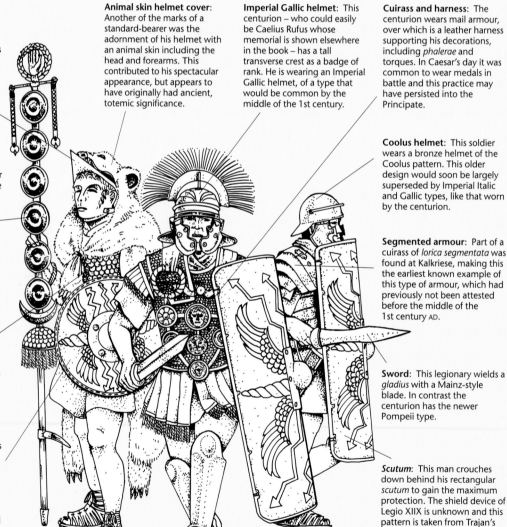

Masked helmet: Although conventionally dismissed as parade armour, a face mask from a helmet was found at Kalkriese suggesting that it was worn in battle. The tombstone of one *signifer* appears to show him wearing such a helmet.

Signum: The essential design of the century standard appears to have changed little over the centuries. The number of discs may have indicated the identity of the century, while the hand was perhaps originally associated with the maniple. Notice the projecting hand grip low down on the shaft. Standards were often planted in the ground and it required some force to pull them out again.

Scale armour: This *signifer* wears a cuirass of bronze scales. When polished such armour would contribute to the splendid appearance of the man carrying this symbol of the century's pride.

Shield: Roman army standards were heavy objects, especially the *signa* which often carried large amounts of decoration. It was therefore impractical for a standard-bearer to carry a normal-sized *scutum*, and they instead seem often to have had a small round shield.

Animal skin helmet cover: Another of the marks of a standard-bearer was the adornment of his helmet with an animal skin including the head and forearms. This contributed to his spectacular appearance, but appears to have originally had ancient, totemic significance.

Imperial Gallic helmet: This centurion – who could easily be Caelius Rufus whose memorial is shown elsewhere in the book – has a tall transverse crest as a badge of rank. He is wearing an Imperial Gallic helmet, of a type that would be common by the middle of the 1st century.

Cuirass and harness: The centurion wears mail armour, over which is a leather harness supporting his decorations, including *phalerae* and torques. In Caesar's day it was common to wear medals in battle and this practice may have persisted into the Principate.

Coolus helmet: This soldier wears a bronze helmet of the Coolus pattern. This older design would soon be largely superseded by Imperial Italic and Gallic types, like that worn by the centurion.

Segmented armour: Part of a cuirass of *lorica segmentata* was found at Kalkriese, making this the earliest known example of this type of armour, which had previously not been attested before the middle of the 1st century AD.

Sword: This legionary wields a *gladius* with a Mainz-style blade. In contrast the centurion has the newer Pompeii type.

Scutum: This man crouches down behind his rectangular *scutum* to gain the maximum protection. The shield device of Legio XIIX is unknown and this pattern is taken from Trajan's Column.

double the normal strength at 160 men, so that the entire cohort mustered 800. In ascending order of seniority, its centurions were known as *hastatus posterior*, *hastatus*, *princeps posterior*, *princeps*, and *primus pilus*. All of these ranks, and especially the *primus pilus*, enjoyed immense prestige, their holders living in substantial houses rather than barrack rooms in a permanent camp. In the Late Roman manual of Vegetius, the author claims that the men of the first cohort were supposed to be taller than the men of the rest of the legion. A modern suggestion is that the cohort included the legion's veterans. Either way, this might suggest that the first cohort provided a strong, élite force within the legion. Yet the evidence is by no means good enough to tell us whether all legions were reorganized in this way or only some. One possibility is that for reasons of prestige, or perhaps the scale of the local military problem, certain legions were selected to be enlarged in this way.

The professional *auxilia*

The Romans had always relied heavily on allied soldiers to supplement their armies. These were known generally as the *auxilia*, since they aided and supported the citizen legions. In the Mid Republic each legion was supported by an *ala*, and many armies also included contingents of non-Italian allies, often fighting in their native style. Usually these men were drawn from the theatre of operations in which the campaign was being waged. During the Punic Wars Roman armies in Sicily were supplemented by troops from the Greek cities of the region, those in northern Italy received aid from the local Gallic tribes, the forces in Spain usually included large numbers of Iberian and Celtiberian tribesmen, and the final defeat of Hannibal in North Africa owed much to Rome's Numidian allies. Local allies were a useful source of additional numbers, but were often even more important in providing soldiers whose fighting styles were particularly suited to the conditions

A 1st-century AD relief from the headquarters of the legionary fortress at Mainz showing an auxiliary infantryman. He brandishes a javelin in his right hand and has two more held behind his flat oval shield.

of the region. However, such allies were not always reliable, and a major disaster occurred in Spain in 212 BC when a Roman army was abandoned by its Celtiberian allies and then overwhelmed by numerically superior Carthaginian forces.

After the Social War the Italian allies (or *socii*) were absorbed into the legions, reducing the proportion of non-citizen soldiers in most Roman field armies. However, the practice of employing contingents from outside Italy continued and in many ways became more important. The post-Marian legions lacked integral cavalry and light infantry, so it was necessary for commanders to find such troops from other sources. During the campaigns in Gaul, Julius Caesar supported his legions with Gallic, German and Spanish cavalry, and Numidian, Cretan and German skirmishers. One of the reasons for the disaster at Carrhae in 53 BC was that Crassus

Known Auxiliary Regiments

Unit name	Additional titles	Formed	Served
Ala I Brittonum	Veterana civium Romanorum	Domitian?	Pannonia Inferior, Syria?
Cohors I Septimia Belgarum	equitata	late 1st century?	Dalmatia, Germania Inferior*
Cohors I Britannica	Milliaria equitata civium Romanorum	Claudius? Or Domitian	Pannonia, Upper Moesia, Dacia
Cohors I Brittonum	Milliaria Ulpia Torquata Pia Fidelis civium Romanorum	Vespasian?	Noricum, Pannonia, Moesia, Dacia
Cohors II Britannorum	Milliaria civium Romanorum Pia Fidelis	?	Germania Inferior, Moesia, Dacia
Cohors II Flavia Brittonum	equitata	Flavians	Moesia Inferior
Cohors II Augusta Nervia Pacensis	Milliaria Brittonum	Trajan	Pannonia, Dacia
Cohors III Britannorum		Flavian?	Raetia
Cohors III Brittonum	Veterana equitata	Flavian?	Moesia Superior
Cohors VI Brittonum	equitata Pia Fidelis		Cappadocia?

* A British origin for this unit has been suggested, but cannot be proven.

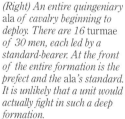

(Right) An entire quingeniary ala of cavalry beginning to deploy. There are 16 turmae of 30 men, each led by a standard-bearer. At the front of the entire formation is the prefect and the ala's standard. It is unlikely that a unit would actually fight in such a deep formation.

lacked sufficient horsemen and missile-armed foot to combat the Parthian horse archers and cataphracts. Very little is known of the allies of this period, so that we cannot tell to what extent these were trained and disciplined. At least some of these units remained essentially the personal followings of a tribal war-leader, fighting for him in the same way that they would have done in inter-tribal warfare.

Under Augustus and his immediate successors, the *auxilia* were turned into a much more regular and professional force. Significantly they were not organized into formations of equivalent size to the legions or old Italian *alae*, but into units of roughly cohort strength. One reason for this was that it was far easier to shift such small units around the Empire as the situation required. Perhaps as importantly, the higher level of the legionary command structure

gave the citizen soldiers a marked advantage in pitched battles should the foreign auxiliaries ever rebel.

There were three types of auxiliary unit – infantry, cavalry and mixed. The infantry were organized into cohorts, either quingenary (500 strong) or milliary (1,000 strong). In spite of their names, a quingenary cohort normally consisted of 480 men divided into six centuries of 80, whilst a milliary

cohort mustered 800 men divided into 10 centuries of 80. The cavalry were also organized into quingenary and milliary units, although in this case these were known as *alae* rather than cohorts. A quingenary *ala* consisted of 512 men divided into 16 troops (*turmae*) of 32 men. A milliary *ala* fielded a formidable total of 768 men in 32 *turmae*. The organization of the mixed units, or *cohortes equitatae*, is far less certain, but the most probable interpretation is that these had the same number of infantrymen as an ordinary cohort and added 120 cavalry and 240 cavalry for a quingeniary and milliary unit respectively. These cavalrymen were not as well mounted or equipped as the men in the specialist cavalry *alae*.

The *auxilia* provided the imperial army with the vast majority of its cavalry. It also provided men armed with longer-ranged missile weapons than the *pilum*, including units of foot and horse archers. There were also slingers amongst the *auxilia*, although as yet we know of no unit exclusively armed with this weapon, and it is possible that small contingents were included in other units. Our literary sources state that some cohorts were lightly armed, although none is specifically attested epigraphically. Most auxiliary infantry were close-order troops who fought in a manner very similar to the legions. They 'supported' the legions more by providing them with extra manpower rather than novel methods of fighting. The smaller units of the *auxilia* were especially useful in providing a cheaper and more flexible force for frontier policing.

A metope from the early 2nd-century AD Tropaeum Traiani at Adamklissi in Romania showing three auxiliary infantrymen. All wear mail, carry oval shields and have swords in their right hands.

Troops stationed in Italy

It was not until the very end of the 2nd century AD that a legion was permanently stationed within Italy itself. Augustus and his successors had not wished their reliance on military support to be too blatant. Nevertheless some troops were required by the emperor in Rome and Italy, and this led to the formation of the praetorian and urban cohorts.

Many Roman commanders had maintained a bodyguard unit known as the praetorian cohort after the headquarters (*praetorium*) in a camp. Augustus maintained such a force even after the end of the civil wars. Its size was kept at nine cohorts of 480 men, just smaller than a legion. At first only three cohorts did duty in Rome at any one time, but under Tiberius all nine cohorts were concentrated in the newly built barracks (the *castra praetoria*) on the edge of the city. Later emperors would also increase the size of each cohort to milliary strength. Each cohort was commanded by a tribune and the entire praetorian guard by two prefects. All of these officers were members of the equestrian order.

The praetorian guard gave the emperor the capacity to enforce his will on the population of Rome. They soon acquired a grim reputation for the arrest and execution of Roman noblemen suspected of plotting against the emperor. The support of the guard could make or break an emperor. Claudius was discovered hiding behind a curtain after the assassination of Caligula by the praetorians, who forced a reluctant Senate to grant him the throne. Nero's position only became hopeless when the guardsmen abandoned his cause. In AD 193 the power of the praetorians was even more blatantly demonstrated. Having murdered the Emperor Pertinax, the praetorian prefect auctioned off the throne to the highest bidder from the walls of the *castra praetoria*.

The praetorians were expected to accompany the emperor to war. This was rare in the 1st century, but became increasingly common later. As a military force the praetorians were trained and equipped as legionaries, although some of their gear was considerably more ornate. We hear of praetorian cohorts being allowed to load their heavily decorated standards onto pack animals when their bearers had difficulty carrying them on a long march.

Attached to the praetorian guard was a cavalry force which steadily grew in size, which along with the emperor's horse guards (*equites singulares Augusti*) reached a peak of 2,000 men at the end of the 2nd century AD. These men were specially chosen from the auxiliary cavalry and trained to a very high standard. There were also two paramilitary forces in Rome. The three (later five) urban cohorts acted as a police force, as well as providing one unit to guard the imperial mint at Lugdunum (Lyons) in Gaul. There were also seven cohorts of *vigiles*, who acted as a fire brigade and night police force in Rome itself. Both groups only ever took the field at times of extreme crisis, usually provoked by civil war.

A close-up view of praetorians on a relief found in Rome and probably dating to the early 2nd century BC. These men have thick crests in long crest-boxes fitted to the top of their classical helmets.

A group of soldiers – who may well be praetorians – on Trajan's Column. These men have somewhat smaller crests than those shown above.

Senatorial Officers under the Principate

(Above) A relief from Holland depicting the Emperor Tiberius offering a ritual popanum cake in sacrifice.

(Opposite) In this scene from Trajan's Column, the Emperor Trajan is shown in the uniform of a senior senatorial officer on campaign.

Whilst the creation of the Principate robbed the Senate of any real freedom and independence, senators as individuals continued to play a central role in the running of the Empire until well into the 3rd century, providing the overwhelming majority of provincial governors and senior army officers. A few served in offices which had long existed under the Republic, although most were in newly created posts which made explicit the fact that their authority came from the Emperor. All now operated in a

completely different political environment which restricted their freedom of action. Men were no longer elected to magistracies which brought them civil and military responsibilities. A successful career depended primarily on influence and patronage and most of all required imperial approval. This was especially true for the more important military commands, for no emperor wanted to give control of legions to a man who might become a rival.

A senator's son who aspired to a public career normally served as a junior magistrate in his late teens. Most became one of the 'board of 20' (*vigintiviri*) in Rome, before receiving their first military experience as a *tribunus laticlavius* in one of the legions. It seems to have been fairly common for men to serve in a unit stationed in a province governed by a family member or close friend. It is distinctly possible that governors were allowed to request such postings, for we certainly know that they were able to appoint men to many lesser positions. Usually a minimum of one year was spent in the post. A minority served for longer than this, and cases are known of men serving in several legions, invariably stationed in different provinces, in succession. Later, usually at 24, although some men were granted exemptions and achieved the distinction at a younger age, a man would be formally enrolled in the Senate and might gain the quaestorship. This involved administering the finances of a settled province and with very few exceptions did not include military responsibilities. In subsequent years a man might hold a succession of magistracies which retained only a shadow of their former importance and involved mainly ceremonial duties.

The next military post was to become a *legatus legionis* in command of a legion, usually achieved around the age of 30. As a *legatus* or 'representative' these officers were clearly marked out as deputies of the emperor acting on delegated authority. These commands were certainly not at the disposal of each province's governor, and were instead direct appointments of the emperor. Some men remained in command of a legion for six to seven years, but the average tenure seems to have been nearer three. It was very rare for a man to be appointed to the legateship of more than one legion. Following this post, a man might go on to govern a settled province – one without a significant military garrison – as a propraetor, before returning to Rome to hold the consulship.

The culmination of a man's career was usually the post of *legatus Augusti proparetore* in charge of one of the military provinces of the Empire. The limited number of such posts and their importance ensured that the majority of senators never achieved this high rank. On average men served about three years in such a post, but there were many exceptions. Tiberius became unpopular with the Senate because he kept governors in office for

(Opposite left) An inscription
set up in honour of the legate
commanding Legio II
Augusta, Tiberius Claudius
Paulinus, providing some
details of his career. After his
tenure as legionary legate, he
was proconsul of one of the
Gallic provinces, and then
imperial legate to another.
This monument probably
dates to before AD 220, for in
that year Paulinus became
legatus Augusti of Lower
Britain.

(Right) An inscription from
Caesarea on the coast of
Judaea recording the
construction of a building
dedicated to the Emperor
Tiberius by Pontius Pilate, the
equestrian governor of the
province. Pilate's title is given
as prefect (praefectus), but by
the reign of Claudius
equestrian governors were
known as procurators. This is
the only inscription to survive
from Pilate's 10-year tenure
in Judaea.

(Opposite right) Trajan's
Column formed the centre-
piece to the Forum complex
constructed to commemorate
the Emperor's victory in
Dacia. It is 100 Roman feet
high (29.8 m or 97 ft 9 in)
and was originally topped by
a statue of Trajan.

exceptionally long periods, frustrating those aspir-
ing to this rank by reducing the number of available
commands. In the 2nd century AD it was not
unusual for a man to serve in a smaller military
province before gaining command of one of the
largest armies in Britain, Upper Pannonia or Syria.
At times of crisis experienced and loyal men might
be sent to take command of an area facing a rebellion or other serious problem.

Only two provinces which contained a legionary
garrison were not governed by imperial legates.
The first, Egypt, was an equestrian command and
will be dealt with in the next section. The second,
Africa, was the only province administered by the
Senate to contain a legion and its governor was a
proconsul who possessed imperium in his own
right. Although this man was chosen and appointed
by the Senate, it is clear that they were expected to
select someone of whom the emperor approved and
under Caligula this senatorial proconsul was
replaced by an imperial legate.

Competence, experience, merit and patronage

Before being placed in command of an army, a
provincial legate had experience of serving as a
military tribune and legionary legate. Pliny the
Younger appears to have spent most of his tenure
as tribune with a legion in Syria in routine
administration, in particular involving a thorough
inspection of unit accounts in that province.
However, Pliny was never to serve with the army in
any more senior capacity. Tactitus claims that his
father-in-law, Agricola, was unlike most military
tribunes in that he did not waste his time as tribune
in debauchery, but took the post seriously and was
given significant responsibilities. Much must have
depended on a man's temperament, that of his
senior officers, and the local situation during his
year or more of service. This is also true to a fair
extent of legionary legates, although their responsibilities were significantly greater. By modern
standards the generals of the Roman army were
amateurs.

Some scholars have argued that from the very
beginning of an aristocrat's career his behaviour,
loyalty and ability were closely scrutinized and his
suitability for higher office judged. This created a
group known as the *viri militares* or 'military men'
who were marked out for the most important
provincial commands. There is no real evidence to
support this view, or any indication of just who
these boards of assessors could have been. As far as
we can tell, it was patronage more than anything
else which dictated whether an individual's career
ended prematurely or would eventually include the
highest offices. Letters of recommendation are by
far the most common form of document to survive
from the Roman world. The Romans did not consider this to be corruption, viewing it as both logical
and proper that a man should use his authority to
benefit his friends. Pliny the Younger expressed the
Roman attitude in a letter written to a governor of
one of the major military provinces:

'For two reasons I have singled you out to approach with a request which I am most anxious to be granted. Your command of a large army gives you a plentiful source of benefits to confer, and secondly, your tenure has been long enough for you to have provided for your own friends. Turn to mine – they are not many.'

The emperor was the ultimate source of all patronage and, as we have seen, his favour was necessary to secure appointment as a legionary legate or provincial governor. Emperors needed capable men to command their armies and rule their provinces, but a delicate balance had to be struck for they did not wish to grant power to men who were too able and so risk creating a rival. The activities of governors were far more closely supervised than had ever been the case under the Republic. Augustus urged caution on his commanders and attempted to curb the traditionally aggressive tendencies of Roman aristocrats when placed at the head of an army. Claudius recalled the legate of Lower Germany, when the latter had begun an invasion of a German tribe to the east of the River Rhine. The legate, Gnaeus Domitius Corbulo, one of the most famous generals of the 1st century, commented on how fortunate the generals had been under the Republic, before obeying orders and returning to his province.

Equestrian Officers under the Principate

On this metope from Adamklissi a senior Roman officer is shown riding down a barbarian. Although the relief is quite badly eroded, it is still possible to make out the officer's muscled cuirass, decorative pteruges *and flowing cloak. This stone may possibly depict Trajan himself.*

Under the Republic there had been very few opportunities for equestrians to rise to positions of authority in the army or provinces. This was all to change under the Principate, when Augustus and his successors created an enormous range of posts for members of the order. This not only provided the Emperor with a far greater number of representatives than the Senate alone could have provided, but it helped to secure the support of the knights for the new regime. Membership of the order was open to all citizens possessing the required value of property and, as the franchise was extended to a growing number of provincials, over time the aristocratic families of much of the Empire became equestrians and were able to have public careers.

There were far more equestrians than senators, and they were able to hold a wider variety of posts in the army or government. As a result, there was no single equestrian career pattern in the same way that there was a senatorial career. It is worth considering the various posts open to equestrians.

Auxiliary commanders

With the formation of the regular *auxilia* as infantry cohorts or cavalry *alae*, several hundred posts came into being. A few cavalry *alae* are known to have been led by former legionary centurions in the very early days of the Principate, but this practice was soon abandoned. Otherwise all auxiliary units were commanded by equestrians. The commanding officers of quingenary cohorts and *alae* were known as prefects (*praefecti*). Milliary units, and also cohorts bearing the title *civium Romanorum*, were led by tribunes. (The *cohortes civium Romanorum* had originally been raised by Augustus from freed slaves during the military crises of AD 6 and 9. Slaves automatically received citizenship on manumission, but the Emperor had not wanted these men to serve in the legions. After the original recruits had been discharged the units became ordinary auxiliary cohorts, recruited from non-citizens even though they retained their titles.)

Auxiliary units often acted independently, giving their commanders considerable freedom and opportunities to display their initiative. Garrison commanders were often the most senior representative of Roman power for some distance around and as a result might become involved in many aspects of local administration.

Legionary officers

There were five equestrian *tribuni angusticlavii* in each legion, performing a variety of staff functions. They might also be appointed to command sizeable detachments (vexillations) of soldiers sent to undertake a project or join a field army. Each legion also had a camp prefect who was a member of the equestrian order, save in cases where more than one unit occupied the same fortress in which case there was only one post per camp. We also hear of equestrians who were directly commissioned as legionary centurions and followed a career within this grade.

Troops in Rome

The loyalty of the military and para-military units in Rome was of fundamental importance to any emperor. Rather than entrust command of such units to senators who might easily see themselves as rivals, they were officered by equestrians. Each cohort of the praetorian guard was commanded by a tribune. With only a few short-lived exceptions, the guard as a whole was led by two praetorian prefects, since few emperors were willing to grant this much power to a single man, even if he were only an equestrian. The command structure of the urban cohorts and the *vigiles* was similar, though each had only one prefect and both he and the tribunes ranked below their praetorian counterparts.

Equestrian provinces

Augustus established some provinces to which he appointed equestrian governors. With the one exception of Egypt, these were smaller areas than the provinces given to senatorial legates. They were not usually frontier provinces and, although some were garrisoned by auxiliary units, none contained legions. One example was Judaea, although after the rebellion under Nero in AD 66 this was felt to require a legionary garrison and was turned into a senatorial legateship. Equestrian governors were at first known as prefects, but this title was changed to procurator before the middle of the 1st century AD.

For much of the Principate Egypt was not faced with significant external threats. However, its population was sometimes unruly and a garrison of two legions was maintained, which was concentrated outside Alexandria, a frequent source of unrest. A highly organized agricultural system based around the annual inundation of the Nile produced a massive agricultural surplus, so that in time Egypt came to supply a high proportion of the grain consumed by Italy and Rome itself. Augustus appointed an equestrian prefect to govern this important province, and forbade any senator from even visiting Egypt without express permission. Even so, the first prefect, Cornelius Gallus, committed suicide when accused of treason following his excessive celebration of his own military achievements.

Uniquely, a legion stationed in Egypt had neither a *legatus* not a *tribunus laticlavius*. Instead it was commanded by an equestrian *praefectus legionis*, who performed exactly the same role as his senatorial counterpart.

Equestrian careers

Equestrians who sought military posts included men born into equestrian families as well as those who had been admitted to the Order at a later stage of their life. A legionary *primus pilus*, most probably at least in his 40s, normally became an equestrian after his year in the post and could go on to hold senior positions. Other men entered the Order at various ages as they acquired sufficient wealth. Felix, who became procurator of Judaea under Claudius, was one of the Emperor's freed slaves. Equestrians therefore entered the army at all sort of ages and with varied ambitions.

The most common career for a man born into an equestrian family was the 'three posts' (*tres militiae*):

(i) Prefect of an auxiliary infantry cohort.
(ii) *Tribunus angusticlavius* in a legion.
(iii) Prefect of a cavalry *ala*.

The Emperor Claudius decided to increase the status of the legionary tribunate, and for a while made this the third, most senior position, but the practice was unpopular and soon abandoned. A cavalry prefect was usually allowed much more independence than a staff officer with a legion and there was a degree of glamour associated with commanding horsemen, even if these were not citizens. There was also the simple fact that the army required more legionary tribunes than it did prefects of *alae*, so that even in normal circumstances some tribunes were unable to make the next step. In the 2nd century, probably under Hadrian, the career pattern was refined still further and a fourth post

Two standard-bearers from Adamklissi depicted in undress uniform, without either armour or helmets. Each carries a square vexillum flag. Unlike many of the legionaries on Trajan's Column who have thick beards, the soldiers on the Tropaeum Traiani are invariably shown clean-shaven.

*A tombstone from Bonn
dating to the middle of the 1st
century AD, commemorating
the cavalryman Vonatorix,
son of Duco. He died aged 45
after 17 years' service in the
Ala Longiniana. Vonatorix is
shown bare-headed but
wearing scale armour and
wielding a spear. He has a
long* spatha *sword suspended
on his right hip.*

created, as commander of a milliary *ala*. There were never more than a dozen or so of these prestigious units in existence, so that such commands were reserved for the ablest, or best-connected, officers.

Unlike ordinary soldiers, who frequently include their age and length of service on their monuments, equestrians rarely mention such things unless they died whilst actually serving in a post. Such as it is, the evidence seems to suggest that many, perhaps most, men from equestrian families began their military careers at the age of 30 and served from three to four years in each post. These men had already served as local magistrates before entering the army and some would return to such posts after one or more military appointments. Other men spent far longer with the army, and might serve in several dif-

ferent appointments at each level, although in most cases such moves were to a unit in another province. Former chief centurions (a group known collectively as *primi pilares*) who had been admitted to the Order rarely became auxiliary commanders after the early 1st century AD. Many went on to serve as camp prefects, to posts with the Roman units, and appointments as procurators.

Patronage was as important in an equestrian as a senatorial career. Pliny, whilst serving as *legatus Augusti* in Bithynia, wrote to Trajan recommending a certain Nymphidius Lupus, son of a former *primus pilus* who had entered the equestrian order and been serving as an auxiliary prefect when Pliny had been a *tribunus laticlavius* some years before. Lupus had already completed a term as a *praefectus cohortis* and evidently hoped for a further position.

It was probably patronage that allowed one Publius Aelius Tiro to command a cohort at the age of 14. It is hard to know whether this post was purely nominal, allowing the youth to draw the pay and gain the prestige without actually spending time with the unit. Men who lacked such influential patrons had far more difficulty. The future Emperor Pertinax tried and failed to gain a commission as a legionary centurion in his youth. It was not until his mid-30s that he was made prefect of an auxiliary cohort instead. In the event he proved a very capable soldier, serving in increasingly senior positions until he was enrolled in the Senate by Marcus Aurelius. Other men, perhaps finding it impossible to advance in the normal way, abandoned the formally equestrian posts and were transferred into the legionary centurionate. The most prestigious positions, commands in the units in Rome, and especially provincial commands, were reserved for especially favoured men.

The tombstone of Longinus Sdapeze from Colchester dates to a little later than that of Vonatorix (opposite) and has the common motif of the horseman trampling an unarmoured – and often naked – barbarian warrior. This man may have adopted or been given the common army name of Longinus when he joined the army in addition to his own tribal name of Sdapeze. He served for 15 years and died at the age of 40. Like Vonatorix he wears scale armour, but in his case has no sword visible and probably wore his on the left.

LON INVSSDAPEZE

Other Officers:
The Centurionate and Below

There were many ranks below the levels exclusively held by senators or equestrians. The most important were the centurions, of whom there were 59 or 60 in each legion and altogether some 1,800 legionary and at least as many again auxiliary centurions throughout the Empire. The centurion commanding each century in a legion was assisted by an *optio*, *signifer* and *tesserarius*, who collectively were known as the *principales*. There were also a number of staff posts, such as *librarius* and *cornicularius* with the HQ of the legion or attached to the governor's staff, as well as ranks such as *beneficiarius*, who usually served on detached duty. Many other posts, varying from weapons' instructors to torturers, are attested, but it is difficult to know whether these appointments were associated with specific ranks. In addition a soldier could be rated as an *immunis*, which meant that he was exempt from many ordinary duties and fatigues. Otherwise *immunes* do not appear to have possessed any more authority than ordinary soldiers.

A considerable number of Roman army re-enactment groups have been formed in the last few decades. These dedicated individuals both provide displays which bring to life the army to the general public, and have contributed a great deal to our knowledge of military equipment by their painstaking reconstruction and testing of armour, weapons and tools. In this photograph we see members of the first serious group, the Ermine Street Guard, outside the reconstructed barrack block at Wallsend. In the centre is a centurion with his tall transverse crest. Over his mail armour he wears a harness bearing decorations including torques and the disc-like phalerae. *Beside him is a standard-bearer* (signifer) *and musician* (cornucen).

Many of these posts and grades, though by no means all, are attested under the same or an equivalent title in the *auxilia*.

The overwhelming mass of our evidence for understanding rank structure and careers at this level comes from the epigraphic record, since junior officers and ordinary soldiers have left little trace in the literary record. Histories were written by and for the élite in society, and present an often contemptuous, and always stereotyped, view of their social inferiors. The great dangers of reconstructing career patterns primarily from epigraphy are that we impose an artificial order on the evidence or force it to conform with our own preconceptions of what an army should be like. It was no coincidence

that the German scholars who pioneered the reconstruction of the Roman army's rank structure in the late 19th century created an image of a force that was remarkably similar to the Prussian and German armies of their own days, especially in the great variety of NCO ranks. Later, British scholars were inclined to see similarities to the British army, coming to view centurions as similar to the experienced warrant officers. We need to be both very careful of imposing anachronistic cultural assumptions on the Romans and aware that there are many things which our evidence cannot tell us.

Legionary centurions

Centurion is better thought of as a grade or type of officer, rather than a specific rank. The centurions of the first cohort, collectively known as the *primi ordines*, were certainly of higher status than the other centurions of the legion. The relationship between the centurions in the other nine cohorts of the legion is less clear. We know that the commander of each of the six centuries in a cohort had a different title and can infer that to some extent the differences in seniority between the three lines of the Republican army were preserved. Much administration was carried out at the level of the century, and soldiers were more likely to describe themselves as members of a particular century than a particular cohort. However, the cohort was the basic tactical unit, as well as playing a significant role in building projects, and cannot have functioned effectively without a commander. There is no evidence for any rank equivalent to the auxiliary prefect, and the conclusion must be that one of the centurions acted as cohort commander. The *pilus prior*, commander of the senior century, would seem the most probable candidate for this role, but it is also possible that seniority and hence command was instead based on length of service.

Caesar talks of promoting centurions from a lower grade in an experienced legion to a higher grade in a newly recruited unit, implying a rise in status, responsibility and perhaps pay, though not admission to the first cohort. The Late Roman theorist Vegetius claimed that promotion for centurions and all other ranks in the legion involved movement between cohorts as well as centuries. According to him the first cohort was senior, followed by the second, third and so on. On promotion a man was immediately posted to the tenth cohort and had to begin to work his way step by step back up the order of seniority. Therefore some scholars believed that a man would normally work his way from being *hastatus posterior* of the tenth cohort, and hence the junior centurion in the entire legion, stage by stage until he reached the post of *primus pilus* in the first. Yet it is very difficult to see how this system could possibly have worked. Unless such a process took an incredibly long time, then no one could have served for more than a few months in

Many legionaries identified strongly with their century and legion, but far less with their cohort. This altar from Chester was dedicated to the genius *or protective spirit of his century by the* optio *Aelius Claudianus in fulfilment of a vow.*

Re-enactors from the Ermine Street Guard representing some of the principales *or junior officers/NCOs of a century. On the right is an* optio *holding his staff of office* (hastile). *It is not known whether distinctive crests and plumes were used as insignia of rank by* optiones *and* tesserarii *as was the case with centurions, but it seems plausible that they were.*

any of these capacities. An alternative view was to see the six century grades in cohorts two to ten as equal, so that promotion was either to a senior century in any cohort, or eventually into the privileged ranks of the *primi ordines*. Other commentators have gone further and denied that there was any distinction between centurions outside the first cohort. This seems too extreme, and whilst we must admit that we do not fully understand the system, it is clear that one existed.

Becoming a centurion

We know of three basic routes to appointment as a legionary centurion:

(i)   After service in the ranks, as a *principalis* or in a junior staff post in the legion: it has been estimated that on average it took a man 15 to 20 years to become centurion in this way.

(ii)   After or in the course of service in the praetorian guard: praetorians served for only 16 years, making their veterans somewhat younger than their legionary counterparts.

(iii)   Direct commission: some equestrians were appointed in this way. Other men who were less wealthy, but still relatively well off, gained appointments after service as magistrates in their local city.

All three methods are reasonably well attested throughout the 1st and 2nd centuries. Unfortunately, it is very difficult to assess which method was most common. One of the first scholars to study promotion in any detail argued that most officers came from the ranks of the praetorian guard. This allowed the emperor to ensure that the bulk of the centurions in the legions were men promoted because of their loyalty to him. However, since a disproportionately large part of surviving inscriptions come from Italy – the main recruiting ground for the praetorians but not the legions – it is likely that Italian centurions, and therefore former praetorians, are too highly represented in the record. Few scholars now accept this view and most instead assume that the vast majority of legionary centurions were promoted from the ranks. Directly commissioned men are assumed to have been only a small proportion of the total even if, with their superior connections, they had a greater prospect of reaching the highest posts.

Yet, even though this view is now generally accepted, it rests on very slender evidence. The overwhelming majority of centurions attested

The 1st-century AD tombstone of the centurion Marcus Favonius Facilis from Colchester provides one of the best images of an officer of this rank. Facilis is shown in mail and holding his vine cane (vitis), which was both a mark of rank and a means of inflicting punishment. As a centurion Facilis wears his gladius *sword on the left. As with most centurions' memorials, this monument records very few details of Facilis' service or even age. All we are told is that he was a centurion in Legio XX.*

make no mention of any service prior to that rank, as indeed many *primi pilares* fail to mention any more junior posts. It is conveniently assumed that this was because men wished to conceal service as ordinary soldiers once they had risen to higher station. Whilst this is possible, it is equally plausible to suggest that those men who specifically mentioned rising from the ranks did so because they were very proud of what was a rare and difficult achievement.

The status of centurions

Centurions were extremely important individuals who might be given positions of considerable responsibility. Some were appointed to administer regions of a province where they were the most senior representative of Roman rule. Such duties, as well as the routine administration required in the daily life of their unit, meant that centurions required a high level of literacy and numeracy. It is very hard to know just how high a proportion of ordinary recruits to the legions were sufficiently well educated. The most senior might have even greater responsibilities, and we know of at least one *primus pilus* who was sent as ambassador to Parthia. Retired centurions were also important men in their own cities, towns or villages.

Rates of pay for centurions, and indeed many other officers, are not known with certainty, but were clearly substantially more than those of the ordinary soldiers. Pliny the Younger, having secured a commission as a centurion – presumably directly from civilian life – for one of his clients, provided the man with 40,000 sesterces to provide himself with the necessary uniforms and equipment. At a time when ordinary legionaries received 1,200 sesterces a year, this was more than they would have earned in their entire 25 years of service. Centurions were clearly men of great status, even if they were still less influential than equestrian and senatorial officers. The sheer fact that some equestrians chose to become centurions is an indication of their importance and prestige. On the whole it seems more likely that most centurions were directly commissioned or promoted after a comparatively short time, probably having served as a *principalis* or in a junior staff post. We know of one centurion who was only 18 when he died, which suggests that patronage had secured his appointment. As with the more senior officers, connections probably did more to shape the speed and success of a man's career than simple ability or experience. Yet, as with the higher posts, the system was not so rigid that able men could not make their way in spite of their lack of connections. Men were able to progress to become *primi pilares*, a few perhaps even of these having first joined in the ranks, and thus enter the equestrian order and hold some senior equestrian posts. Their sons were able to pursue a full equestrian career, in

the same way that some equestrian families were eventually able to enter the Senate. Usually such advancement was spread over a generation or so, although in a few rare cases individuals were able to do this. Social mobility was always possible at Rome.

Two Examples of Centurions' Careers

A: The career of the centurion Petronius Fortunatus (late 1st/early 2nd century AD; died aged 80 years) as recorded on his tombstone found at Lambaesis in North Africa:

1   Enlisted in Legio I Italica (Lower Moesia). Over four years held in succession the posts of *librarius*, *tesserarius*, *optio*, and *signifer*.
2   Promoted to centurion in the same legion by the vote of his comrades.
3   The next 46 years spent as centurion with Legio VI Ferrata (in Syria), I Minervia (Lower Germany), X Gemina (Upper Pannonia), II Augusta (Britain), III Augusta (Numidia), III Gallica (Syria again), XXX Ulpia (Lower Germany again), VI Victrix (Britain again), III Cyrenaica (Arabia), XV Apollinaris (Cappadocia), II Parthica (probably Italy), I Aduitrix (either Upper or Lower Pannonia). During this time he was decorated with a mural crown (given to the first man over the wall of an enemy town), as well as other decorations including torques and *phalerae*.

4   His tombstone also mentioned a son, who died aged 35 and had served for six years as a centurion in the army (and was therefore probably directly commissioned), successively with Legio XXII Primigenia and Legio II Augusta.

B: The career of Caius Octavius Honoratus (1st/2nd century AD; age at death unknown) as recorded on his tombstone found in Thuburnica in Africa:

1   Directly commissioned as centurion from the equestrian order in Legio II Augusta (Britain).
2   Service successively in Legio VII Claudia pia fidelis (Upper Moesia), XVI Flavia firma (Syria), X Gemina (Upper Pannonia). Ended his service as a *princeps posterior* (the fourth senior grade of centurion in an ordinary cohort) in the fifth cohort of X Gemina. No details of age or length of service given on monument.

(Left) A 2nd-century AD relief from Turin appearing to show a centurion – note the sword worn on the left – and another soldier. His armour is either a traditional muscled cuirass or was originally painted silver to suggest mail. He is carrying what appear to be writing tablets, which suggests he had an administrative role.

Auxiliary centurions

Far less is known about centurions in the *auxilia*, although again it has often been assumed that they were promoted from the ranks and therefore usually of the same ethnic background as their men. There is some evidence from papyri to suggest that a man usually became a decurion in charge of a *turma* of cavalry after between eight and 25 years in the ranks. However, many centurions do appear to have been directly commissioned and to have come from the wealthier families and local aristocracies. This may well have been the most common practice. The evidence suggests that a significant proportion of auxiliary soldiers were illiterate, making them unsuitable for promotion. As far as we can tell none of the texts from Vindolanda near Hadrian's Wall were written by anyone lower in rank than a *principalis*.

This memorial to the family of Voconius from the Colonia Augusta Emerita (modern-day Merida in Spain) makes no mention of any connection with the army. However, above the inscription there is a depiction of a centurion's harness and two types of military decoration – torques and armillae. *It is therefore probable that someone in the family had served as a centurion.*

The professional Roman soldier spent much of his adult life – 25 years for most of the Principate – in the army. This was the soldier's world, set apart from the mass of the civilian population, where he formed part of a rigid and clearly defined hierarchy, his life governed by military law and regulation. For much of the time he would be stationed at one of the army's permanent bases, which varied in size from small way-stations or outposts accommodating a handful of men to auxiliary forts with garrisons of some 500–1,000 soldiers and the massive legionary depots which could house more than 5,000 troops. Barracks life was dominated by routine, the days occupied with parades and ceremonies, training and drill, fatigues and a whole range of other duties.

Roman soldiers came from a wide variety of backgrounds. Apart from the major distinction between the citizen legionaries and the non-citizen auxiliaries, recruits were drawn from virtually every province of the Empire, and even from outside its borders. Some soldiers were conscripts, but probably far more volunteered. Once in the army all were subjected to the same discipline, ate the same rations and were paid according to the same system. From the moment he came before a recruiting officer to his discharge, the life of each soldier was recorded by the army's bureaucracy. Only a fraction of this paperwork has survived, but it provides us with many insights into the daily routine of the army. Other sources tell us about the more private aspects of soldiers' lives, such as the gods and goddesses they chose to worship, and the families which they raised in spite of an official bar on marriage.

Some of a soldier's time was spent preparing for war, yet they were also called on to perform a broad range of more peaceful activities. Soldiers sometimes acted as administrators and policemen, or as craftsmen, engineers and builders. Others were occupied not with full-scale war, but with the low-level patrolling and skirmishing on the frontiers and in some of the more lawless regions inside the Empire.

A scene showing a group of soldiers in a marching camp. The eight men of a contubernium lived in their leather tent and prepared their meals together. A mule was allocated to each contubernium to carry the tent and any other heavy equipment.

III   The Life of a Roman Soldier

Joining the Roman Army

Most recruits to the army of the Principate were volunteers. Legally, all Roman citizens were still obliged to undergo military service whenever the state required, but conscription was hugely unpopular, especially in Italy. Augustus held a levy (*dilectus*) on only two occasions, following disasters in Pannonia in AD 6 and Germany in AD 9. There were many attempts to avoid enlistment and the Emperor sold one equestrian into slavery for cutting the thumbs off his two sons and so making them medically unfit for service. In the main, Augustus' successors avoided imposing conscription on Italy. Elsewhere, the method was sometimes used to raise auxiliary forces, and there are occasional references to a *dilectus* being held to bring the legions of a province up to strength, almost always in preparation for a major war. It is difficult to know whether this meant a full or partial conscription of eligible citizens in the area, or simply a more active recruiting drive using more normal methods.

Whilst serving as governor of Bithynia and Pontus, Pliny the Younger was faced with the problem of two slaves who had illegally enlisted in the army, and wrote to the Emperor Trajan seeking advice. Trajan's reply made it clear that there were three categories of recruits, volunteers (*voluntarii*), conscripts (*lecti*), and substitutes (*vicarii*). The conscripts seem to have been chosen either by Roman officers sent to supervise a levy, or by the local authorities within a province, although it is also possible that at times something as simple as a press-gang may have operated. Substitutes were presumably provided by unwilling conscripts, or their families, as the price of their discharge. Preparations for Trajan's planned Parthian expedition were almost certainly already taking place in these years, and it may be that the Emperor was aware that levies of conscripts were being raised to bring the units in the eastern provinces up to strength. Yet it is certainly an indication that forms of the *dilectus* still provided the army with some of its manpower. However, the army of the Principate was tiny in comparison to the population of the Empire, and it does seem that the number of volunteers was adequate to supply its needs most of the time.

The attractions of a soldier's life

In the main, service in the ranks seems to have been most attractive to the poorer sections of society.

(Left) A bronze statuette apparently depicting a war god in the uniform of a Roman legionary. The segmented cuirass is heavily stylized.

(Right) An inscription providing details of the career of Quintus Pompeius Falco, who was legatus Augusti *of Britain in the early years of Hadrian's reign. The experience of ordinary soldiers enlisting in the army was very different from that of a senatorial officer whose military service was interspersed with civil posts.*

The army assured a man of food, clothing, better medical facilities than he could probably otherwise have afforded, and a steady wage. The soldier's salary was not especially high, and an unskilled and uneducated labourer may well have been able to earn as much or more, especially in the big cities. Yet such work was by its nature uncertain, whilst the army offered the security of a definite annual income. For those with ability and sufficient education, there was the prospect of promotion with the better pay and conditions which this brought, and perhaps even for social advancement. Financial records preserved on papyrus suggest that at least some soldiers were able to amass considerable sums of money. All soldiers had certain advantages under the law, a theme taken up by the late 1st-century satirist Juvenal, who spoke of the difficulty for a civilian to gain redress for abuses committed by a soldier. Soldiers were uniquely permitted to make wills even if their father was still alive – normally all property of any children was legally assumed to belong to their father. On discharge from the army, legionaries usually received either a bounty or the grant of a plot of land.

Yet although the soldier enjoyed these advantages, they came at the price of 25 years of service.

During that time they were subject to an extremely harsh system of discipline, both corporal and capital punishment being imposed almost at the whim of their commanders. Probably for this reason, desertion seems to have been a constant problem. Promotion was possible, but required a level of education and influence which many recruits may have lacked. Nor was the legal position of soldiers unambiguously favourable. They were forbidden to marry, and any marriage contracted prior to service was declared illegal on enlistment. Even so, many men clearly did develop long-term relationships and begin to raise a family during service. This was one of the main reasons for allowing soldiers to make wills, for this was for a long time the only way they could bequeath property to their children or 'wife'. Yet in the eyes of the law such children remained illegitimate and therefore were not entitled to citizenship.

The standard of recruits

Vegetius described the ideal recruit in some detail, although some of his views had more to do with the racial prejudices and medical myths of his day. Therefore men raised in a temperate climate, rather than the hotter eastern provinces, were supposed to prove steadier soldiers. The preference for recruiting men from rural areas rather than the towns was in part a legacy of the old hoplite ideal of a farmer soldier, but also had some practical basis. Soldiers raised in the country had generally led a harsher life and become accustomed to hard physical labour, so that it was necessary for recruits drawn from the towns to undergo a much longer period of fitness training before their proper military training could begin. The former profession of a potential soldier was equally important, and Vegetius claimed that more physical occupations such as those of the hunter, butcher, or blacksmith should be preferred to the unmanly tasks of pastry-cooks, weavers or fishermen. Recruiting officers were to examine each man's size and physical fitness very closely. Height was important.

Traditionally – and probably Vegetius is here referring to the Principate – recruits for the first cohort of a legion or a cavalry *ala* were to be, in Roman measurements, 6 ft, or occasionally 5 ft 10 in tall (just over 5 ft 10 in (1.77 m) and 5 ft 8 in (1.7 m) by modern measurements). However, he argues that shorter men of good build could also be accepted, since strength was more important to a soldier than mere height. Some educated recruits were also desirable, for the army needed a great number of clerks and administrators at all levels. Vegetius says little about the age of recruits, but other evidence suggests that the vast majority were in their late teens or early to mid-20s.

Some scholars have rather naively assumed that the vast majority of recruits actually met Vegetius' high standards, but theoretical manuals are dangerous guides to the normal. The Emperor Tiberius once complained that the legions were having trouble finding recruits of sufficient quality, and that in Italy only the poorest vagrants were drawn to military service. Men who had been condemned to be thrown to the wild beasts, deported to an island or exiled for a fixed term not yet expired were barred from joining the army and, if discovered in the ranks, were to be immediately discharged. The same was true of men who had joined up to avoid prosecution. It is noticeable that only men convicted of the most serious crimes were barred from service, and there may have been many petty criminals in the ranks of the legions.

The enlistment process

Recruiting parties appear to have been supervised by the governor of a province. The first stage, or *probatio*, consisted of an inspection of the potential recruits. Each man's legal status was supposed to be made clear at this point, for only citizens were permitted to enlist in the legions, and slaves were not allowed to join any part of the army under normal circumstances. When Trajan replied to Pliny's letter concerning the two slaves found to have enlisted, he stated that the men would be subject to full punishment if they had falsely claimed to be free men. However, if they were substitutes, then the blame rested with the men who had provided them, and if conscripts then the recruiting officer was at fault. Citizenship and status were very important in the Roman Empire, but records of such things were not always readily available. An Egyptian papyrus dating to AD 92 records the case of an *optio* in Legio III Cyrenaica who was accused of not being a Roman citizen, and thus faced at the very least dismissal. The man cited three witnesses to prove his status, two of them legionaries from other centuries and the last a veteran.

The *probatio* also involved a medical examination. Another papyrus records the discharge on 24 April AD 52 of a certain Tryphon, son of Dionysius, weaver, due to weak eyesight caused

A scene from Trajan's Column showing a group of ambassadors from a range of different barbarian peoples. Some have hair knots, a style associated with the Germanic Suebi, while those on the left have the long, kaftan-like robes characteristic of the Sarmatians. Roman auxiliaries were recruited from a broad range of peoples within, and sometimes outside the provinces.

by a cataract. In this case it is not certain that Tryphon was being discharged from the army, rather than some other form of service, but it is unlikely that a military discharge on medical grounds would have been very different. The late 3rd-century AD account of the *Martyrdom of Maximilianus* probably gives a fair reflection of the normal process of a *probatio*, although in this case it was clearly a matter of conscription. Maximilianus was brought before the representative of the governor, and it was formally stated that he had the required qualities for a soldier and that his height, 5 ft 10 in (1.77 m), was satisfactory and that therefore he ought to be enrolled. Throughout, Maximilianus claimed that as a Christian his beliefs did not permit him to serve as a soldier or do any evil. It was for this repeated refusal that he was eventually executed.

A more enthusiastic recruit to the army could find his path greatly eased by bringing letters of recommendation. The higher the status of the referee and the closeness of the bond between him and the presiding officer added to the power of such documents, so that Juvenal could joke about a recruit armed with a letter from the goddess Venus to her lover, the war god Mars. Letters could make clear a potential recruit's status and abilities, and might lead to rapid promotion. In AD 107, a certain Julius Apollinarius enlisted in a legion and was able to gain an almost immediate appointment as a clerk (*librarius*). In a letter to his father he congratulated himself on being able to work at such light duties whilst his fellow recruits were outside breaking rocks, presumably for some building project. On the other hand, unsatisfactory recommendations could lead to disappointment. Around the same period

Claudius Terentianus tried and failed to enlist in a legion, before joining the far less prestigious navy. Even there he was discontented with his prospects, and complained that 'nothing could be done without money, nor will letters of recommendation be of any use, unless a man helps himself'.

After the *probatio*, those recruits accepted for service would be sent on to their unit. Probably at this time they were given the *signaculum*, an inscribed lead tablet worn around the neck in a leather pouch which served much the same function as the identity disks of modern soldiers. Already the recruits had probably taken the military oath (*sacramentum*), swearing loyalty to the emperor. Then they received travelling money (*viaticum*) which seems always symbolically to have consisted of three gold coins, whose total value was 75 *denarii*. Although a substantial sum of money, much of this was consumed during their journey, and relieving the recruits of their new wealth may well have been one of the perks of the regular soldiers escorting the party. On average a large party of recruits who arrived to join Cohors I Lusitanorum in AD 117 had less than a third of their *viaticum* left to deposit with the *signifers* of their centuries. Another document describes a draft of recruits:

Copy C. Minucius Italus to Celsianus
Give instructions that the six recruits approved by me for the cohort under your command be entered on the records with effect from 19 February. I have appended their names and distinguishing-marks to this letter.

C. Veturius Gemellus	aged 21	no distinguishing marks
C. Longinus Priscus	aged 22	scar on left eyebrow
C. Julius Maximus	aged 25	no distinguishing marks
-. Julius Secundus	aged 20	no distinguishing marks
C. Julius Saturninus	aged 23	scar on left hand
M. Antonius Valens	aged 22	scar on right side of forehead

Received 24 February AD 103, through Priscus, *singularis*. I, Avidius Arrianus, *cornicularius* of Cohors III Ituraeorum, state that the original letter is in the records office of the cohort.

These were recruits to an auxiliary cohort, and therefore unlikely to have been citizens, but nevertheless all are listed with three 'Roman' names and would be referred to in this way in all the vast documentation which would accompany them throughout their military career. An Egyptian called Apion who had enlisted in the fleet and been posted to Misenum in Italy wrote to his family to tell them that he was now to be known as Antonius

Maximus of the Athenonican century. The same man assured his father of his good health, and thanked him for giving him an education which should be a great asset in his career.

On arrival with a unit, the recruits would be added to its nominal roll and allocated to a century or *turma*, but would undergo a period of rigorous training before becoming a fully qualified soldier.

Auxiliary recruitment and the ethnic composition of units

All legionaries were supposed to be Roman citizens, although in a few, exceptional cases at times of civil war or military crisis, foreigners were permitted to enrol and given an immediate grant of citizenship. Auxiliaries were normally non-citizens, and gained citizenship only at the end of their 25 years of service. Most auxiliary units included a regional or ethnic distinction in their title. This name usually referred to the composition of the unit when first raised, but the Romans seem to have made no particular effort to continue finding recruits from the same ethnic group. Wherever possible, the army recruited from the nearest available sources of manpower. This was true to a great extent of the legions, as during the Principate the number of recruits from Italy steadily declined. Instead citizens were found from the communities in provinces nearer to each legion's home base. The same was true of the *auxilia*. If they happened to remain stationed near their place of origin, then a cohort or *ala* might well continue to be predominantly composed of men from that same region. Otherwise they would over time mainly be composed of men from the most local recruiting grounds. Some units, especially ones which were moved from province to province, might contain soldiers from a mixture of different regions and peoples. An inscription from Hadrian's Wall singles out the Germans within a particular cohort. It is hard to tell whether the different groups would be formed into distinct centuries or simply be mixed up. The word of command, and the language of the administration which ran the army, was in Latin. Recruits would have to acquire at least a rudimentary understanding of the language, although it is much harder to estimate how many auxiliaries – or indeed legionaries – were literate.

Basic training

A recruit's training at first focused on physical fitness and accustoming the new soldiers to discipline. Close-order drill was an especially important element, and the men were taught to march in step and keep formation. They also underwent route-marches to improve their stamina. Vegetius claims that they were expected to complete a march of 20 Roman miles in five hours at the ordinary pace, and 24 miles in the same time at the quick step. There was also great emphasis on running and jumping. At least some of these exercises were performed in

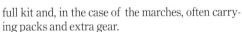

full kit and, in the case of the marches, often carrying packs and extra gear.

Weapons' training employed a system copied from the gladiatorial schools. A 6-ft (1.82-m) post was erected and the recruit taught to fence by aiming blows at it. He was issued with a wooden sword and a wicker shield, both of the normal size but considerably heavier than the real thing. Therefore, as he practised the regulation cuts, thrusts and parries, the heavy equipment also helped to strengthen his arms. *Pila* would also be thrown, using the post as a target, and it is possible that there was basic instruction in other weapons, such as slings, bows and the various forms of artillery. Vegetius also recommended that all troops be taught to ride and swim.

The level of training gradually increased. Recruits would then begin to fight mock battles, using practice weapons or real weapons with their points covered with leather discs to prevent serious injuries. At first pairs would fight each other, and then larger groups until exercises involved entire units. In all, basic training probably lasted for several months, until the recruit became a fully qualified member of the unit. Training did not end,

(Above) Two re-enactors show how Roman troops were often exercised by fencing with blunt-tipped weapons. In the early phases of training, recruits used wooden swords and carried wicker shields – both heavier than the equipment actually used in battle. Later they would employ proper kit, the tips of weapons being made safe by leather tips.

(Right) An ox skull found at Vindolanda. Visible are a number of square section holes made by bolts from a light ballista, *suggesting that the skull had been used for target practice by soldiers.*

but was a continuous activity throughout the remainder of his service, and Roman commanders were supposed to keep their units well drilled and prepared for actual war.

Daily Routine

Much of a soldier's life was spent in barracks, and it is worth now considering this environment. For recruits from the towns and cities, life in a crowded military base will not have been entirely unfamiliar. Those men from rural areas, especially many auxiliaries who came from the less settled provinces, can only have found it a new and strange place.

It is conventional to refer to the largest of the army's permanent bases, and in particular the establishments capable of housing an entire legion, as fortresses, whilst the smaller installations suitable for a single auxiliary unit are referred to as forts. Temporary bases, regardless of size, are known as camps. None of these terms is entirely appropriate, and they conceal the enormous variety of function within each group. Fortress and fort inevitably suggest a position which was primarily defensive, something akin to a medieval castle. In fact, the army's bases were rarely provided with especially strong fortifications. Instead they were first and foremost barracks providing accommodation for large numbers of soldiers and storage space for the supplies required to support them.

The Legionary Fortress

Even after the Marian reform, the Roman army did not have permanent bases. It was still essentially a field army, designed to carry out mobile operations. This was a time of conquest, and the Empire continued to expand rapidly until AD 14. Yet active campaigning was normally confined to the spring, summer and early autumn, for it was exceptionally difficult for armies to find adequate food and forage in the winter months. At the end of each season of operation, a legion would retire and settle into winter quarters (*hiberna*). In urbanized areas this might mean being billeted on a town or city, but elsewhere it involved the construction of a far more substantial version of the marching camp. The fortifications were made more formidable, the earth and timber ramparts made higher and strengthened with towers, whilst tents were replaced by huts. Such camps provided the troops with a measure of comfort during the winter months, which should have resulted in lowering the losses to sickness. They also often had a strategic function, serving to hold down recently conquered territory or positioning the army in readiness for the next season's campaign.

Under Augustus the army took on a new permanence and, whilst expansion continued, many legions began to spend longer periods stationed in the same part of a province. Over time, the old winter quarters evolved into more permanent bases, which acted as the legion's depot, housing much of its records and administration, even if the bulk of the unit was away on campaign. At first such bases were simply slightly better constructed versions of the winter camp, with timber buildings and earth ramparts, but over time these were rebuilt in more substantial form. Eventually, tiled roofs replaced thatch, and wooden walls were replaced by stone. The rebuilding in stone usually occurred in stages, and the choice of buildings reflected a unit's immediate priorities. The pace at which this process occurred was influenced by the state of the existing timber structures and the local availability of suitable masonry.

A legionary fortress was big, covering some 50–60 acres (20–25 ha). A small number, such as

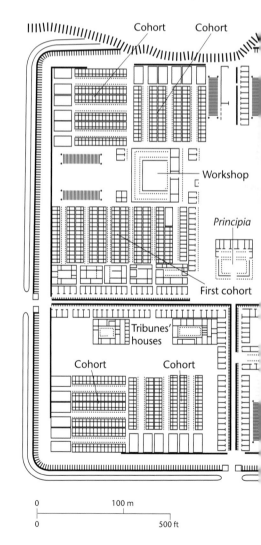

Cohort · Cohort · Workshop · *Principia* · First cohort · Tribunes' houses · Cohort · Cohort

| 0 | | 100 m |
| 0 | | 500 ft |

Vetera (modern day Xanten) on the Rhine, were even bigger, housing two legions on the same site. Many legionary fortresses now lie beneath modern towns, such as Chester or York in Britain, and this, combined with their sheer size, has meant that detailed excavation has only been possible in small fractions of most sites. This means that our picture of a legionary fortress must to a great extent be an amalgam of many different sites. Since there appears to have been a great degree of uniformity in plan and layout, this may not present too much of a problem, but it is important to remember that each site so far excavated has displayed a few peculiar features. Some were occupied for several centuries and during that time passed through numerous phases of development.

Defence was rarely of prime concern in the siting of legionary fortresses. It was far more important for these bases to have access to very good communications by road, and especially by water, so most are located next to navigable rivers. There is some variation in the earliest period, but virtually all fortresses conform to the classic playing card shape – a rectangle with rounded corners – common to marching camps. Two roads were central to the layout of any Roman base. The first, or *via principalis*, ran between the gateway in each of the longer sides of the fort. Joining this at a right angle was the *via praetoria*, which led from the most important gate of the camp, the *porta praetoria*, up to the headquarters building or *principia* which lay behind the *via principia*. There were other roads within the fortress, most notably the *via decumana*, which led from beyond the range of buildings surrounding the *principia* out to the *porta decumana* gate in the rear wall.

Internal buildings

The principia: The headquarters was the administrative and spiritual heart of the legion. Its main entrance, usually constructed on a monumental scale, lay on the line of the *via praetoria*. This

(Below left) A plan of the legionary fortress at Inchtuthil in Scotland, which was built in the late 1st century AD and abandoned before it had been completed.

(Below) A plan of the legionary fortress at Caerleon (Isca Silurum) in South Wales was occupied for more than two centuries by Legio II Augusta. There are many similarities with the layout of Inchtuthil, but no two fortresses appear to be absolutely identical.

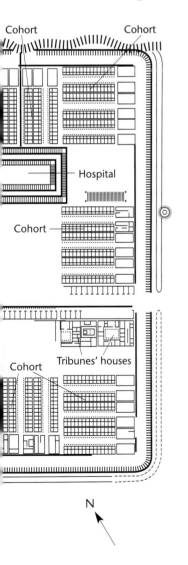

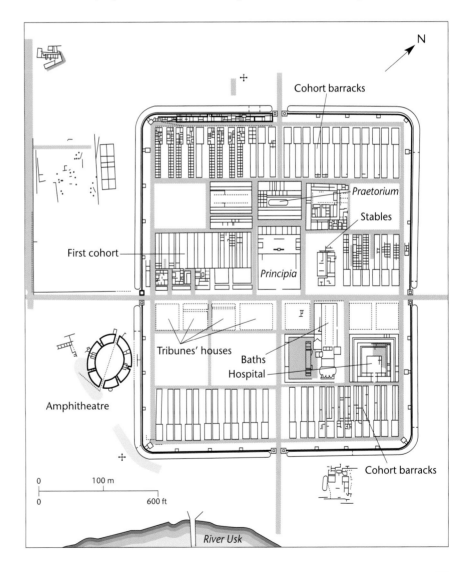

opened into a colonnaded courtyard, usually paved, surrounded by rooms which may have served as offices. Behind this was an enormous transverse hall or basilica, some 30–40 ft (9–12 m) wide with a double row of massive columns running along its length to support the high roof. There is evidence from excavations at Caerleon and York that the hall often contained larger-than-life-sized statues of the emperor and members of his family. This area appears to have been used for formal parades and ceremonies and at one end there was a raised tribunal from which the senior officer presiding over such affairs could address the gathering.

In the centre of the far wall was the entrance to the shrine (*aedes* or *sacellum*) where the legion's standards, the 59 or 60 *signa*, the *imagines* (busts) of the imperial family, the *vexilla* (flags) used by detachments and most of all the *aquila* or eagle, were kept. Screens, often in part of stone, separated the shrine from the main hall, but still allowed the precious standards to be glimpsed. On either side of the shrine were ranges of offices, whilst beneath was often a cellar housing the legion's treasury.

Although the actual dimensions and details vary from site to site, it seems that the *principia* in most fortresses conformed to this pattern. One exception was at Lambaesis, the depot of Legio III Augusta in North Africa, where the functions of the main hall were fulfilled instead by an open colonnaded square.

The praetorium: The commander of a legion, with the exception of the units stationed in Egypt who were led by equestrian prefects, was a Roman senator, and thus a man of considerable wealth and standing. The accommodation provided for the legate, along with quite possibly his wife and family and certainly a large household of slaves and freedmen, had therefore to be on a grand scale. The legate's house, or *praetorium*, was modelled on a Roman aristocrat's town house and consisted of a range of buildings around a central square courtyard, which provided rooms for public and social functions as well as private living space. Quite often there were other small courtyards, and the legates' houses at both Xanten and Caerleon had on one side a long colonnaded area with semi-circular ends, most probably a garden. These houses were luxurious, with under-floor heating and their own bath houses, and were also very big. Estimates of the size of the *praetorium* at Caerleon suggest that it was substantially larger than the biggest house in Pompeii, which was in keeping with the status of legionary legates as senators, members of an imperial élite numbering a few hundred. Their houses were also unequivocally Roman in design and style, even when the legionary fortress lay in regions with a very different climate from the Mediterranean.

Other houses: The other senior officers of a legion were also provided with houses of their own. The

(Left) The principia *at Lambaesis in North Africa is one of the best-preserved examples of these buildings which formed the spiritual and administrative heart of a legion. Unlike the headquarters in the colder, damper climates of Europe, much of the space was taken up by an open-air courtyard in which parades could be held.*

(Below) A scene showing the fort at Vindolanda as it would have appeared near the end of the 2nd century AD. In front of the gateway is the vicus, *the civilian settlement that grew up to support any permanent army base. Notice the design of the strip houses, whose very narrow front facing the road was intended to provide as many dwellings as possible with road access. Many of these buildings may have had shops or bars in front.*

tribunus laticlavius was also a senator, and lived in a smaller version of the Italian courtyard house. Similar, if possibly slightly less fine, accommodation was provided for the equestrian tribunes, and probably the *praefectus castrorum*. The centurions of the first cohort, the *primi ordines*, in turn enjoyed a higher status than the rest of the centurionate, and were allowed to live in small houses, rather than a suite of rooms at the end of a barrack block.

The barracks: The most common type of building within the fortress was the barrack block, providing accommodation for a century of 80 men and its officers. A legionary fortress would contain 60 such blocks, or 64 if its first cohort was milliary. In a temporary camp each century pitched its tents in a line, and the long thin barrack buildings preserved this arrangement. Instead of a tent, each eight-man *contubernium* (squad) was given a pair of rooms. One seems to have provided living and sleeping quarters, perhaps in bunk beds although there is no direct evidence for this. The other room, probably used to store equipment, was about the same size, around 50 sq. ft (4.6 sq. m) or a little smaller. There was no internal corridor, but a colonnade ran along the front of the building with perhaps a door for each pair of rooms. Finds of window glass are reasonably common around barracks, suggesting that most had windows, but it is probable that the inside of these buildings was gloomy. This was especially true of the rooms at the rear, since it was common for two blocks to be built back to back separated by a very narrow alley.

At the end of each block was a wider range of rooms, whose plan varies to a far greater extent from site to site. These seem to have provided some office and administrative space for the daily running of the century, and also a suite of rooms for the centurion. There is some evidence that these officers lived in a degree of comfort, with the walls of their rooms plastered and painted in decorative patterns. They also usually included a private lavatory and wash room with its own under-floor drain. Usually it seems that the bigger and better rooms were at the end of the block furthest from the main street and so presumably a little more peaceful.

Theoretically each barrack block ought to have consisted of the centurion's rooms and offices, and 10 pairs of rooms for the 10 *contubernia*. However, excavated blocks rarely if ever have 10 pairs of rooms, and 11 or 12 is far more common. The purpose of these extra rooms is uncertain, and various uses such as storage space or accommodation for the *principales* have been suggested. The front room in some barrack blocks were provided with hearths, although at other fortresses, such as Caerleon, ovens were built into the inner side of the main ramparts. When units were at full strength, life in barrack blocks may well have been crowded and gloomy, but such living conditions were unlikely to have been much worse than those of poorer civilians living in the blocks of flats (*insulae*) of the cities.

The hospital (valetudinarium): Another of the larger buildings in the fortress was the hospital, built to conform with the medical wisdom of the day. Once again, these tended to be rectangular buildings based around a central courtyard. At Inchtuthil in Scotland the hospital measured some 300 ft by just under 200 ft (91 by 56 m). It was divided into 64 wards, each about the size of a *contubernium* room in a barrack block. If, like the latter, these rooms were expected to accommodate from four to eight soldiers, then this would have meant that the hospital was capable of coping with a 5–10 per cent sickness or injury rate for the entire legion. The wards were built in two separate ranges, one inside the other, joined at intervals by short corridors. Hospital buildings found in fortresses in

(Right) The reconstructed timber granary at the 1st-century AD Lunt fort near Coventry. Note the windows to provide ventilation and the raised floor.

(Below) The granaries at Housesteads fort on Hadrian's Wall show one of the methods of raising the floor level of such buildings to control the temperature of stored goods and protect them from vermin. Notice the great thickness of the walls. Granaries were extremely substantial buildings.

Germany lack this detail, but are otherwise similar, although the ones at Neuss and Xanten also have a single larger room at their main entrance.

The granaries (horrea): Although conventionally referred to as granaries, these massive buildings were in reality storehouses containing a range of foodstuffs and other items apart from grain. Their remains are distinctive, because invariably the floor was raised above ground level, either by low walls or rows of posts or pillars. This helped to make the stored food less accessible to vermin, and even more importantly, along with ventilators set into the walls, permitted a freer flow of air. In stone granaries the walls are usually buttressed, in part a reflection of the height of the building, but probably also an indication that the roof projected for some distance beyond the wall, helping to ensure that rainwater drained away from the building. In these ways the grain was kept cool and dry, allowing its storage for long periods without significant loss.

The bath house: A bath house was more than simply a place to wash for the Romans, it was an important social environment. Some of the most sophisticated technology ever developed by the Romans was employed in regulating the temperatures of the different rooms in a bath house. All military bases had a bath house, and in the case of legionary fortresses these were constructed on an enormous scale, being something akin to modern sports centres.

Other buildings: Legionary fortresses were very large and included a range of other buildings. At Inchtuthil a large workshop (*fabrica*) was discovered. At Lambaesis a building was tentatively identified as the *scholae* or guild houses associated with particular ranks such as centurions. A number of buildings are known only through their plan revealed by excavations and it is impossible to do more than guess at their function. A strange elliptical building has been discovered in the fortress at Chester which is unlike any structure known from either civilian or military contexts elsewhere. In some cases there were large open spaces, perhaps because the original plans were altered. Although many legionary fortresses were occupied by the army for several centuries, this does not mean that all parts of the base were constantly maintained to a high standard. At Chester for instance, much of the fortress was

The reconstructed stone gateway at Arbeia fort (modern-day South Shields overlooking the mouth of the Tyne) was built on the foundations of the original Roman structure. Recently discovered evidence from Egypt suggests that the towers probably had an extra storey.

abandoned during the 2nd century AD, with buildings in some areas being demolished, before the fortress was subsequently reoccupied. There is no reason to suppose that this was unique.

Fortifications

The walls surrounding a Roman base were not especially high or formidable. In the 1st and 2nd centuries AD, towers normally did not project beyond the wall and so could not be used to deliver enfilading fire against attackers pressing the main wall. The height of walls is difficult to calculate, but the walkway was probably not more than 12–15 ft (3.6–4.5 m) above ground. The towers may well have been twice as high again, or higher, and it is certain that the towers forming part of the main gateways were deliberately made tall and impressive.

Outside the walls was invariably at least one ditch, and it was rare for auxiliary forts and other small outposts to have fewer than three ditches. These were usually v-shaped in section, some 6 ft (2 m) in depth, and with a small rectangular trench at the bottom to facilitate cleaning out spoil as well as making it easy for anyone attempting to cross to twist their ankle. In some cases the area in front of the ditches was covered with concealed pits, each with a sharpened stake in the middle, known to the soldiers as 'lilies' (*lilia*).

The defences of most Roman forts would have posed few problems for an army with some knowledge of siegecraft. However, for much of the Principate only the Romans possessed this technology. Against a less skilled opponent, the ditches and other obstacles would certainly have served to slow down and break up an attack, robbing it of momentum. All the while the defenders would also have been bombarding any attackers with a hail of missiles, from javelins and arrows to simple hand-thrown stones. Experiments by modern re-enactors have suggested that ditches were sighted so that they could be covered by thrown missiles from the walls and towers of a fort. Some bases may also have included artillery as part of their defences, although this perhaps only became more common in smaller forts during the 3rd century.

The Romans possessed the knowledge and skill to construct far larger and greater fortifications around their bases, but under the Principate chose not to do so. Even so, an attack on a fort would have been a difficult and risky operation for most of Rome's enemies. The defences were not made even stronger, because the army remained primarily an army for mobile operations. The Romans expected under most circumstances to move out from behind their fortifications and defeat the enemy in the open.

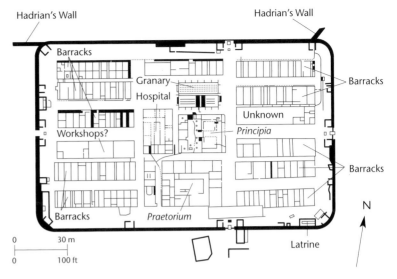

(Above left) The reconstructed gateway built at the Lunt fort gives an impression of the entrances to earth and timber forts. Once again the height of the original structure is impossible to establish.

(Above right) A plan of the fort at Housesteads on Hadrian's Wall, giving a good impression of the layout of auxiliary forts and their scale in comparison to the vast legionary fortresses. Housesteads was a little bigger than some auxiliary forts; it appears to have been constructed for a miliary cohort.

An aerial photograph of Housesteads today shows the praetorium, principia *and* hospital *in the centre. A few buildings of the civilian* vicus *are visible outside the gateway, but this settlement was in fact far bigger, covering most of the slope to the south and west.*

Auxiliary Forts

In many respects auxiliary forts were a smaller-scale version of the great legionary depots. Their plan was essentially the same, with the main *via praetoria* and *via principalis* meeting at a t-junction, behind which lay the *principia* building, itself a smaller version of a legionary headquarters. Beside this was the *praetorium*, in size more like the tribune's houses in a legionary base, and probably a smaller version of the hospital, sometimes as a single range of rooms rather than a courtyard building. Barrack blocks were much the same size as their legionary equivalents, but there were fewer of them – a mere six for a quingeniary cohort and 10 for a milliary unit. Mixed cohorts and *alae* also added stable blocks, roughly similar in dimensions to the barrack buildings. Bath houses were also smaller and normally lay outside the walls of the fort.

Barracks Life

Like many other standing armies throughout history, the Romans believed in keeping their soldiers busy. The massive military bureaucracy, of which only the most minute fraction has survived, recorded where each soldier was and what he was doing. A duty roster survives for a century of one of the Egyptian legions, perhaps Legio III Cyrenaica, from the late 1st century AD. Covering the first 10 days of the month of October, it lists the tasks assigned to each of the 31 legionaries available for duty. Tasks range from guard duty at the *principia*, on the gates and rampart of the fortress, to patrols around and outside the base. At different times, two men spent a day with the artillery, although whether this involved training in its use or simply cleaning the weapons and their ammunition is impossible to know. There were also fatigues, such as being assigned to the bath house, presumably assisting in its running and maintenance rather than enjoying its facilities, and, even less pleasantly, cleaning out the latrines. Some men were assigned to 'boots', which either meant looking after their own kit, or perhaps some role in repairing the century's footwear. Assignment to clean the centurion's boots most probably involved acting as batman, and the men 'in century' may simply have been at the immediate disposal of the centurion and *principales*.

In many ways this duty roster would be readily familiar to the soldiers of many regular armies. It should not surprise us that the century appears to have done little or nothing as a unit whilst in camp. The men were assigned as individuals to wherever they were required. Several were posted to other centurions for tasks both inside and outside the camp. Initially there were 31 men available for duty, although this was subsequently increased to 35. The remaining nine soldiers of the century, which was thus at little more than half its theoretical strength of 80, were *immunes* or exempt from normal duties. These were also listed along with their specialist tasks, including a wagon repairer, keeper of weapons, and a range of administrative posts. Men with such positions, just as Julius Apollinarius had gleefully written to his father, were able to avoid heavy labour and many of the more unpleasant tasks. It was also recognized that in many units some soldiers bribed their centurions to avoid any disagreeable duty. Though obviously detrimental to discipline, this problem appears never to have been wholly eradicated.

Some documents listed the activities of every soldier in the unit. Documents survive listing the names of every soldier in Cohors XX Palmyrenorum at Dura Europus and listing their current assignments. Once again, men tended to be posted as individuals to perform a very wide range of tasks, rather than operating in their centuries or *contubernia*. Units also appear to have kept records of each individual, listing periods spent away from the unit. Another late 1st-century papyrus from Egypt records the absences of four soldiers of Legio III Cyrenaica over the course of seven years. During this time Marcus Papirius Rufus had been sent twice to the granary in the Mercurium quarter and once to the granary at Neapolis in Alexandria. Another man, Titus Flavius Saturninus, had spent some time dredging a harbour, and then been assigned to the centurion Timinius, and subsequently the freedman Maximus.

Parades and religious ceremonies

Although soldiers spent much of their time assigned as individuals to specific tasks, the corporate life of the unit continued, once again much as it does in many modern armies. When in barracks, the day seems to have begun with a muster parade, when the roll was called. Quite probably a senior officer would deliver the orders for the day, perhaps from the tribunal in the *principia*. As men were then despatched to their tasks, other parades took place after which men were enrolled as sick or returned to normal duties. At some point the guards throughout the camp would be changed and a new password for the day issued. It seems probable that this process involved considerable ceremony.

On some days further parades were required to mark important occasions. One document, known as the *Feriale Duranum*, from Dura Europus, lists the formal calendar of Cohors XX Palmyrenorum in the late AD 220s. Written in Latin, the calendar includes many traditionally Roman festivals, when offerings were made to the Capitoline triad of Jupiter, Juno and Minerva, as well as other important Roman deities, such as the war god Mars.

Duty Roster for a Century in Legio III Cyrenaica, Egypt, Late 1st Century AD

Name	1 Oct.	2 Oct.	3 Oct.	4 Oct.	5 Oct.	6 Oct.	7 Oct.	8 Oct.	9 Oct.	10 Oct.
C Domitius Celer					Latrines?				Leave by Prefect's Permission	
C Aemilius Valens		Batman to Helius					Cotton guard?	Armoury	Baths	In century/or with cattle?
C Julius Valens	Area/ training	Tower?	Drainage	Boots	Armoury		Baths	Orderly	In century	Baths
C Julius Octavianus	as before				In century	Baths	HQ guard	Road Patrol	In century	?
P Clodius Secundus	Camp market duty?						Gate guard	Boots	Helius' boots	
M Arrius Niger			In century		Duty in the lines/side streets of the camp					
L Sextilius Germanus	Gate Guard	Standards	Baths	Tower?	Duty in D Decrius' century					
C Julius F…		Artillery?	Watch tower		Duty with century of Serenus					
Q Cassius Rufus	Island								Boots	
C Julius Longus Sido	Camp market duty?					In century of Helius				In century
C Julius Longus Avso	As before		On detachment with Asinius for boots?							
T Flavius Priscus					Rampart Guard					
T Flavius Niger	Left with tribune									
M Antonius Crispus	Baths	Stretchers	In century	Plain clothes	In century		Tribune's escort			
M Num…		On guard at *principia*			In century			Road Patrol	In century	
Q Petronius		?		Baths		Camp Market duty?				
. Car…s										
C Aemilius …		Escort to centurion Serenus				Camp market duty?				
C Valerius…	Escort to primus pilus					Duty in D Decrius' century				
T Flavius …				Baths			Gate guard			
Q Fabius Faber	Baths	Gate guard		Baths						
M Marcius Clemens	On detachment to harbours with Aelius or discharged on medical grounds?									
C Valerius Felix	Duty in century of Caecilius?									
C Cerficius Fuscus				Gate guard		Baths		In century		
T Furius …			Road patrol		In century	In century	Armoury			
L Gall…			Tower?					Road patrol		
Q Annius	Street cleaning									
Q V…co	On guard at *principia*						Gate guard			
M Longinus										
M Domitius …			On detachment to the granaries at Neapolis							
M Longinus A…						Latrines				
M Julius Felix	Escort to Serenus?					Gate guard				
T Flavius Valens										
C Sossius Celer										
L Vi…eius Serenus										
M Julius Longus										

(Right) A view across the late 1st-century AD fort guarding the desolate Hardknott Pass in the Lake District. Nearest to the camera is the granary – note the thick, buttressed walls – while beyond is the principia.

(Below) Outside Hardknott fort, which can be seen in the distance, is a wide area of flattened land, which appears to have formed the garrison's parade ground.

Events of purely military significance were rare, being limited to the day of *honesta missio*, or demobilisation, on 7 January, and the *rosaliae signorum*, or decoration of the standards, on 10 and 31 May. A high proportion of festivals were associated with the imperial family, in this case the Severi, and evidently intended to remind the soldiers of their loyalty. Deified emperors such as Augustus, Claudius and Trajan were also remembered, as was the divine Julius Caesar and, curiously enough, Germanicus the grandson of Augustus who died in AD 19 and was neither emperor nor deified, but extremely popular with the army. Most of these occasions are likely to have required a formal parade of most or all of the unit and were accompanied by a sacrifice, usually of bulls, cows or oxen. Probably this was followed by feasting, when the sacrificial meat was eaten, a practice certainly followed when Titus and his army celebrated the capture of Jerusalem in AD 70.

Unit training and exercises

Vegetius declared that soldiers should train constantly so that they were always prepared for war. Josephus also contrasted the never-ending and arduous exercises undergone by the Roman army with the lack of preparation of all other nations. So hard did the Roman army train and so perfect did their skill and discipline become, that the Jewish historian claimed that 'it would not be wrong to describe their drills as bloodless battles, and their battles as bloody drills'. It was also one of the most important features of the ideal Roman commander that even in peacetime he imposed upon his men a hard programme of fitness training and drill.

The reality often failed to live up to this perfect image. A common theme in the literature of the period was the belief that the army in the eastern provinces lived a luxurious and soft life in garrisons in or around the prosperous cities of the area, so that its soldiers were ill-disciplined and utterly unprepared for the rigours of campaigning. This was largely a myth, but what was certainly the case throughout the Empire was that the army's other duties frequently hindered its training for war. We have already seen that surviving duty rosters suggest that soldiers spent little time within their unit training together, but were assigned to a host of tasks in and out of the camp. Other surviving documents, which we shall examine later, confirm the picture of an army whose units were often divided into many penny packets (small detachments), which can only have reduced the opportunity for them to drill together, confirming the bonds, trust and mutual understanding between officers and men. The army was required to fulfil very many roles and at times, these could become more important than maintaining a thorough preparation for war. Even so a good provincial governor, and the officers in the hierarchy at all levels, were expected to find the time to ensure that military training did occur on a regular basis, and most Emperors made it clear that this was an important part of their task. Some went beyond admonition. Hadrian spent much of his reign touring the provinces, inspecting the army in each area and looking closely at its state of training, drawing upon his own extensive knowledge of weapons and tactics.

In AD 128, Hadrian visited the army in North Africa, and observed a series of large-scale exercises performed by Legio III Augusta and the auxiliary units of the province. Afterwards, the Emperor addressed the army at a formal parade and an inscription bearing the text of his highly complimentary speech (*adlocutio*) was subsequently set up to commemorate the event. The language and style of such pep talks has changed little over the centuries. Hadrian spoke in a direct manner, referring to 'my legate' and 'my legion', and showed detailed awareness of the unit's recent history. He mentioned that one cohort was away on detached service with the proconsul of Africa, and that two years earlier another cohort, along with four men from every other century, had been sent to reinforce another Legio III – either Gallica or Cyrenaica – and so they were under strength. In addition

Aerial view of Woden Law hillfort, Scotland. The Roman camps and siegeworks outside this Iron Age settlement have variously been interpreted as traces of training exercises or a genuine siege.

the legion had recently shifted its base on at least two occasions, and spent a lot of its time dispersed in small outposts. Having declared that these factors could have provided an excuse for poor performance, Hadrian said that no excuse was necessary for he was entirely satisfied with them, paying particular compliments to the *primi ordines* and other centurions. Throughout the speech the Emperor was especially keen to praise his officers, and the diligence of the Legatus Quintus Fabius Catullinus was continually noted.

In front of Hadrian the Ala I Pannoniorum had performed a series of manoeuvres, the cavalrymen demonstrating their skill at throwing different types of javelin. They were followed by the cavalry contingent of Cohors VI Commagenorum, who, in spite of their fewer numbers and lower-grade horses and equipment, still acquitted themselves well. There were occasional criticisms, for instance that some of the cavalry had charged and pursued too rapidly and so fallen into disorder, but on the whole the comments were extremely positive.

The exercise had included elements of a mock campaign and battle. Hadrian complimented a *cohors equitata* on moving to a position, rapidly constructing a camp, using stone for the walls and hewing out the ditch in hard ground, setting up its tent lines and cooking a meal, before forming up again and moving off once more. Several sites in Britain, notably at Llandrindod Common in the Brecon Beacons where at least 15 small camps have been located, have revealed traces of temporary camps which were almost certainly dug by troops on exercise. There is therefore at least some physical evidence for military training, but we cannot know how common training at unit and army level was. Much must have depended on the local situation and conscientiousness of unit commanders and provincial governors. Most if not all camps had a parade ground outside their perimeter, but larger-scale exercises were carried out elsewhere, perhaps in designated training areas.

Unit Exercises

'It is difficult for the cavalry of a (mixed) cohort to put on a pleasing display anyway, and especially difficult not to displease after an exercise performed by an *ala*; the latter fills a greater expanse of plain, has more riders to throw javelins, makes frequent wheels to the right and performs the Cantabrian ride in close formation, and, in keeping with their higher pay, has superior horses and finer equipment. However, you have overcome these disadvantages by doing everything you have done energetically, in spite of the hot temperature; Added to this, you have shot stones from slings and fought with javelins and everywhere mounted quickly. The special care taken by my legate Catullinus is very obvious…'

Part of the Emperor Hadrian's speech to Cohors VI Commagenorum after exercises, North Africa, AD 128.

The Rewards of Service

Pay Parade, AD 70

For the appointed day having arrived for the distribution of the soldiers' pay, he ordered his officers to parade the forces and count out the money to each man in full view of the enemy. So the troops, as was their custom, drew forth their arms from the cases in which till now they had been covered and advanced clad in mail, the cavalry leading their horses which were richly caparisoned. The area in front of the city gleamed far and wide with silver and gold, and nothing was more gratifying to the Romans, or more awe-inspiring to the enemy than that spectacle'.
Josephus, *The Jewish War* 5. 349-351 (Loeb translation).

Josephus' account of the Roman army's pay parade during the siege of Jerusalem, AD 70.

In this scene from Trajan's Column the Emperor is shown rewarding auxiliary soldiers for conspicuous service. Under the Principate all decorations came nominally from the Emperor even if they were actually presented by the provincial legate.

Legionary pay

Tradition maintained that the Roman Republic first began to pay its soldiers during the 10-year siege of Veii at the beginning of the 4th century BC. Polybius provides us with the rates of pay for Roman cavalrymen and infantrymen in the mid-2nd century BC. Cavalrymen received higher pay than the infantry, which in part reflected their higher status, but was also intended to cover the cost of fodder for their horse, for some pay was deducted to cover the cost of grain issued to each man. Allied soldiers were not paid by Rome, but received their grain ration free. Polybius gives equivalent values in Greek currency and says that a centurion received 4 obols, an infantryman 2 obols, and a cavalryman 1 drachma per day. It is now very difficult to calculate the original sums in Roman coinage, since we do not know on what basis Polybius made his calculation, but it is possible that he assumed a rate of 1 drachma = 1 *denarius*. This pay was not intended to provide a soldier with his main income, but to cover his expenses until he returned to civilian life.

Caesar doubled the pay of his legionaries so that they received 225 silver *denarii* (9 gold *aurei*) a year, which implies that before this reform they were receiving something like 112.5 *denarii*. The rate set by Caesar was maintained until the end of the 1st century AD. It was issued in three instalments (*stipendia*), each of 75 *denarii* (symbolically 3 gold coins or *aurei*, but probably paid in more practical silver), probably on 1 January, 1 May and 1 September. On campaign such regular issues were not always possible, but Titus called a pause in the siege of Jerusalem in AD 70 to pay his army. This was done with great ceremony, the troops parading in their finest equipment, and lasted for four days, one for each of the four legions in the army. The pay was probably overdue, for the parade was held at the end of May and beginning of June. It occurred when a series of reverses had shaken the legionaries' confidence and was intended to boost their morale.

At the end of the 1st century Domitian increased legionary pay to 300 *denarii* (or 12 *aurei*). This probably involved adding a fourth *stipendia*. Just over a century later, Septimius Severus increased legionary pay once again, perhaps to 450 *denarii*, which seems to have been paid once again in three *stipendia*. His son, Caracalla, increased pay by a further 50 per cent, an indication of the spiralling inflation of the 3rd century AD.

The pay received by officers of all ranks in the legion is not known with any certainty. Dio tells us that under Augustus praetorian guardsmen received double the salary given to legionaries, but it is more than possible that this is a rough approximation.

Auxiliary pay

It is clear that not all auxiliary soldiers were paid at the same rate. We know that a cavalryman received higher pay than an infantryman, so that a transfer to the cavalry section in a *cohors equitata* was considered promotion. Hadrian's speech from Lambaesis further tells us that the men of an *ala* received higher wages than the horsemen of a mixed cohort. Some men, including the *principales* and those in other junior posts, received pay and a half (*sesquiplicarii*) or double pay (*duplicarii*). However, there is no clear evidence for the amount of basic pay for any branch of the *auxilia*. Opinion is divided over whether non citizen infantrymen received the same salary as legionaries, or were paid less. One of the most recent studies arguing for a lower rate of pay suggested that under Augustus, when a legionary received 225 *denarii* per year, an auxiliary infantryman got 187.5 *denarii*, a cavalryman in a cohort 225 *denarii* and a cavalryman in an *ala* 262.5 *denarii*. All commentators seem to believe that each branch of the *auxilia* – the cavalry in an *ala*, the horsemen of a mixed cohort and the ordi-

nary infantryman – were paid at a universal rate throughout the Empire. This may have been true, but it is also possible that rates of pay sometimes varied from unit to unit, and was influenced by each unit's origins.

Stoppages and savings

All of these figures represent gross pay, and the amount actually received by the soldier was considerably less. In Tacitus' description of the mutiny in the Rhine army following the death of Augustus in AD 14, he has the mutineers complain of their low pay, from which was deducted charges for clothes, equipment and tents. A small number of surviving documents dealing with the pay, stoppages and savings of individual soldiers provide more concrete examples. One of the best-preserved documents lists the accounts of two soldiers in Egypt in the year AD 81. Their unit is unknown, but it is usually assumed that they were auxiliaries, since each instalment of pay is less than a legionary *stipendium*. Payment was made in drachmas, one of which was probably equivalent to 1 *sestertius*. This has been taken to mean that their standard *stipendium* was 250 *sesterces* (or 62.5 *denarii*), but that 2.5 *sesterces* were deducted as a charge for converting the pay into locally used drachmas. The account of the first man is as follows:

In the consulship of Lucius Asinius (AD 81)
QUINTUS JULIUS PROCULUS from DAMASCUS
received the first salary instalment of the third year of the Emperor, 247.5 drachmas, out of which:

hay	10 drachmas
for food	80 drachmas
boots & straps (poss. socks)	12 drachmas
Saturnalia of the camp	20 drachmas
?	60 drachmas
expenditure =	182 drachmas
balance deposited to his account	65.5 drachmas
and had from before	136 drachmas
making a total of	201.5 drachmas

received the second instalment of the same year 247.5 drachmas, out of which:

hay	10 drachmas
for food	80 drachmas
boots & straps (poss. socks)	12 drachmas
to the standards	4 drachmas
expenditure=	106 drachmas
balance deposited to his account	141.5 drachmas
and had from before	201.5 drachmas
making a total of	343 drachmas

received the third instalment of the same year 247.5 drachmas, out of which:

hay	10 drachmas
for food	80 drachmas
boots & straps (poss. socks)	12 drachmas
for clothes	145.5 drachmas
expenditure=	247.5 drachmas
balance deposited to his account	343 drachmas

The other man's account is similar, but he suffered an additional charge of 100 drachmas for clothing in his first *stipendium*, and also started off with less money saved so that his final savings were only 188 drachmas. Most of the other entries were identical, which suggests that the charges, such as 80 drachmas for food per *stipendium*, were standard and incurred by all soldiers. It is unclear why the men paid for hay, since they do not appear to have been cavalrymen. Perhaps it was used for bedding, as in some form of palliasse, or required by the *contubernium*'s mule. Both men paid 145.5 drachmas for clothing in the third *stipendium*, which suggests that certain items were issued annually in the expectation that they would wear out in this time.

A similar document was found at Masada in Judaea and appears to record the expenses incurred by a soldier serving as part of the fortress garrison after its recapture. The man, Gaius Messius, was a Roman citizen, most probably serving in Legio X Fretensis. In this case all sums are in *denarii*, 20 of which – equal to 80 drachmas – were deducted for food, which once more suggests a standard rate. The document also appears to record the purchase of items, in one case a cloak and in the other a white tunic, from other named individuals, probably fellow soldiers. The man also paid for barley, which has led some to believe that he was a legionary cavalryman, although it may instead equate to the hay in the Egyptian papyrus. What is curious is that his salary is listed as 50 *denarii* in the first instalment and 60 in the second. This has variously been interpreted as referring to the total deductions, or implying earlier stoppages made before the unit's *signifer* came to issue money. Both views are plausible enough, but this oddity should warn us against generalizing about pay from a tiny sample of specific documents.

Domitian banned soldiers from banking more than 250 *denarii* with the unit funds, after a provincial governor had tried to employ these to fund a rebellion. Other records on papyrus suggest that at least some men were able to save as large, or even larger, sums, and it is more than probable that this restriction soon lapsed.

Donatives

On his death, Augustus bequeathed 250 *denarii* to every praetorian, 125 to soldiers in the urban cohorts, and 75 to legionaries and the members of the *cohortes civium Romanorum* (units of freedmen raised in the crises of AD 6 and 9). Successive emperors repeated this practice, and other substantial donatives were made on accession or to mark key events. The loyalty of the praetorians was essential, and as a result these men always received considerably more money than any other part of the army. Claudius owed the throne entirely to the praetorians and as a result gave each guardsman 3,750 *denarii*. In the second half of the 2nd century, Marcus Aurelius and Lucius Verus marked their accession and confirmed the support of the praetorian guard by presenting them with 5,000 *denarii* apiece. The amounts given to legionaries increased, though not as rapidly. Auxiliaries seem to have been excluded from such bounties until Late Antiquity.

Decorations

Not all rewards given to soldiers were financial. Polybius believed that one of the most important reasons for Rome's military success was the care she took to reward brave soldiers. At the end of a campaign the army was paraded and the general addressed them from a tribunal. He then 'calls forward those he considers to have shown exceptional courage. He praises them first for their gallantry in action and for anything in their previous conduct which is particularly worthy of mention and then distributes gifts.' Josephus

The 1st-century AD tombstone of Gnaeus Musius, aquilifer (eagle-bearer) of Legio XIV Gemina, shows him wearing a harness decorated with a large number of dona, *including* phalerae *and* torques.

described how Titus presided at such a parade after the fall of Jerusalem in AD 70:

'Calling up each by name he applauded them as they came forward, no less exultant over their exploits than if they were his own. He then placed crowns of gold upon their heads, presented them with golden neck-chains, little golden spears and standards made of silver, and promoted each man to a higher rank; he further assigned to them out of the spoils silver and gold and raiments and other booty in abundance.' (Loeb translation)

Listed are some of the most common decorations (*dona*), including the blunt-headed, miniature spear (*hasta pura*), the miniature standard (*vexillum*), and a torque worn around the neck. Smaller, torque-shaped medals, along with disc-shaped decorations (*phalerae*), were often worn on a harness over a man's armour, whilst arm-bands (*armillae*) were worn on the wrists. The most important decorations were various types of crowns. The oldest, and most hallowed, was the civic crown (*corona civica*), which was awarded for saving the life of a fellow citizen. Traditionally, that man had to acknowledge the debt he owed to his comrade, and himself make a simple crown from oak leaves. The siege crown (*corona obsidionalis*), made from twisted grass, was only awarded on a handful of occasions to men who had relieved a besieged garrison. The other crowns were of gold – the mural crown (*corona muralis*) and the rampart crown (*corona vallaris*), given to the first man over an enemy wall or rampart respectively. Leading an assaulting party on an enemy-held fortification was extremely dangerous, but brought a man considerable fame. After the capture of New Carthage in 209 BC, Scipio Africanus had to arbitrate between rival claims from the fleet and legions that one of their men had been first over the wall. Ultimately, he gave both claimants the crown.

It was extremely rare for the Romans to make any sort of posthumous award, although Caesar seems to have honoured one of his centurions who fell at Pharsalus in 48 BC. A soldier had normally to survive to claim a tangible reward. Perhaps inevitably, officers were more likely to receive recognition for their bravery. The regular pattern of awards to senior officers such as tribunes and legates under the Principate suggests that most were automatic decorations and did not require any conspicuous behaviour.

At Jerusalem, the soldiers receiving decorations were also promoted and given a larger share of the spoil. These tangible rewards were doubtless very important, but we should not underestimate the deep emotional importance of the medals themselves. Soldiers who won such awards had proved their gallantry and received the respect and admiration of their comrades. In 47 BC, during the civil war between Caesar and his enemies, the general Metellus Scipio initially refused to present gold *armillae* to a cavalryman because the man was an ex-slave. The soldier's immediate commander, Labienus, offered to reward him instead with gold coins. When the soldier refused this, Metellus relented and delighted the man by presenting him with silver *armillae* of considerably less intrinsic worth. *Dona* were important, so much so that they were frequently mentioned, and often physically depicted, on the recipient's tombstone. Understanding the deeply emotional importance of decorations, all emperors ensured that these were presented in their name, helping to confirm the loyalty of the army.

By the late 1st century AD, decorations were rarely if ever presented to ordinary soldiers in auxiliary units, although they were still received by officers. Instead, conspicuous gallantry was rewarded by honours paid to the unit. In some cases the soldiers received Roman citizenship before their discharge, as happened with Cohors I Brittonum milliaria after active service in Trajan's Dacian Wars. Such units usually kept the title *civium Romanorum* (of Roman citizens), even after all the men who had actually received the grant had left the army. Several of the battle honours awarded to auxiliary units echoed the names of individual *dona*, so that units received such titles as *torquata* or *bis torquata*, *armillata*, or *coram laudata* (usually abbreviated to C.L.). The unit of Britons mentioned earlier eventually gathered a long list of such honours, to become Cohors I Brittonum milliaria Ulpia torquata p.f. (pia fidelis) c.R. (civium Romanorum).

Diet and rations

During a campaign, the need to keep his army adequately supplied was one of the greatest concerns of a Roman commander. Even in peacetime, considerable effort was needed to provide for the army in its garrisons. As we have seen, the cost of his food was a standard deduction from a soldier's pay, and it was important both for morale and the health and efficiency of the army that proper rations were actually issued. Literary sources suggest that the basic components of the military diet were grain (usually wheat), meat (especially bacon), cheese, and sour wine (*acetum*) as opposed to proper, vintage wine (*vinum*), often vegetables and notably lentils.

Much of the ration was issued unprepared, for there were no real equivalents to the communal canteens or mess-halls of modern armies. Soldiers were issued with their individual ration and then prepared it with their *contubernium*, either in ovens set into the fortress walls or built into the barrack blocks. The army had two basic meals in the day, breakfast (*prandium*) in the morning and dinner (*cena*) at the end of the day. The grain ration was usually issued in its basic form – although on campaign it might be provided in the form of hard-tack biscuit (*bucellatum*), and was then ground by the soldiers into flour. The Emperor Caracalla was

The north-east corner of the legionary fortress at Caerleon. On the right is a barrack block and on the left the rampart, between them the roadway or intervallum. Set into the rampart are ovens while in the corner is a tower.

eager to live the simple life of an ordinary soldier when on campaign, and it is said that he used an army hand mill to grind his own grain ration. Quern stones have been found at some military sites. Once turned into flour, the ration was frequently baked into wholemeal bread (*panis militaris*). A bread-stamp from the legionary fortress at Caerleon suggests that a baker and two assistants were responsible for making a century's bread in an oven. There seems also to have been a higher-quality military loaf, which was perhaps eaten by officers. Alternatively, the grain ration could be used to make porridge or soup, the latter possibly in combination with vegetables and meat, or turned into one of the forms of pasta known from Pompeii.

There is an enduring myth that Roman soldiers were essentially vegetarian. It rests largely on the misreading of a few passages where a historian notes that Roman soldiers were reluctantly forced to exist on an overwhelmingly meat diet. Yet it is clear that whenever possible the troops wanted a balanced and varied diet. Bacon and pork are often mentioned in our literary sources, and formed an important part of the diet of Italian civilians. Interestingly, pig bones turn up far more frequently in the excavation of legionary fortresses than auxiliary forts, especially in northern Europe, which suggests that citizen soldiers had a greater fondness for this meat. They are especially common in early legionary bases such as Nijmegen in Holland, occupied under Augustus, when the legions consumed pork in similar quantities to Italians. Thereafter, probably reflecting the decline in the number of Italians serving in the legions, the proportion of pig bones from legionary sites drops,

although it rarely falls below 20 per cent and on the Upper Danube tends to be considerably higher.

Instead of pork, the legionaries seem to have eaten a good deal of beef. Cattle provided not only meat, but leather which the army required for a range of purposes, most notably the manufacture and repair of tents. The bone finds from auxiliary forts also suggest that these troops consumed large numbers of cattle, but there is usually a much higher proportion of sheep and goat bones from these sites in comparison to legionary bases. It may be that this difference had as much to do with availability as dietary preference. In Britain the inhabitants of the simpler villages and farms which changed little from the pre-Roman Iron Age seem to have kept and eaten more sheep and goats, whereas the more 'Romanized' sections of the population dwelling in towns or villas ate far more beef. Auxiliary forts tended to be located in the less developed areas and the meat component of their diet reflected that of the local population in type, although it was usually greater in quantity. It is also probable that the difficulty of transporting pigs, as opposed to cattle or sheep, over long distances made these more readily available in the centrally located legionary bases.

The rations issued by the army appear in general to have been adequate, if inclined to be somewhat monotonous, and were evidently often supplemented by private purchases. Food is a common theme in the surviving correspondence of Roman soldiers. One document from Vindolanda appears to be an account from a firm of civilian traders who supplied both grain and loaves to units and individuals, both military and civilian. Letters from Egypt

A scene from Trajan's Column showing a row of Roman fortlets and watchtowers along the River Danube. On the left two auxiliaries unload stores from a boat. In the ancient world it was usually far easier to transport bulky items over water than on land.

reveal soldiers writing to their families requesting that they send them extra food. Food is the main theme of the many *ostraka* (potsherds with messages on them) written in the 1st century by soldiers garrisoning the rather desolate post at Wadi Fawakhir on the road from Coptos to the Red Sea. These mention bread, barley, oil, various vegetables, including onions, radishes and cabbages, salted fish, wine and meat. Inevitably officers with their higher pay were able to purchase a great number of luxury items, from oysters to sauces and fine wines. Some of the Vindolanda tablets give an impression of the requirements of the household of a senior officer, although the actual purchasing was usually the task of slaves. One slave, Severus, wrote to another slave, Candidus owned by the prefect Genialis, arranging for him to purchase goods which included radishes. Another letter, again probably from slave to slave, gave instructions for the purchase of a range of goods needed by a large household, including 'bruised beans, two *modii* [17.5 litres, or 30.8 pints], chickens, twenty, a hundred apples, if you can find nice ones, one hundred or two hundred eggs, if they are for sale at a fair price … 8 sextarii [4.4 litres, or 7.7 pints] of fish sauce … a modius of olives….'

Apart from purchase, additional food could be supplied by hunting and there is considerable evidence for soldiers indulging in this. Deer, especially red and roe dear and elk, were commonly hunted for food as well as sport in the northern provinces. The German provinces seem to have offered better hunting grounds than Britain, for the bone evidence from military sites in this area attests to the hunting of a very wide range of animals, many of which, such as bear, wolf and aurochs, are now extinct in the region. Fishing was another source of additional food, and bones and fishhooks have been found at a number of sites.

Beer (*cervesa*) is mentioned on several occasions at Vindolanda, and may well have formed part of the basic ration. There is some evidence to suggest soldiers brewing beer at Caerleon, and this drink was probably very common, especially in the northern and western provinces. It is likely that there were other regional and period variations affecting the military diet, but such trends are hard to discern. Certain foods may have been taboo on religious grounds to men recruited from some ethnic groups. The garrison of Bearsden on the Antonine Wall appears to have eaten little meat, but we cannot say who they were or why this was so.

Apart from the soldiers, the army had also to meet the needs of the many animals they maintained as mounts or beasts of burden. A late 1st-century AD document from Carlisle lists the allocation of wheat and barley to the 16 *turmae* of a cavalry *ala*. Wheat was intended for the soldiers and the barley for their horses. The huge quantities of grain, as well as meat, required by the army were provided from a range of sources, which included taxation. Local supply was not always possible, and indeed could rarely provide all the requirements of a unit, and large quantities of grain and other material were often transported considerable distances. Depots, consisting primarily of rows and rows of large granaries, were often established at ports or on navigable rivers, such as the base at Arbeia (South Shields) near the mouth of the Tyne in the 2nd and 3rd centuries. From such points, grain could be distributed as required to individual units.

Health and medical facilities

The continued good health and fitness of its soldiers was essential for maintaining the army's effectiveness. Roman bases and temporary camps were supposed to be sited in as healthy a location as possible. Bath houses were provided to keep the soldiers clean, and drains and latrines to ensure reasonable standards of hygiene. The latrine at Housesteads is particularly well preserved. Men sat on wooden seats above stone lavatories, the waste dropping into a drain which was kept constantly flushed by flowing water. Other channels of flowing water were provided to wash out the sponges which the Romans used instead of lavatory paper.

Some temporary camps may have included a sizeable tented hospital, usually laid out as a square around a central open space, a design which was to a great extent preserved in the permanent buildings of the later fortresses. Even when there was no large-scale campaigning, the base hospitals seem often to have been occupied. A strength report of Cohors I Tungrorum stationed at Vindolanda

A view of the internal buildings at Housesteads, showing the hospital on the far right. A strength report from nearby Vindolanda includes men hospitalized because of unspecified illnesses, eye inflammation, and wounds.

(Right) A range of Roman
medical equipment. Some
army doctors were highly
skilled by the standards of the
day, and the Medical Manual
of Celsus contains much
information about the
treatment of wounds. Soldiers
received better medical care
than was available to the
poorer classes in civilian life.

(Below) In one of the battle
scenes on Trajan's Column, a
legionary and an auxiliary are
shown having their wounds
treated by medical orderlies.

around AD 90 listed 31 men as unfit for duty, namely
15 sick, six wounded and 10 suffering from inflammation of the eyes. This represented almost 12 per
cent of the 265 men actually at the base, and just
over four per cent of the entire unit. Records from
units elsewhere usually include a number of men
incapacitated by disease or wounds. One of the
letters written by the legionary Claudius Terentianus to his father apologized for failing to meet
him. He explained that 'at that time so violent and
dreadful an attack of fish poisoning made me ill,
and for five days I was unable to drop you a line, not
to speak of going to meet you. Not one of us was
able to leave the camp gate.' After returning to duty
he seems to have been injured whilst policing a riot
in Alexandria and returned to hospital.

There were a range of medical staff supporting
the legions. The most important was the doctor
(*medicus*), at least some of whom seem to have
ranked with centurions (*medicus ordinarius*). A
good number of these men appear to have been
from the Hellenistic provinces, and some at least
were highly skilled. The great medical writer Galen
mentions with approval a headache cure devised by
an army doctor called Antigonus, as well as an eye-
salve made from a range of ingredients including
mercuric sulphide which was the work of an oculist
in the British fleet (*classis Britannica*) named Axius.
Another army doctor, Pedanius Dioscurides, had
written *Materia Medica*, a text which was cited by
Galen and used for a considerable period of time.
Such men were clearly amongst the best army

doctors, and the skill of the average *medicus* may well have been far lower, although another medical writer, Celsus, notes that they, like the surgeons at the gladiatorial schools, had far more opportunity to study anatomy than their civilian peers.

Beneath the *medici* were a range of personnel, including the *optio valetudinarii*, who seems to have overseen the administration of the hospital. Men known as *capsarii*, after the round first-aid/bandage box or *capsa*, provided more basic treatment than the senior medical staff. Celsus' manual provides detailed descriptions of treating various wounds, methods which were only a little less advanced than any employed until recent centuries. Some surgical implements have also survived and attest to quite sophisticated operations. The army provided a level of medical care which was far greater than that normally accessible to poor civilians.

Discipline and punishment

The Roman army's system of discipline had been severe even when the legions were raised from wealthy citizens serving out of their sense of loyalty to the state. If anything, its punishments became even more brutal when the army became a professional force. From the very beginning of a recruit's training, the army made it clear how they expected a soldier to behave. Those who conformed to this pattern of behaviour were rewarded, but those who failed to do so faced punishment. A Byzantine military manual, the Strategikon, dates to well after our period but preserved drill commands in Latin which probably had changed little from the days of the Principate. Silence and rigid discipline were constantly stressed, and the *optiones* walking behind the rear rank of the formation had long staffs with which to strike any man who dropped out of place or spoke. The *vitis*, the centurion's vine cane, was frequently used to inflict beatings, leaving scars on many a soldier's back. This corporal punishment appears to have been inflicted entirely at the whim of these officers, and such martinets were invariably the first targets in a mutiny. Tacitus tells us that in AD 14 the mutinous legions on the Rhine lynched a centurion nicknamed 'Fetch me another!' (*cedo alteram*) from his habit of snapping his cane over a legionary's back and bawling out for another to continue his punishment.

The death penalty probably required the sanction of more senior officers, but was inflicted for a range of offences. Sentries found asleep on guard – the old soldiers' trick was to prop up their long shield with their *pilum* and then lean on it, dozing off whilst still standing up – were, as under the Republic, clubbed to death by the comrades whose lives they had put at risk. Soldiers who fled from battle could be condemned to be crucified or thrown to the wild beasts, penalties reserved normally for criminals from the lowest sections of society, and not inflicted on

An altar dedicated to Disciplina, *the personified deity of military discipline, by Legio II Augusta. The cult of* Disciplina *flourished for a while in some provinces during the 2nd century.*

citizens. Probably the most famous punishment was decimation imposed on a unit which had fled ignominiously from battle. One tenth of the soldiers were selected by lot for execution. The remaining 90 per cent of the unit suffered a more symbolic penalty, for they were ordered to set up their tents and sleep outside the rampart of the camp, and were issued barley instead of wheat. As with the medals which demonstrated a man's warrior status, these public humiliations were deeply felt. Augustus is said to have punished not only soldiers but even centurions, by ordering them to stand at attention outside his tent for an entire day, wearing only their unbelted tunic and perhaps holding a pole or clod of earth.

Soldiers had no opportunity to appeal against any penalty. In the 4th century AD the historian and soldier Ammianus Marcellinus claimed that avoidance of punishment was the commonest reason for a man to desert. This may well have also been true under the Principate, and certainly our sources attest to desertion as an ever-present problem for the professional army. Many enemy leaders, including Jugurtha, Tacfarinas and Decebalus are said to have recruited their best men from Roman deserters. In the 1st century AD Corbulo, renowned as a strict disciplinarian, routinely executed men captured after deserting for the first time. Normally, only men who had run two or three times suffered the death penalty. Yet even so, he did not eradicate the problem altogether, and his army simply suffered a lower than average rate of desertion.

Off Duty

(Right) A stone found near the fortress at Caerleon commemorating a soldier's wife, Tadia Vallaunius, who died at the age of 65, as well as her son Tadius Exuperatus.

(Below) The tombstone of the freedman Victor, who died aged 20, was set up by his former master, Numerianus, a trooper in Ala I Asturum. The high quality of the tombstone suggests Numerianus' affection for his freedman.

Marriage and families

From Augustus onwards, Roman soldiers were forbidden to marry. If already married when they joined the army, then the union was immediately declared invalid. The state felt that armies would operate more effectively if unencumbered by soldiers' families, and even more importantly was reluctant to accept any responsibility for these dependants. This ban endured for more than two centuries, until it was finally lifted by Septimius Severus, although the precise nature of this reform is uncertain. Yet soldiers served for 25 years, the bulk of their active adult life, and it was unrealistic

to expect them to wait until discharge before forming a long-term liaison with a woman. In fact, in spite of the official position, there is ample evidence to show that soldiers took women as their 'wives' and raised families in a union which both parties considered to be a proper marriage. Probably always common, this practice became even more so as the army's units settled into more permanent garrisons by the late 1st and early 2nd centuries. Many of these women were natives of the provinces, and not a few were former slaves, freed and then married by their soldier owners. By the 2nd century AD a growing number of soldiers declared themselves as having been born 'in the camp' (*in castris*), showing that they were offspring of just such a relationship. A tombstone found outside the fortress of Legio II Augusta at Caerleon commemorates not only a woman, Tadia Vallaunius, but her soldier son, Tadius Exuperatus, who had died on a military campaign in Germany. The monument was erected by her daughter, Tadia Exuperata, and mentions that it lay next to the tomb of her husband, himself perhaps also once a soldier.

The reality of the situation was tacitly acknowledged by the wording of the *diplomata* presented to auxiliary soldiers at the end of their 25 years service. This granted Roman citizenship not only to the soldier, but to his wife and children or, if he was still single on discharge, to a wife (but only one wife) married subsequently. On some early *diplomata* the soldier, his wife and children are all specifically named. By the middle of the 2nd century AD the wording changed and the grant of citizenship to children was no longer included.

Legionaries were already citizens and so received no grant of the franchise at the end of their time in the army. Many had begun to raise a family, but the legal position of both wife and children was highly insecure. Most wives were non-citizens, and even if they were the marriage was not recognized and so the children were legally illegitimate and would not gain the franchise. It was often difficult for families to inherit. In many respects a soldier's legal status was peculiar. Forbidden to marry, he was liable to the penalties imposed upon citizens who had no children until Claudius exempted soldiers from these laws. Appreciating the desire of soldiers to bequeath property to their families, and yet reluctant to remove the ban on marriage, successive emperors granted them concessions, allowing them to make wills – something not normally possible for a man whilst his father was alive, since technically the latter owned all the property of his household. Hadrian confirmed this right, allowed soldiers to make bequests to non-citizens, and even permitted soldiers' children to make claims on his property if he had died without making a will. Papyri from Egypt attest the deep concern felt over many of these issues. One, dating to AD 131, consists of a declaration by Epimachus, son of Longinus, that the baby girl Longinia born to his wife/concubine, Arsus, was his daughter. Such formal statements of paternity, made before witnesses, could help the child to prove her identity and succeed in any claims on inheriting her father's property. The difficulty of securing such rights is demonstrated by surviving legal decisions. In AD 117 the 'widow' Lucia Macrina tried to recover money from her late husband's estate by appealing to the prefect of Egypt. The latter, deciding that the money she had given to her soldier husband was understood as a dowry, but knowing that legally a soldier could not marry, refused to allow its return to her. A few years before, a Roman citizen serving in an auxiliary cohort who was cohabiting with a citizen woman and had had two sons by her, tried to get them the franchise. The prefect permitted the boys citizenship but refused to remove their status as illegitimate. In another case, the woman Chrotis sought recognition for her son by the soldier Isodorus, who had made the boy his heir without formally declaring himself the father. The prefect once again stressed that a serving soldier could not have a legitimate child, but was willing to allow the boy to inherit since he had been named in Isodorus' will. The legal situation of soldiers' families was confused and precarious at best.

Although we know that a high proportion of soldiers – some scholars have estimated as many as 50 per cent – married and started families, it is not at all clear where these families actually lived. It has been conventional to assume that the women and children dwelt in the *canabae* around a fort, which would presumably mean that married men were able to spend a good deal of time, and perhaps sleep, outside the ramparts. However, there is some evidence, chiefly consisting of finds of artifacts and clothing associ-

A late 2nd-century AD monument from Germany commemorating a sailor's daughter. Whatever the official attitude towards military personnel raising families, the troops themselves clearly took such bonds very seriously.

ated with women or children inside excavated barrack blocks, which may mean that wives and children lived inside the fort with their husbands. Although to the modern mind this would suggest that the *contubernium* rooms were terribly crowded and that families had no privacy, such practices were common in many European armies until well into the 19th century. Families may not have been the only civilians to live within military bases. Some soldiers kept slaves as personal servants, whilst the army owned many more, known as *galearii* (or 'helmet-wearers'), who wore a simple uniform and performed service functions such as controlling the baggage and pack animals on campaign.

Officers' wives

The ban on marriage did not apply to senior officers from the senatorial and equestrian classes, nor to legionary centurions, and probably not to auxiliary centurions and perhaps also decurions. There is certainly some evidence to suggest that these auxiliary officers were also permitted to marry. During his term as governor of Bithynia and Pontus, the Younger Pliny successfully entreated the Emperor Trajan to grant citizenship to the daughter of an auxiliary centurion and there is no mention of any bar on his having married. Decurions' wives sometimes appear on inscriptions, for instance Aelia Comindus who died at the age of 32 and was commemorated by her husband Nobilianus at Carrawburgh on Hadrian's Wall. Another decurion, Tiberius Claudius Valerius, who died at the age of 50 after 30 years service with Ala II Hispanorum et Aravacorum, had his tombstone set up in Teutoburgium in Pannonia by his wife and daughter.

Senators, and many equestrian officers, spent only part of their public career with the army.

Although it appears to have been normal for their wives and children to accompany them during their military service, it is very rare for the presence of the latter to be recorded unless they or their husbands died and were commemorated. Rufinus, prefect successively of Cohors I Augustae Lusitanorum and Cohors I Breucorum died aged 48 at High Rochester. The memorial to her 'well-deserving husband' was set up by Julia Lucilla, herself from a senatorial family. An altar found outside the fort demonstrates that the couple were accompanied to the frontier by their household. It was set up by one of their freedmen, Eutychus and his family, fulfilling a vow to the god Silvanus Pantheus, to whom he had prayed for the welfare of his master and mistress. The Vindolanda tablets help to give some idea of the social life of the wives of garrison commanders. One of the most famous is an invitation sent to the wife of Flavius Cerealis, the commander of Vindolanda, by the wife of another auxiliary prefect:

'To Sulpicia Lepidina, wife of Cerealis, from Severa.

'Claudia Severa to her Lepidina greetings. On 11 September, sister, for the day of the celebration of my birthday, I give you a warm invitation to make sure that you come to us, to make the day more enjoyable for me by your arrival, if you are present… Give my greetings to your Cerealis. My Aelius and my little son send him… their greetings. I shall expect you, sister. Farewell, sister, my dearest soul, as I hope to prosper, and hail.'

Although the main text was doubtless written by a slave or freedman, the last line was added in Severa's own hand. In another letter, Severa mentions having to ask her husband's permission to visit Lepidina, reflecting the dangers of travelling on the exposed northern frontier.

Senatorial and equestrian officers were expressly forbidden to marry women from the province in which they served, but the same did not apply to centurions, many of whom married locals. Depending on the size of the garrison, the community formed by the officers' wives might be substantial or tiny. In an auxiliary fort only the commander's wife was an equestrian, and the perhaps half-dozen or so centurions' spouses were her clear social inferiors. In a legionary fortress, both the legate and the senior tribune were senators, and if married their wives would come from a similar background. There were also the equestrian tribunes and their families, the camp prefect and senior centurions who achieved equestrian status during their career, as well as a large number of centurions, many of whom were probably married. At times the provincial governor – or even occasionally the emperor and empress – and his family passed through a military base or came to one of the towns in the area, either on a tour of inspection or to oversee a campaign. Septimius Severus' wife Julia Domna accompanied her husband to Syria, where she was granted the title 'Mother of the Camp' (*mater castrorum*) in AD 195, and also to Britain. From AD 14 to 16 Agrippina and her children lived in the army camps whilst her husband Germanicus, the Emperor Tiberius' adopted son, campaigned across the Rhine. The couple dressed their young son Gaius in a miniature version of the soldier's uniform, earning him the nickname Caligula or 'little boots'. Agrippina took her role very seriously, visiting the sick and wounded in hospital and even famously taking charge of the Rhine bridges when false rumours spread of a disaster.

Governors' wives did not always behave in such exemplary fashion. A few years later Plancina, wife of Lucius Calpurnius Piso, a Syrian governor sacked by Germanicus and rumoured to have subsequently engineered the latter's mysterious death, had presided over military exercises and tried to build up a body of supporters amongst army officers. However, when one senator tried to ban governors' wives from following their husbands to their provinces, he found little support for the measure.

Alongside the formal military hierarchy, army bases of any size also enclosed the narrow world of wives and families. Sometimes large, sometimes isolated, this community was also at times rocked by scandal. During Caligula's reign the wife of the legate Calvisius Sabinus began an affair with the *tribunus laticlavius* and noted rake Titus Vinius. On one occasion she disguised herself in military uniform and accompanied the tribune as he inspected the guards on duty in the fortress that night. The couple were later discovered to have gone on to make love inside the *principia*. Although Vinius was arrested on Caligula's orders, the latter's assassination soon afterwards brought him pardon. The Younger Pliny was involved as a prosecutor in a trial resulting from another such scandal, in this case when Gallitta, a tribune's wife, had carried on an affair with one of the centurions under his command. The centurion was dismissed from the army and exiled, whilst the husband, who according to Pliny was 'apparently satisfied once he had got rid of his rival', was reluctantly forced to divorce his wife.

Canabae and *vici*

Civilian settlements quickly grew up around almost every Roman base. Caesar's description of a surprise attack on one of his legion's winter camps in 53 BC mentions as an aside the presence of traders camping outside the fortifications. The little stone huts scattered outside the Roman siege camps at Masada in Judaea may show that merchants and camp followers stayed with the army during the siege in AD 74 even in the harsh conditions of the desert. These temporary settlements were known as *canabae*. We cannot know if this was where soldiers' families lived, although it seems most probably that this was the case until barracks were built in a

substantial and permanent fashion. It is certain that the people who followed the army and lived around its bases provided many service-industries for the troops. Merchants could sell them additional food or drink to supplement their rations, and many of the other luxuries which could make a soldier's life more pleasant. Paid regularly in coin, military garrisons provided a ready market for a whole range of goods and services. The *canabae* also provided entertainment ranging from music to bars and brothels. One veteran of Legio II Augusta paid to set up a monument to a certain Polla Matidia, also known as Olympia, a dancer or entertainer at Asciburgium in Germany. Titus Aelius Iustus, a musician from Legio II Aduitrix skilled on the water-organ, was married to Aelia Sabina, herself a singer and musician, and even better player.

At first the settlements around camps appear as shanty towns, and suggest a somewhat rough-and-ready frontier community. One of the houses near

Aerial view of the fort at Vindolanda with the civilian vicus *in the foreground. The writing tablets from this site have given some insight into the social life of senior officers' wives.*

(Right) The amphitheatre at
Caerleon lies actually on the
edge of the ditch surrounding
the fortress rampart. The
stonework here would have
been greatly heightened by
wooden structures supporting
tiers of seats capable of
accommodating at least the
entire legion of some 5,000
men. An amphitheatre
provided an area for parades
and displays by troops, but its
primary role was the staging
of gladiatorial games and
other violent entertainments.

the southern gate of Housesteads fort was discovered to have had the skeletons of a man and woman buried beneath its floor, something which only the builder can have done. In time, most *canabae* grew into something more formal, and villages or *vici* were established. The ordered plan of many *vici* suggests that the army was involved in at least some stages of their initial planning. Usually the settlements are linear or ribbon-like in shape, with rows of houses running along a road near, leading up to or surrounding a base. In a number of sites an existing road was widened to create an open area which probably served as a market place. Space along the roadsides was at a premium and most buildings are strip houses, narrow-fronted but very long, of a type known from many Roman towns. Usually the front of the house was partially open providing a commercial space, probably a shop or bar.

The *vicus* and the fort had a symbiotic relationship benefiting both parties, but it is clear that the *vicus* was seen as a community in its own right and may have had magistrates overseeing its affairs. The populations of these settlements were often highly cosmopolitan with soldiers, serving and discharged, locals and traders from all over the Roman world rubbing shoulders. Barates, a native of Palmyra, the great oasis city on the silk road in the far east of the Empire, set up a memorial to his wife outside South Shields fort on the northern frontier of Britain. She was a Briton, although from a tribe living in the south of the island, and once his slave, but then freed and married. Barates himself may be the same man whose tombstone was found further along Hadrian's Wall at Corbridge, where he is described as either a standard-bearer or, less plausibly, a seller of flags. Whether soldier or merchant, this family testifies to the considerable mobility of some parts of the population of the Roman world.

Entertainment

There was usually an amphitheatre outside any legionary fortress, and in a few cases even outside the much smaller auxiliary forts. These structures were built by the army primarily for its own use and in some cases a timber structure predates a later more permanent stone arena, suggesting that these were often constructed in an early phase of the base. Excavations at the amphitheatre outside the base of Legio II Augusta at Caerleon revealed centurial stones marking out sections of the building built by a particular century. One, commemorating the 'Century of Rufinus', was especially finely carved and clearly intended as a permanent display. This practice of dividing the task up between working groups based on the units was commonly employed in major projects, most notably the construction of Hadrian's Wall. The Caerleon amphitheatre measures 81.4 m (267 ft) along its longest axis and 67.7 m (222 ft) in width. A massive and heavily buttressed external wall, 1.7 m (5 ft 6 in)

thick, supported the earth bank on which the seating was built. Estimates of the original height of the tiers of seats suggest a seating capacity of at least 6,000, so that it could have accommodated more than the entire legion at full strength. Other legionary amphitheatres, for instance at Chester and especially Carnuntum on the Danube, were even bigger than this.

Amphitheatres were primarily designed to mount the range of spectacular blood sports which so fascinated the population of the Roman Empire. It is unlikely that provincial garrisons could afford the massive displays staged at Rome, and there were in fact limits on the amount communities elsewhere were permitted to spend on such entertainment, although the military arenas doubtless put on periodic gladiatorial bouts or beast fights. The amphitheatre also provided a stage and viewing arena for other activities, including formal parades and displays of drill and weapons' handling put on by the legion itself.

Baths and bathing

The bath house provided a range of services far beyond simple hygiene. For the Romans bathing was an important ritual, a process which involved passing through a series of bathing areas maintained at different temperatures. There was the cold room (*frigidarium*) with its plunge bath, hot room (*laconicum*), warm steam room (*tepidarium*) and the hot steam room (*caldarium*). Temperature was regulated by a combination of underfloor heating and hot flues inside the walls. Excavations at Vindolanda revealed wooden sandals worn to protect a bather's feet from the often too hot floor in parts of the bath. Bathers rubbed down with oil and then

scraped off the dirt using a tool called a *strigil*. Taking a bath was an experience to be savoured and not hurried, but even after a soldier had bathed he might choose to remain in the bath house. In the larger establishments there were facilities for further exercise, but in all baths there was space and opportunity for relaxed socializing. Men could drink and talk, or play at the various gambling games, most of all dice, with which the Romans were obsessed.

Apart from the bath houses built by the army itself, there were often other baths in the *vici*. At Caerleon a bath house was discovered near to the amphitheatre. It is impossible to know whether these establishments were ever frequented by troops as well as civilians. Finds from several military baths show that these were used by women as well as soldiers, although it is possible that there were set times for different groups. The Roman army also appears to have taken a keen interest in the development of baths at spa sites, such as Bath (Aquae Sulis) in Britain. This complex was constructed relatively soon after the conquest of the area and it is likely that the legionary garrisons at Exeter and Gloucester were closely involved in its construction. The healing power of hot springs was highly valued by the Romans, and almost certainly employed for aiding the recovery of the sick and wounded. One altar from Bath recording the reconstruction of a 'religious place' (locus religiosus) was set up by Caius Severius Emeritus, a centurion charged with the administration of a region.

(Above) The bath house at Chesters fort on Hadrian's Wall is sited near the river. The danger of fire ensured that the baths in cramped auxiliary forts were built outside the walls.

(Below) A reconstruction of the bath house at Vindolanda shows the various rooms with water heated to different temperatures. For the Romans bathing was a very sociable experience.

Religion

Official religion

Mention has already been made of the *Feriale Duranum*, the calendar of Cohors XX Palmyrenorum milliaria sagittariorum equitata, a text found at Dura Europus and most probably dating to *c.* AD 225–27. The following are some extracts from the text which give an indication of the variety of festivals marked by the unit:

3 January. Because vows are fulfilled and made both for the welfare of our lord Marcus Aurelius Severus Alexander Augustus and for the eternity of the Empire of the Roman People, to Jupiter Optimus Maximus and ox, to Queen Juno a cow, to Minerva a cow, to Jupiter Victor an ox, to Juno Sospes a cow…, to Father Mars a bull, to Mars the Victor a bull, to Victoria a cow…

19 March. For the festival of the Quinquatria, a supplication; similar supplications until 23 March…

4 April. For the birthday of the divine Antoninus the Great, to the divine Antoninus an ox…

9 April. For the imperial power of the divine Pius Severus, to the divine Pius Severus an ox…

21 April. For the foundation day of the Eternal City of Rome, to the eternal City of Rome a cow…

Two of the 17 altars dedicated to Jupiter Optimus Maximus (almost invariably abbreviated to IOM) found outside the auxiliary fort at Maryport on the Cumbrian coast. The altar on the left was dedicated by the commander of Cohors I Baetasiorum civium Romanorum, while that on the right was erected by Cohors I Hispanorum equitata.

The Quinquatria was a ceremony dedicated to Minerva and she, along with the remainder of the Capitoline triad of Rome's most important deities, Juno and Jupiter, figure prominently in the calendar. Many of the festivals such as this and the celebration of Rome's foundation had no specifically military associations and were simply part of the normal Roman year. No local deities are mentioned in the text, nor anything else specific to Cohors XX, and it is generally supposed that army units throughout the Empire celebrated the same round of sacrifices, supplications and feasts. Apart from the dates associated with subsequent emperors, especially the current dynasty, there is little in the calendar which could not have been established by Augustus.

Whether or not the *Feriale Duranum* in its preserved form was followed by every unit in the army, it is clear that many of the festivals mentioned were celebrated elsewhere. Outside the fort at Maryport on the Cumbrian coast in northern Britain, a series of altars was discovered buried near what is thought to have been the garrison's parade ground. No fewer than 17 were devoted to IOM – Jupiter Optimus Maximus or 'Jupiter Best and Greatest'. The texts carved onto the stone are very similar, for instance 'To Jupiter Optimus Maximus, the First Cohort of Spaniards (Cohors I Hispanorum), commanded by Marcus Maenius Agrippa, tribune, set this up' or 'To Jupiter Optimus Maximus, for the welfare of Antoninus Augustus Pius, Postumius Acilianus, prefect of the First Cohort of Dalmatians (Cohors I Delmatarum), set this up.' Maenius Agrippa appears on three altars as leader, whilst Postumius Acilianus figures on two. Other commanding officers occur only once, whilst the tribune Caius Cabillius Priscus dedicated four altars. It is most likely that this series represents annual dedications of an altar to Jupiter for the good of the emperor, quite possibly on 3 January as at Dura Europus. As an aside, this then gives some idea of the length of postings held by equestrian officers with auxiliary units.

At such ceremonies the commanding officer represented the unit and his name is the only one to appear on the altar, but it is clear that he acted on behalf of the entire cohort. A fresco from Dura Europus seems to depict a ceremony of this sort. It shows a file of soldiers on parade, watching as their tribune, Julius Terentius, sacrifices before three statues. Although the latter have sometimes been identified as local deities, it seems more probable that they are members of the imperial family. The occasion appears much like a modern-day military church parade, an important means of confirming the soldiers' sense of corporate identity as much as purely an act of worship. The days when the unit's standards were formally decorated were another confirmation of esprit de corps, and the early Christian writer Tertullian felt that the army's veneration of its standards amounted to religious worship.

A reconstruction at the Senhouse Museum in Maryport of the shrine or aedes *which was at the heart of the* principia *in each auxiliary fort. Here the standards were carefully guarded. The statue is of Hadrian.*

The regular marking of dates significant to the imperial family, and the close association of the family with the worship of Rome's traditional gods and goddesses, was obviously intended to confirm the loyalty of the soldiers. In the first half of the 2nd century AD, a cult to military discipline (*Disciplina*) developed, quite possibly introduced by Hadrian during his inspections of the provincial armies. Such abstract concepts were not infrequently the object of formal worship in Roman society, and in this case it was clearly expected to promote not merely loyalty, but also military efficiency. The military oath (*sacramentum*) had distinctly religious associations, so much so that the spirit of the oath (*genius sacramenti*) was occasionally venerated.

Personal religion

Religion was everywhere in the Roman world, to a degree that is difficult to imagine from a modern perspective. Many activities of daily life involved some form of worship or ritual. Apart from the many gods and goddesses, including the deities of such abstractions as Fortune or Health, Romans might also revere even vaguer spirits, such as the *genii* or guiding spirits associated with a place, an occupation or, in the case of the army, a unit or rank. In the main our evidence for this important aspect of life comes from the physical remains, temples, altars with their inscriptions, and dedicated items. Whilst these tell us a great deal about the range of deities worshipped by soldiers, they are far less revealing about just what such cults meant to the participants. It is also evident that only the wealthier soldiers could afford to perform such rituals; and it will be virtually impossible to detect the presence of cults whose practices did not produce any physical remains.

Although soldiers took part in acts of worship organized by their unit, they enjoyed a good deal of freedom to perform religious acts as individuals. The Roman form of polytheism was very open, and able to accommodate without difficulty most other cults it encountered, including very often the religions of conquered peoples. It was not infrequent to combine a dedication to several deities, so that for instance an altar set up at Housesteads by a detachment of Legio II Augusta was to 'Jupiter Optimus Maximus, the god Cocidius, and the Genius of this place'. Cocidius was frequently worshipped on Hadrian's Wall, and appears to have been a Celtic war god, sometimes associated with Mars. Individuals sometimes of their own accord took part in what we might consider as official cults, associating themselves closely with Rome, its leaders, and the guiding spirits of the army. A remarkable series of four altars was erected in the second half of the 2nd century in Scotland by the same centurion:

'To Jupiter Optimus Maximus, and to Victorious Victory for the welfare of our Emperor and the welfare of himself and his family, Marcus Cocceius Firmus, centurion of Legio II Augusta, [set this up].'

'To Diana and Apollo, Marcus Cocceius Firmus, centurion of Legio II Augusta, [set this up].'

'To the Genius of the Land of Britain, Marcus Cocceius Firmus, centurion of Legio II Augusta, [set this up].'

'To Mars, Minerva, the Goddesses of the Parade-ground, Hercules, Epona, and Victory, Marcus Cocceius Firmus, centurion of Legio II Augusta [set this up].'

Dedications were made by soldiers to an immense variety of cults. Some men chose to worship essentially Roman gods, whereas others worshipped deities local to the places where they were stationed, or continued to revere the gods of their own homeland. Various aspects of Mars the war god were commonly worshipped, as were other local deities associated with martial virtues. Hercules enjoyed a particular popularity in the 3rd century AD, but was worshipped in various forms for most of the period as a personification of manly virtues of strength and courage. There is evidence for Roman soldiers, both legionaries and auxiliaries, making dedications at the Batavian temple of Hercules Magusanus at Empel. Yet at other times soldiers worshipped gods and goddesses with no obviously military associations. The cult of Covventina, based around the goddess's sacred spring, was revered by many soldiers from the garrisons in northern Britain. The army appears to have made little or no attempt to restrict this religious activity, and soldiers were free to worship as they wished in private, as long as they participated in the corporate religious life of the unit. Cult practices common in the pre-Roman Iron Age, such as the offering of pieces of metalwork, often military equipment such as helmets, by casting them into rivers or lakes, appear to have continued into the Roman period and been practised by soldiers. The burying of ritual objects, often in disused grain pits recorded at pre-Roman sites, for instance in the hillfort at Danebury in Britain, has parallels in Roman army bases such as Newstead. The practice of religion in the Roman world was extremely diverse.

Sometimes an ethnic group from within a unit chose to worship together. Amongst the altars set up by Cohors II Tungrorum at Birrens fort in southwest Scotland was a dedication to 'Mars and the Emperor's Victory' by the 'Raetian tribesmen', another to the goddess Ricagambeda by the 'men of the Vellavian district', and one to the goddess Viradecthis by the soldiers from the 'Conductian district'. Both Ricagambeda and Viradecthis were German deities, worshipped in the homelands of the two groups. At Carrawburgh in northern Britain an altar was erected 'To the Genius of this place (by) the Texandri and Suevae, from a detach-

An altar dedicated to the goddess Covventina in honour of a vow made by Coscianus, the prefect of Cohors I Batavorum.

ment of cohors II Nerviorum.' It is interesting to note that within a single auxiliary cohort there was a range of sub-groups consisting of men from the same ethnic groups. An early 3rd-century AD altar found near Housesteads was set up by the German tribesmen of Twenthe 'To the god Mars Thincsus and the two Alaisiagae, Beda and Fimmilena, and to the Deity of the Emperor.'

Eastern cults and mystery religions

A number of cults which originated in the eastern Mediterranean spread remarkably widely throughout the Roman Empire. The storm god Dolichenus, worshipped since the Hittites at the cult centre of Doliche in Commagene (in modern Turkey), was associated with Jupiter by the Romans. A great number of inscriptions were set up to the god by

Auxiliary Cavalrymen of the Late 1st Century AD

This scene shows three auxiliary horsemen making an offering of an ornate helmet to a local deity in fulfilment of a vow. The practice of dedicating objects by throwing or placing them into water – perhaps a river, lake, pool or spring – was common amongst many Celtic and Germanic peoples in the late, pre-Roman Iron Age. Only rarely did the Roman Empire actively suppress any religion, and it seems clear that many auxiliaries continued to follow the cult activities of their own societies. A very high proportion of existing Roman helmets have been found in rivers. For a long time such finds were explained as due to accidental loss, but it seems more probable that they were deliberately thrown into the river as part of a ritual. Although the practice was probably initially more common amongst non-citizen soldiers, this, along with many other religious practices, seems in time to have spread more widely throughout the army.

Mail cuirass: This man wears a mail shirt with shoulder doubling in the more traditional style copied from the Gauls.

Helmet: This iron helmet is similar to an example found at Heddernheim in Germany. It provides good protection to the face with very wide cheek-pieces which cover the ears – in a whirling mêlée when two cavalry units inter-mingled, a rider might well come under attack from the sides or rear.

Mail cuirass: This soldier wears a shirt of mail (*lorica hamata*) which reaches down to his thighs. The bottom and the arms of the coat end in a decorative jagged fringe, a style depicted on Trajan's Column. Mail was widely worn by all units of the army of the Principate.

Helmet: This helmet with a face mask and hair decorating the top is of a type usually considered to have been employed solely for parades or the cavalry sports. However, it is more than possible that helmets fitted with masks were more widely used for general service by soldiers – and perhaps especially officers – who wished to cut a dash. Such an expensive and magnificent object would appear a likely item for sacrifice.

Spear: The main armament of most cavalrymen was a spear thrust over-arm. Lighter javelins were also carried for throwing. A small proportion of units were armed instead with the bow, or a two-handed spear known as the *contus*.

Helmet: Many cavalry helmets are decorated with a representation of curls of hair. Often this takes the form of thin tinning over the bronze bowl. A small number of helmets have been found with real animal hair replacing this decoration. This may have been a fashion peculiar to Germanic auxiliaries such as the Batavians.

Helmet: This iron helmet is based on an example found at Ely in East Anglia. It is ornate and covers the ears, but, like that worn by the standing soldier, it has no extra protection for the front or top of the head.

Scale cuirass: This sort of scale armour is very similar in basic shape to the mail shirt worn by the cavalryman from the *ala*. Scales from such shirts are comparatively common finds, and vary in size and detail. Scale armour was less flexible than mail, but looked very impressive. It seems to have been worn by cavalry in the cohorts and *alae*, and also in some infantry units.

Shield: This soldier carries a flat oval shield with insignia taken from Trajan's Column. Some cavalry units carried long hexagonal shields.

Tunic: This tunic has long sleeves, a rather Gallic style which is depicted on the tombstones of a number of cavalrymen. His comrades' tunics conform to the more conventional military design.

Sword: Both of the kneeling soldiers are shown with *spatha* swords worn on their left hip. In spite of their length – up to a foot more than the *gladius* – such weapons are also shown being worn on the right hip.

The Mithraeum *(temple to the eastern deity Mithras) at Carrawburgh on Hadrian's Wall lies a short distance outside the ramparts of the fort. The three altars at the far end were each dedicated by the equestrian commanders of the garrison.*

units and especially individual soldiers in the 2nd and early 3rd centuries AD. The cult seems to have reached the height of its popularity under the Severi. It is difficult to say how it was originally introduced and spread, but it is clear that veneration of Jupiter Dolichenus went far beyond troops recruited from Commagene.

A number of eastern cults required adherents to undergo a series of initiation ceremonies and bound them by solemn oath never to tell of the mysteries of their worship. Of these 'mystery' religions, several of which, for instance the cult of Egyptian Isis and Serapis, won many converts throughout the Empire,

the cult with greatest appeal to soldiers was that of Mithras. Like many of these cults, Mithraism appears to have offered a stronger promise of an afterlife and encouraged a very personal relationship with the god. Also like the other mystery religions, the bar on recounting any of its core beliefs makes it very difficult to reconstruct the cult's theology, although this has not stopped various scholars from attempting to do this. Mithras was an Iranian god, normally depicted wearing a phrygian cap and associated with the sun. Apparently with the assistance of several creatures, which later gave their names to the grades of devotees in the cult,

Mithras killed a bull in what appears to have been a creation myth. Temples, several of which have been discovered outside Roman forts, were poorly lit, narrow buildings constructed to resemble caves. Strength, courage and endurance were important aspects of the rites, and had an obvious appeal to soldiers. A high proportion of known altars were set up by officers, notably the equestrian commanders of auxiliary units, and it is quite likely that Mithraism was often the preserve of senior ranks. Apart from its religious importance for these men, it may also have helped to develop friendships and connections useful in their careers.

This reconstruction of a Mithraeum gives some impression of the cave-like interior of these buildings. The worship of Mithras was a mystery cult, its adherents bound by solemn oaths not to reveal its practices. One result of this is that we have only the sketchiest idea of its doctrines and rituals.

After Service

After service auxiliaries were granted Roman citizenship, proof of which came in the form of the diploma, *a bronze copy of the document registering their citizenship in Rome. This one was presented to a Spanish cavalryman.*

The Roman army recognized three different types of discharge. Soldiers who became unfit for service through sickness or injuries were released from service (*missio causaria*). This was not done lightly, but only after thorough medical examination had confirmed that it was extremely unlikely that they would ever recover sufficiently to serve again. Dis-

honourable discharge (*missio ignominiosa*) was the penalty for soldiers committing a serious crime. Such men were barred by law from living in Rome itself or from entering imperial service in any form, and may at some periods have been branded or tattooed with a symbol of ignominy. In addition they enjoyed none of the rights and privileges granted to soldiers honourably discharged (*honesta missio*) at the end of their service. In most respects men discharged for medical reasons were treated as honourably discharged, although the size of any grants made to them was usually scaled in accordance with their length of service.

Thorough documentation accompanied a soldier throughout his military career and inevitably marked this final transition back to civilian life. The type of discharge was marked against a man's name in his unit's records as he was removed from their strength roster. The soldier probably received a written statement of his release from military service, such as the statement found in Egypt and dating to 4 January AD 122 confirming the discharge of Lucius Valerius Noster, cavalryman from the *turma* of Gavius in Ala Vocontiorum. There were also cases when an entire group of soldiers discharged at the same time chose to commemorate this important event by erecting a monument. Such inscriptions list from around 100 to some 370 names, and various calculations have been made in attempts to show what percentage of legionaries lived long enough to leave the army. Unfortunately, the sample of evidence is tiny, and anyway so many factors determined the number of men eligible for discharge in a single year that it would be rash to generalize.

Praetorian guardsmen and men from the *auxilia* each received a copy of a bronze *diploma*, which listed in detail their new legal status as veterans. Legionaries did not receive similar tablets, but it was very important for all men to have proof of their membership of a particular branch of the service and honourable discharge from it, to ensure that they actually gained the status and legal rights to which they were entitled. The text of a petition recording the case of 22 Egyptian veterans in AD 150 has been found at Caesarea in Judaea. These men had originally enlisted in the fleet, but had at some point been transferred to Legio X Fretensis, perhaps when it was in need of manpower during the Jewish Rebellion under Hadrian. The men wanted and were granted written confirmation of their service in the senior branch of the forces, for legionaries enjoyed far higher status than sailors.

At some periods discharged soldiers, especially legionaries, were settled together on land in military colonies. Augustus claims in the Res Gestae – a long inscription set up outside his Mausoleum recounting his great achievements – that he settled some 300,000 veterans in colonies or sent them back to their home communities. Such massive programmes of settlement were required to ensure that

the vast numbers of troops raised during the civil wars could be re-integrated into civilian society and so did not threaten the stability of the Augustan regime. The limited archaeological evidence for the colonies of this period suggests that housing consisted of small blocks or *insulae* of the type common in Roman towns, each divided into several flats occupied by an individual veteran and his family In many cases the colonists lived not in a central settlement, but on individual farms. In some recently conquered areas, colonies served a strategic purpose. During the initial stages of the conquest of Britain under Claudius, the tribal capital at Camulodunum was one of the army's most important targets. After its occupation a legionary fortress was built nearby to control the region, but when this unit, Legio XX, was moved west to rejoin the field armies in the late AD 40s, a veteran colony was established to take its place. There is some evidence to suggest that barrack blocks were rebuilt to provide housing for the veterans. Something similar may well have happened at Gloucester, where another colony was created on the site of a legionary base, although the chronology and relationship between the two is unclear. Farms were provided for the veterans by surveyors dividing the land into large squares, a traditional Roman practice known as centuriation. One of the complaints of the mutineers in the Pannonian legions in AD 14 was that when finally discharged they were given a farm consisting of swampland or barren mountain. In most cases the land had been confiscated from the conquered peoples and its location was not necessarily determined by its suitability for agriculture. Inevitably, the Roman veterans were resented by the native population which had suffered defeat and the requisition of their territory. When the British tribes rebelled under Boudicca in AD 60, the first target of the Trinovantes was the colony of Camulodunum established in their land. The town was burned to the ground and the settlers massacred.

Twenty-five years of military service represented at least half the lifetime of most soldiers, and even the shorter 16-year term served by praetorians was still a major part of their lives. Such long spells in the army, living within a closely defined hierarchy, his daily routine closely regulated and ordered, must have had a big impact on a man. Certainly, veterans continued to define themselves as members of their old unit even when they lived on for several decades. A good number of men lived near their old base, taking up residence in the *vicus*. Since soldiers often married local women this acted as another incentive to remain in the province where they had served. Often their sons went on to join the army, their daughters to marry soldiers or veterans. However, in other cases men did return to their homeland. This trend is especially visible in Egypt because of the survival of correspondence and records from

The tombstone of Longinus of the Ala Sulpicia civium Romanorum shows the soldier reclining on a couch in the Roman manner. Beneath is another scene showing him walking behind his horse and carrying two spears. The top of his helmet appears to be shaped in a stylized portrayal of hair, a feature of many surviving cavalry helmets. The horse's saddle and harness is shown very clearly on this relief.

several villages. Such a move was obviously especially likely for men who had corresponded with their families during service. Army veterans had some privileges, for instance exemption from certain types of punishment and restrictions on their liability for public service in the local communities, and were also Roman citizens. To an extent they formed a privileged sub-group within the wider population, but in most cases they were not the only such privileged group. The society of the Roman world was a good deal more complex and multi-layered than many modern commentators allow.

Auxiliary veterans

Much of what has already been said applies as much to auxiliary soldiers as to legionaries. Such men acquired Roman citizenship as a result of service and tended to be drawn from the less urbanized and developed parts of the Roman Empire, and in some cases from tribes outside the formally organized provinces. Service in the Roman army can only have been a dramatically different experience from their former lives, and many scholars have wondered to what extent they became 'romanized' through this experience. If they returned home after discharge as many, perhaps most, appear to have done, they would return as citizens, a distinc-

(Left) The tombstone, from Mainz, of Lucius Valerius Verecundus, who served in the first cohort of the fleet and died at the age of 25 after four years service. Even such comparatively simple monuments as this were expensive items.

(Right) A 3rd-century monument from the province of Dacia showing the retired soldier reclining on a couch at a feast. The spots on the garment draped around him may be intended to represent some kind of animal fur.

tion which was likely to have been rare in their native communities. Auxiliary recruitment could then be seen as a means of spreading Roman culture and ideas throughout the provinces, and so helping to consolidate Rome's power. It is possible that it did, consciously or not, perform such a role, although the evidence is really insufficient to reach a firm conclusion, but it would be unwise to see this as the main purpose of the *auxilia*. These existed because the army needed manpower to serve as an effective fighting force. Yet in one respect the Romans were convinced that service with the *auxilia* changed a man and that was by giving him an understanding of the Roman way of warfare. It was a common Roman conceit that their most dangerous enemies were men who had served with their own armies. Arminius and Gannascus in Germany, Tacfarinas and Jugurtha in North Africa, and even according to one source the leader of the slave rebellion Spartacus, learned their trade with the *auxilia*.

Death and burial

One of the deductions from a soldier's pay was a standard contribution to the burial club organized by the century, a highly important ritual for most peoples in the Roman world. Should the soldier die during service, this would then cover the costs of a basic funeral. After a major battle, the need to dispose of large numbers of corpses normally led to the mass cremation of the bodies, but in peacetime a greater ceremony was observed. A funeral procession, carrying the corpse on a couch, would leave the fort or camp, for like many contemporary societies the Romans insisted that burial take place outside the settlement. Once outside, and often on a

site running alongside the main road leading to the fort, the corpse would be laid on its couch on top of a funeral pyre. There it would be burnt and, once consumed by the flames the ash of both corpse and pyre gathered into a funerary urn, made sometimes of marble or metal, but most often of glass or pottery, which was then buried. Around the grave site the mourners took part in a funeral banquet.

This was a common form of ceremony during the Principate, but the army included men from many cultures and with an immense range of religious beliefs, and there was a considerable variety in funeral practices. In Egypt the practice of mummification continued throughout this period, and in general inhumation became more common than cremation in Late Antiquity. The chief mourners were

a man's comrades and, as the practice of taking an unofficial wife became widespread, his family. It is doubtful that the burial club paid for more than the most rudimentary of markers for the grave, but many soldiers set aside money to pay for expensive stone monuments. Many tombstones state that they were erected by a man's heirs in accordance with his will. Some consist of a simple inscription, which often details a man's age, rank, unit and length of service – details which even veterans frequently felt appropriate to add. The most elaborate were carved with a picture of the soldier. There is considerable variation in this, with legionaries tending to have themselves shown with minimal military equipment, whilst auxiliaries, especially auxiliary cavalrymen, are shown armed for battle and in

warlike poses. A common type of cavalry tombstone shows the deceased riding a rearing horse and brandishing his weapons as one or more seminaked barbarians cower beneath its hoofs. Some monuments also depict a man's slaves or freedmen.

Some things are rarely mentioned on a man's tombstone. The cause of his death, whether battle or sickness, is usually omitted, making it especially interesting when this detail is included. The senior centurion Marcus Caelius Rufus died with Varus' army in the Teutoburg Wald in AD 9, and was commemorated in a lavish monument by his brother, who added on the inscription the clause that 'should they ever be found, his bones may be interred here'. Later in the 1st century AD Aulus Sentius, veteran of Legio XI, was killed in the territory of the Varvarini in Dalmatia, although it is unclear if he was a discharged veteran or still serving his five years with the legion when this occurred. Lucius Flaminius of Legio III Augusta was killed in battle in North Africa at the age of 40. A fragmentary tombstone from Chester commemorates an *optio* marked out for promotion to the centurionate (*optio ad spem ordinis*) who had drowned in a shipwreck. There is also an intriguing reference on another tombstone from Britain to a soldier killed by an enemy in the camp, which could mean either by a sudden attack which penetrated the fort or murder by a comrade. Yet such details are so rare that we cannot possibly calculate the chances of a man being killed in action or dying of illness or accident during his term of service. Probably, with the exception of occasional major disasters and in common with all armies until the 20th century, the latter was always far more likely.

Military tombstones rarely record how the man died, but this fragmentary tombstone from Chester to an optio *from* Legio XX Valeria Victrix *tells us that he died in a shipwreck. This event cut short a promising career, for the man was awaiting a vacancy as centurion* (optio ad spem ordinis). *Although the man's name has been lost, the surviving part of the inscription states that he was from the century of Lucilius Ingenuus.*

Equipment

As on many military tombstones, this man, Marcus Julius Sabinianus, is depicted in undress uniform, without helmet or cuirass, but carrying shield and weapons. He was a sailor in the Italian fleet stationed at Misenum.

Clothing

The tunic: In the Greco-Roman world the principal garment of a male civilian was a short-sleeved, knee-length tunic, since trousers were considered a barbarian fashion. In the old militia army, soldiers provided their own clothes as well as their own armour, making it unlikely that the legions of this period displayed much uniformity in dress or equipment. Gradually, as the army became a professional force, the state began to issue clothing, armour and weapons to the troops, and by the early Principate regular deductions were made from a soldier's salary to cover the cost of each of these items. A document survives from Egypt which mentions the army ordering large consignments of clothing from civilian suppliers and insisting on a standard design and quality. A version of the civilian tunic remained the normal dress of the Roman soldier until the beginning of the 3rd century AD.

The military tunic was somewhat longer than the type normally worn by civilians, stretching halfway down a man's calves. Normally, however, it was gathered up by a belt so that it hung above the knee. There seems to have been a fashion at some periods for gathering the sides of the tunic higher than the front and rear, so that its bottom edge forms a curve. The tunic's design was simple, consisting essentially of two matching squares of material – usually wool or linen – sewn together at the sides and shoulders, whilst leaving openings for the arms and neck. Some tunics had sleeves, usually fairly short, although some depictions of cavalrymen suggest that their tunics were long-sleeved. At least some infantry tunics could be worn with the right shoulder and arm left bare, which appears to have been more comfortable for heavy labour. Tunics of this sort had a slit down from the neck opening at the centre of the back. Normally this was tied into a knot by a leather thong, or occasionally perhaps held by a brooch, and only unfastened when the soldier wanted to free his right arm. Modern re-enactors have found that this knot can be uncomfortable if this type of tunic is worn with armour. Evidence is limited, but it is possible that each soldier possessed more than one pattern of tunic, different patterns being worn for specific activities.

Cloaks and capes: There were two basic patterns of cloak worn by ordinary soldiers. The first was the *sagum*, a simple rectangle of heavy wool, although sometimes its fringe was decorated. The two sides of material were held together by a brooch on the right shoulder in a way that left a man's right side, and his sword-arm, free. The alternative to the *sagum* was the *paenula*, worn more like a poncho.

In this scene from Trajan's Column, the Emperor and a group of senior officers are shown on campaign, with cloaks over their ornate cuirasses. The cloak was the sagum, *a simple rectangle of material fastened at one shoulder with a brooch. These could be worn in various styles.*

It was probably oval in shape, with an opening for the head, and sometimes an attached hood. The front of the cape fastened with a row of buttons and toggles, so that it could be left partially open. The neck opening tended to be loose-fitting, so that a scarf was essential in cold or wet weather. Senior officers, including the Emperor Trajan, are sometimes depicted wearing a version of the *sagum*, although it seems more than likely that such garments were of superior quality to the ones worn by the ordinary soldiers. On other occasions, officers from the centurionate upwards are shown wearing the more formal *paludamentum*, which could be worn draped over the left arm, rather like the formal civilian toga.

Belts: The military tunic required a belt to be worn properly, so much so that Augustus was known to have symbolically punished centurions by making them stand at attention outside his tent without wearing their belts. A soldier's belt, from which his sword and – at least at some periods – dagger were suspended, was also an important symbol of his identity. Even in undress uniform, without armour or helmet, the belted tunic marked a man out as a soldier. This was reflected in the ornate plates and buckles which covered the functional leather belts. In the early 1st century at least two belts were normally worn, one for the sword, whose scabbard was fastened to it by cords from the four scabbard rings, and the other for the dagger whose scabbard

hooked onto a frog on one of the belt plates. The two belts were worn in a criss-cross pattern, rather like the double holster of the gunfighters depicted in many Western movies. By the end of the 1st century, fashion changed and it was more common to wear a single, broader belt supporting both sword and dagger. Even so, some men appear to have continued to wear multiple belts and one soldier on Trajan's Column is shown with no less than four.

During the 1st and 2nd centuries AD, an apron was often attached to a soldier's belt. This might consist of from one to nine straps, usually studded and with decorative metal terminals. Four to six such straps are most common. These may have served a defensive function, even if the protection offered to a soldier's groin was more psychological than real. However, the experience of modern re-enactors has suggested that they could be a hindrance to a running man if allowed to swing freely. The aprons certainly made the soldier's belt even more decorative and also jingled as he moved, adding to a soldier's presence.

Boots: Apart from the tinkling of apron fittings and the noise produced by any metal armour, the sole of the military boot (*caliga*) was heavily studded. Josephus tells us that the centurion Julianus was pursuing the enemy across the Temple Court in Jerusalem in AD 70 when the metal studs of his boots skidded on the flagstones and he fell, only to

The tombstone, from Mainz, of Publius Flavoleius Cordus, a soldier in Legio XIV Gemina. The subject is once again shown wearing only a tunic. It clearly shows his sword on his right side and dagger on his left, while he holds a pilum in his right hand and has an oval shield on his back. He holds a scroll in his left hand which may indicate that he held a clerical post. Having served for 23 years, Cordus was not too far away from discharge when he died aged 43, in the early 1st century AD.

for a larger allowance of boot-money (*calciarium*) because of the wear suffered on frequent long marches from Puteoli or Ostia to Rome. In reply the Emperor ordered them to march barefoot, a practice which appears to have continued at least to the end of the century.

Although the open appearance of *caligae* makes them look rather like sandals, their construction was considerably sturdier. Made in three parts – a sole, insole and upper – the straps could be tightened to fit more closely. The apparent lack of protection against the weather is also deceptive, since it seems clear that *caligae* were normally worn with socks, and one monument depicting praetorian guardsmen actually shows an open-toed and open-heeled sock being worn on parade. During the 2nd century AD, other types of footwear with more enclosed uppers appear to have become increasingly common, and may well have supplanted the traditional pattern of *caligae* altogether. Most, if not all, footwear worn by the army continued to have hobnailed soles.

Other clothes: One of the most famous letters from Vindolanda records a soldier being sent some 'pairs of socks (*udones*) from Sattua, two pairs of sandals/slippers (*soleae*) and two pairs of underpants (*subligares*) … '. This is one example of the ample evidence which is gradually eroding the persistent myth that Roman soldiers spent their time in northern Britain wearing garb more suited for the Mediterranean. Instead, troops adapted to the local climate, however extreme. Breeches and, especially amongst cavalry, longer trousers were worn beneath the tunic, as were socks and perhaps leggings of various sorts.

Later changes: Both civilian and military fashion began to change again in the 3rd century AD. From this period a long-sleeved tunic became normal. Depictions in wall-paintings and mosaics suggest that these often had a different coloured border and sometimes round or lozenge-shaped decorative patches. Sleeves were usually fairly tight to the wrist. Examples from Dura Europus suggest that these woollen garments were woven in one piece, with a slit for the neck and sometimes also on each hip. Trousers, usually tight fitting, also became increasingly common. In many respects these styles endured until the collapse of the Western Empire and for much longer in the East.

The problem of colour

Fabrics such as wool, linen and leather survive only under exceptional circumstances in the archaeological record. Much of our evidence for military costume comes from the depictions of soldiers on great monuments such as Trajan's Column and on the funerary memorials left by soldiers. Originally these reliefs were brightly painted, a colour often

be surrounded and killed by the enemy. This was a possible danger, but in most circumstances and on less smooth surfaces, the studs gave the boots better grip. The studs tended to wear out and needed to be replaced. On one occasion Vespasian received a demand from sailors of the Italian fleet

The tombstone of an optio *from Chester shows him wearing a* paenula *cloak and holding his* hastile *staff. The paint is modern, although traces of paint were found on this tombstone and it is probable that most were originally painted. The inscription reads: 'To the spirits of the departed: Caecilius Avitus, from Emerita Augusta [modern day Merida in Spain],* optio *of Legio XX Valeria Victrix, of 15 years service, died aged 34; his heir had this erected.' The texts of most military tombstones are extremely formulaic.*

for different orders of dress. It is equally possible – though there is no positive evidence for this – that at some periods some units wore distinctively coloured tunics, either through choice or because of local availability. There is some direct evidence for soldiers wearing white, or off-white tunics, and a little, though far less, for red. A papyrus from Egypt records a unit ordering pure white tunics for its use, and white is the most common colour for soldiers appearing in paintings or on mosaics. Undyed tunics, which would therefore be anything from white to light grey to light brown in shade, were probably also the most common form of civilian dress. Soldiers may well have worn a purer white woollen tunic than could normally be afforded by poor civilians. Tacitus' description of the triumphal march of an army into Rome during the civil war following the death of Nero speaks of camp prefects, tribunes and senior centurions in dazzling white uniforms, which suggests that the higher ranks had brighter, better-quality tunics than ordinary soldiers. This is similar to the system in the 19th-century British army, when the soldier's redcoat was a duller shade than that worn by a sergeant, which in turn was less bright than, and a different cut from, an officer's jacket. An alternative suggestion is that centurions were marked out from ordinary soldiers by wearing red as opposed to white tunics. Although this is possible, it does seem to go against the evidence of Tacitus.

Cloaks are normally shown in paintings as a dull yellowish brown. They were essentially practical items, intended to guard against the wind and weather, so such an unimpressive colour is less surprising. However, several funerary portraits from Egypt dating most probably to the 2nd century AD show bearded men wearing sword belts. These men may well have been veterans or, since the quality of their burial suggests a degree of wealth, former officers. All wear white tunics, but cloaks range in colour from dark blue to dark olive green. It is therefore possible that individuals or particular ranks may have had cloaks in differing shades and that the apparent uniformity of yellow-brown is deceptive. It is also known that Roman generals normally wore a red cloak as a mark of rank, and in the 1st century BC Crassus caused a stir when he appeared wearing a black cloak, since the colour was considered to be unlucky.

Legionary helmets

The study of Roman helmets, as with many other types of military equipment, has often been hindered by emphasis on external fittings which have more to do with decoration than either design, manufacture or function. Most British scholars follow Russell Robinson's categorization of helmets according to type and pattern, whereas those on the continent employ a completely different labelling system associated with find spots. Therefore the

being used to indicate detail which was difficult to carve, such as mail armour or socks, but these pigments have not survived in any useful way. Some Roman sites have produced colourful mosaics or wall-paintings but in the main these have rarely featured extensive scenes involving soldiers in the uniforms of the day. Our literary sources rarely talk in much detail about clothing or equipment either, and on the rare occasions when colour is mentioned it is hard to be too specific about shade. Therefore, although we can with some confidence reconstruct most aspects of the appearance of Roman soldiers, we can be far less certain when it comes to the fundamental question of colour. Reconstructions of military scenes, whether by artists or re-enactment groups, inevitably involve a fair degree of conjecture in this respect.

It is often assumed that all soldiers wore tunics of a standard colour. In fact there is no positive evidence for this and it is possible that different colours as well as different patterns of tunic were employed

same helmet would be either an Imperial Gallic Type A according to Robinson's system or a helmet of the Weisenau/Nijmegen type under the continental system. However, in most respects, there is broad agreement between the two schools over the development of Roman infantry helmets.

In the last century of the Republic the most commonly used helmets were all derived originally from Gallic designs. At first, the most frequently used pattern was the Montefortino which had been in use since at least the 3rd century BC. Over time the neck-guard on this pattern gradually became larger. The Coolus helmet was very similar in appearance and by the end of the 1st century BC had supplanted the other type in popularity. Most, though by no means all, Coolus helmets had a crest knob or spike on the top of the bowl. They also tended to have wider neckguards than Montefortino helmets and from

The Soldier of the 1st Century AD

This scene shows two legionaries from Legio XIV Gemina on campaign in Britain in AD 60 during the suppression of Boudicca's rebellion. This legion played a distinguished role in Rome's eventual victory and was awarded the titles Martia Victrix by a delighted Emperor Nero. Both men wear segmented cuirasses (*lorica segmentata*) and helmets of the type known as Imperial Gallic. The conditions of active service are likely to have resulted in a somewhat different appearance from the classic image of Roman soldiers. These men have slightly ragged and patched tunics, and have adapted their uniform to make it more suitable to a north European climate. Some of the details shown remain conjectural, but all are based on interpretations of the surviving evidence.

Apron: A soldier's belt was an important symbol of his status, marking him out from civilians. Most were highly ornate and had an apron formed by several straps attached to them.

Such straps ended in a metal pendant and were decorated with a row of discs. These fittings rattled and clinked when a man moved, adding to his presence. However, they may have been impractical and awkward and this man has rolled them around his belt for convenience rather than letting them dangle freely.

Pilum: Standing upright with its butt spike driven into the ground, the iron head of this *pilum* is attached to the wooden shaft by a wide tang. It is based on examples found at Oberaden dating to the early 1st century AD.

Shield (*scutum*): This soldier is pulling the leather cover over his shield. Visible is the symbol of his legion, based on the tombstone of an *aquilifer*. The legion's numeral was often written on inscriptions as XIIII instead of the more normal XIV and is shown in this form.

Socks and boots: For additional warmth, these soldiers wear socks. Once again these are mentioned in the Vindolanda tablets. Toeless socks may also be shown on a monument depicting a parade of praetorian guardsmen. By the 2nd century AD the open *caligae* boots seem generally to have been replaced by various types of enclosed boots in the colder provinces.

Pack: Unlike modern soldiers, the Roman infantryman's pack was not fitted to his belts and worn on his back. Instead it was suspended from a pole which he carried over his shoulder. One theory suggests that the pole may have been tied to the shaft of the *pilum* on the march as is shown here. The precise shape and design of the pack is unknown, as is the method of attaching it to the carrying pole. In this case the soldier has a bronze cooking pot (*trulleus*) tied to the cross shaft of the carrying pole.

Leather shield cover: Shields normally had a leather cover, which was only removed in battle or for a formal parade. A number of examples of such covers have survived, providing us with valuable information regarding the size of Roman shields. Many have some form of decoration, usually shaped pieces of leather sewn onto the main cover. Apart from the name of his legion, there are two capricorns, symbols of Augustus who founded XIV Gemina.

Breeches: Underneath their tunic, these soldiers wear woollen breeches. Such garments are depicted on a number of monuments and are mentioned in the Vindolanda tablets.

the middle of the 1st century BC most had a reinforcing peak mid way up the front of the bowl. By this time both patterns of helmets had acquired broader cheek-pieces offering more protection for the face. These seem to have developed from patterns of Gallic iron helmets, such as the Agen type.

Both the Montefortino and Coolus helmets, as well as the later Imperial types, had the helmet bowl and the neckguard made from the same piece of metal. There were two principal methods of manufacture, forging, which involved beating the metal into shape over a former, and spinning, where the metal was shaped using a revolving former (a shaped piece of wood or stone). Iron helmets could only be beaten into shape, because the iron available to the Romans was not sufficiently pure to undergo the spinning process without cracking. However, the alloy – a mixture mostly of copper with about a

This example of a late-pattern (1st century BC) **Montefortino helmet** has wider cheek pieces and a broader neckguard than earlier types. It offered reasonable protection from a blow to the top of the head.

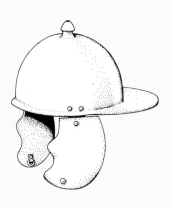

The **Coolus-pattern helmet** (early 1st century AD) was in many ways similar to the Montefortino, but tended to have even wider cheek pieces and neckguard. It also added a reinforcing peak to the front of the helmet to ward off an attack from this direction.

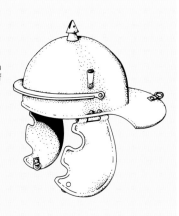

In the **Imperial Gallic helmet** (middle to late 1st century AD), the trends evident in the Montefortino and Coolus helmets are taken further. The neckguard is not only broader, but it is now lower, ribbed for greater strength and angled to deflect a blade.

The **Imperial Italic helmet** (early 2nd century AD) differed only slightly from the Gallic types in shape, although they are usually less ornate. Many later examples have reinforcing cross pieces over the top.

This **iron helmet** found at Heddernheim in Germany was probably used by a cavalryman, but shows many of the same trends apparent in infantry helmets.

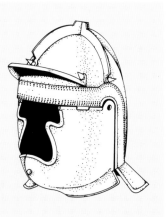

The **Intercisa-type helmet** differed radically from earlier helmets in design. The bowl was composed of two separate sections joined by the ridge in the middle, small neckguard and no reinforcement to the front and top of the helmet.

quarter zinc – used in bronze helmets could be spun, and this production method became common for Montefortino and Coolus helmets in the 1st century BC. The metal in the bowl of a spun helmet was not as well hardened as in a forged helmet and proved brittle, surviving examples often showing damage to this area. It may be that the addition of a peak to the Coolus pattern was at first an attempt to counteract this weakness, although it clearly also conformed with the longer-term trends in Roman helmet design.

Later-pattern Coolus helmets had increasingly wide cheek-pieces and neckguards. These trends, combined with others taken from the tradition of iron Gallic helmets, eventually produced the Imperial Gallic and Imperial Italic helmets, the vast majority of which were made of iron. The earliest types of Imperial helmets have cut-outs for the top of a soldier's ears, which soon developed into ear guards. Neckguards soon ceased to project straight out from the back of the helmet and became increasingly lower and deeper, the guard itself at the same time becoming wider. In time these offered some protection not just for the back of the neck, but also for the shoulders. Rows of ribbing usually strengthened the back of the helmet. The front of the bowl was protected by a peak, much like the Coolus patterns, but increasingly thick. Imperial helmets might be made of either bronze or iron, although the latter is far more common for the Imperial Gallic type. The principal differences between Gallic and Italic helmets is stylistic, although the quality of the latter's finish is also generally superior. Distinctive features of Imperial Gallic helmets are the heavily stylized raised eyebrows on the front of the helmet bowl, the brass piping edging much of the helmet and the brass or enamelled bosses used as decoration. Neither these, nor Italic patterns, tend to have crest knobs, and instead crests were slotted into forked crest holders. In the late 1st century AD, further efforts were made to strengthen the front and top of the helmet. Two reinforcing bands were attached, in some cases to existing helmets as well as in new models, forming a cross on the top of the bowl, so that sometimes this pattern is referred to as the 'hot-cross bun' helmet.

Whilst it would probably be wrong to depict the development of Roman helmets as a steady evolution, the long-term trends do reveal the preoccupations of the makers. Protection to the top of the head was always the highest priority. This area was exposed to the enemy, especially an enemy armed with a slashing weapon such as a sword and able to cut down onto the top and front of the bowl. The peaks on the front of the helmet, as well as the thick reinforcing bands, were all intended to protect against such blows. Equally interesting is the development of deeper and broader neckguards. An enemy in front aiming a blow at the top of the helmet could very easily miss or find his blow

deflected down. Neck guards not only protected the neck itself, but also gave some defence to shoulders. Another notable feature of all Roman infantry helmets before the 3rd century AD was that they left the face and ears uncovered. It was important for a soldier to see what was going on and to be able to hear orders, and both vision and hearing were seriously impaired by closed helmets such as the Corinthian helmet associated with Greek hoplites or the Great Helms of the Middle Ages. However, as much protection as possible was offered by the large cheek-pieces and earguards on Roman helmets.

Helmets, crests and ranks

According to Vegetius, centurions were distinguished from ordinary soldiers by wearing a wide transverse crest. Although depicted on only two monuments, and not yet confirmed by any extant example of such a helmet, it is generally accepted that this applied throughout the Late Republic and Principate. Standard-bearers wore animal skins over their helmets, and it is just possible that this practice was also followed by some auxiliary units. In Caesar's day it was clearly normal practice for soldiers to mount crests or plumes in their helmets during a battle, for he mentions an occasion when the suddenness of an enemy attack denied the soldiers time to do this, as well as remove the leather covers from their shields. Many helmets until the end of the 1st century AD were fitted with the mountings to take a crest. Some helmets, especially of the Coolus pattern, additionally have tubes on either side of the bowl which presumably supported tall plumes. It is unclear whether these represented a badge of rank, perhaps for *optiones*, or were the insignia of a particular legion or legions, or even of a sub-unit within the legion. Julius Caesar formed a legion from Gallic recruits to whom he subsequently gave Roman citizenship. There is an attractive, if unsubstantiated, suggestion that this unit, Legio V Alaudae or 'the Larks', may have worn larks' feathers either side of their helmet in this fashion. On Trajan's Column, and other contemporary monuments, crests are rare, associated only with parades. The reinforcing cross bars on the tops of helmets made it impossible to mount a crest in any of the traditional ways, but whether this, or simply fashion, was the reason for this change in practice is unclear.

Linings and headgear

Some surviving Roman helmets, for instance an Imperial Gallic helmet from Brigetio, show traces of a lining inside the bowl. This ensured that the helmet was a more comfortable fit and was most likely padded so that it helped to cushion any blow delivered to the helmet. Such cushioning was essential if the wearer was not to be at least stunned, and possibly more seriously injured by non-penetrating

In Caesar's day it had been normal to wear crests and plumes in battle, but this practice appears to have become rare in the army of the Principate. However, many helmets could be fitted with crests and such ornamentation was still common for parades and ceremonies. A group of re-enactors display a range of different decorations to their Imperial Gallic helmets. In the centre the centurion's transverse crest (which was probably worn even in battle) marks him out as an officer. It is not known whether other ranks, such as optiones, *were also distinguished by crests and plumes of specific shapes or colours, as is suggested here, but it is certainly plausible that they were.*

strikes to the helmet. If the helmet lacked an integral liner, then the soldier would certainly have worn some sort of headgear beneath it to perform this function.

Later developments in helmet design

The 3rd century saw significant changes in many aspects of the Roman army's equipment. Whilst some Imperial-pattern helmets continued to be used in the first decades of the century, a new type of infantry helmet, heavily influenced by the design of cavalry helmets, seems to have become common. A good example of this type was found at Heddernheim in Germany. Unlike earlier infantry helmets, the ears are almost entirely covered and the neckguard is steeply angled down. There were a few elements of continuity, notably in the continued manufacture of bowl and neckguard from the same piece of metal, but this tradition was soon to be broken by the adoption of several types of helmets made in sections which supersede most other types by the later 3rd century AD. In simple designs such as the 'ridge' type found at Intercisa in Hungary and elsewhere, the top of the helmet consisted of two halves joined by a ridged strip across the top. Several examples show traces of a lining. Although generally cheaper and quicker to make, some of these helmets are decorated with false eyeholes. Many of the Heddernheim-type helmets were exceptionally ornate, and this trend continued with some later designs, most notably the two examples from Berkasovo. The cheaper Intercisa-type ridge helmets or the equally crude spangenhelms – the bowls made from four pieces of iron – were probably infinitely more common in everyday usage, especially by ordinary soldiers. The spangenhelm may well owe its origin to helmets employed by nomadic races from beyond the Danube, such as the Sarmatians and the related Alans. Such simple helmets were not of the quality of earlier types. Nevertheless, the Roman army's ability to provide all, or virtually all of its soldiers with such gear, continued to give them an advantage over barbarian peoples where helmets were the preserve of only the wealthiest warriors.

Body armour

Mail (lorica hamata): Mail armour was in regular use by the Roman army throughout the period covered by this book. In the 1st century BC the vast majority of legionaries wore a mail cuirass, and at least some continued to do so after the famous segmented plate armour came into use. Although some shirts may have been made of copper alloy, the vast majority consisted of iron rings, on average about 1 mm thick and 7 mm in diameter. Each ring was normally connected to four others, the ring being either riveted or welded whole. It was common for legionary mail shirts in particular to have shoulder doubling and extend down onto the hips. A mail

A close-up of an auxiliary soldier from Trajan's Column showing him wearing mail armour, helmet, tunic and breeches. The tunic is a little unusual in that its lower fringe is decorated, while his sleeves are covered in a row of leather strips. Like all auxiliaries on the Column, he carries a flat oval shield.

cuirass is flexible and essentially shapeless, fitting more closely to the wearer's body than other types of armour. In this respect it is comfortable, whilst the wearing of a belt helps to spread its considerable weight of 10–15 kg (22–33 lb) which would otherwise be carried entirely by the shoulders. Mail offered reasonable protection, but could be pene-

trated by a strong thrust or an arrow fired at effective range.

Scale (lorica squamata): Scale armour was sometimes employed by legionaries, and is shown several times on the Adamklissi metopes in Romania. Unlike mail, which was relatively easy to maintain and repair, scale was more prone to damage so that individual scales appear relatively frequently in the archaeological record. Scales were usually of copper alloy or occasionally of iron. The former might be tinned to present a silvery finish and this type of armour could be polished to a high sheen. The size of the individual scales varied from

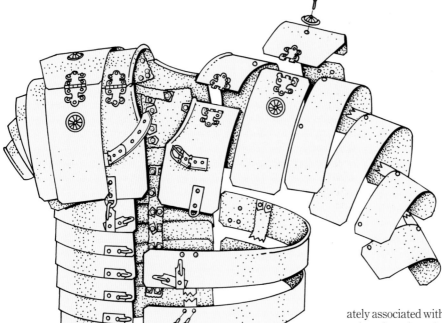

(Above) Pieces of scale armour found at Newstead in Scotland date to the end of the 1st century AD. Scales can be of iron or bronze and vary in size, although their basic design is broadly consistent. Broken scales were less easy to repair than rings of mail, so finds of broken scales are more common.

(Left) A diagram showing the construction of lorica segmentata *based upon the finds at Corbridge, south of Hadrian's Wall. Leather straps support the articulation of the iron plates. The many bronze fittings from these cuirasses were very prone to breakage and are comparatively common finds as a result.*

shirt to shirt, although most were relatively small, no more than a few centimetres long and narrower than they were deep. Rows of scales were wired together and then sewn onto a fabric backing. The scales themselves were thin, and the main strength of this protection came from the overlap of scale to scale, which helped to spread the force of the blow, or from the smooth surface deflecting a hit in the first place.

Plate (lorica segmentata): The segmented plate cuirass is the type of body armour most immedi-

ately associated with the Romans, although it seems only to have been in use under the Principate. Part of an early version of this armour was discovered in the excavations at Kalkriese, the probable site of Varus' military disaster in AD 9, pushing back the assumed date of its adoption by about half a century. Its use became less frequent in the 3rd century AD and the type was soon altogether abandoned. Although depicted on Trajan's Column, it was not until Russell Robinson successfully reconstructed the fragments of three cuirasses found in the hoard of military equipment at Corbridge, south of Hadrian's Wall, that its design became intelligible. The cuirass consists of a series of iron plates articulated by leather straps running underneath. Especially good protection was provided for the shoulders. The iron plates appear not to have been hardened by forging, probably so that the 'soft' metal absorbed a blow, spreading its force. Modern tests have confirmed the efficacy of segmented armour, suggesting that it would deflect or stop most strikes from arrows or spears. Weighing in at some 9 kg (20 lb), a segmented cuirass was a little lighter than mail armour, but its shape made it less comfortable to wear and could restrict deep breathing. The complexity of its design, with the numerous plates linked by copper-alloy buckles, hinges and hooks and the leather harness underneath presented many maintenance problems. Chemical reactions between the bronze fittings and the iron plates fostered corrosion, whilst many of the fittings broke or fell off far too easily. Fittings from segmented cuirasses are fairly common finds on Roman military sites. Although simpler versions of the armour were developed, for instance the 'Newstead pattern' named after the site in southern Scotland where the example was found, these problems were never adequately solved and, combined with the technological skill required to construct the armour in the first place, probably explain its eventual fall from favour in the difficult conditions of the 3rd century AD.

All types of armour at all periods would have been worn over some sort of padded garment and not directly on top of the tunic. Little is known about this item, since it was certainly made of perishable textiles and no example or unambiguous depiction has survived. Apart from making the wearer more comfortable, this extra layer complemented the protective values of each type of armour, and helped to absorb the shock of any blow striking the outer armour. Some of these jerkins may well have ended in a row of leather straps hanging down almost to the edge of the tunic and providing a measure of protection for the lower body and thighs. A very late, and generally unreliable source, refers to such a padded garment as a *thoramachus*, whilst another History speaks of a *subarmalis*. The second term probably appears on a text from Vindolanda describing some sort of textile, although a roughly contemporary document from Carlisle has confused the issue by speaking of a type of javelin known as a *subarmalis*. In some cases an additional, waterproof layer, most probably of leather, may have been worn either between the *thoramachus* and the cuirass or on top of the armour to guard against the weather.

The legionary shield (*scutum*)

In many respects the legionary shield changed little from the Mid Republic through to the early 3rd century AD. It remained a long, body shield, semi-cylindrical in shape and of plywood construction. Before the Marian reform legionaries carried an oval shield, both the tops and sides curving, like the example from Kasr el-Harit in Egypt. Oval shields of much the same pattern remained in use well into

the Principate, both with the legions and, perhaps especially, the praetorian guard. Yet by the beginning of the 1st century AD the vast majority of legionaries carried rectangular shields. These were a little shorter, though of similar width to the earlier pattern. Most were flat-topped, with curved or straight sides, but a leather shield cover from Caerleon was intended for a shield with a curved top and straight sides so there was evidently some variation. The evidence for the shape of legionary shields in the Late Republic is exceedingly poor and it is difficult to know when and why this change occurred. The shorter rectangular shield was a little lighter than the old oval type, and was perhaps more attractive to the professional legionaries in the post-Marian army who had to carry their weapons and equipment on the march. This is conjecture, but there is equally little basis for the common assumption that the rectangular shield did not come into use until the end of the 1st century BC.

No example of a legionary *scutum* survives from the 1st to 2nd centuries AD (although one 1st-century shield may now have turned up at Masada), but one well-preserved rectangular, semi-cylindrical shield was found with the 3rd-century AD remains at Dura Europus. The shield was 1.02 m (3 ft 3 in) long and 0.83 m (2 ft 8 in) wide. It was made of three layers of strips of wood glued together, the back and front set laid at right angles to the longitudinal middle layer. Its thickness was about 5 cm (2 in), but unlike the Kasr el-Harit shield it was not thicker in the centre than at the edges. A rectangular gap in the centre of the shield had been prepared to take the shield boss, although in fact this had not been fitted. The back of the shield was reinforced with a framework of wooden strips glued or pegged into place. The shield had a horizontal handgrip. Both back and front were covered with a thin sheet of leather, over which were stitched reinforcing leather pieces for the corners and a wide binding to protect the edge. This appears to have been a later, cheaper alternative to the brass binding which was normally used on these shields. Examples of this metal shield trim are common finds, suggesting that they were subject to frequent damage. A reconstruction of the Dura Europus shield with an added iron boss and bronze binding weighed in at 5.5 kg (12 lb). A shield of the same dimensions but with the increased thickness of wood in the centre would have weighed something like 7.5 kg (16.5 lb), which was still lighter than the reconstructed Kasr el-Harit shield at 10 kg (22 lb).

When not in use, shields were protected from the weather by leather shield covers, fragments of which have survived from several sites. The front of the shield was normally decorated with the unit's insignia – usually in paint – and some of these symbols were highly elaborate. The sculptors of Trajan's Column took great care to carve devices onto shields, but it is now impossible to identify these with specific units, and only a handful of unit symbols are clearly shown on tombstones. It is not clear whether the entire legion shared a common shield device, or whether each cohort was distinguished in some way, perhaps using colour, but it is clear that some sort of system existed. Tacitus recounts an incident during the civil war after Nero's death when two soldiers picked up shields from the enemy dead and, using this disguise, were able to infiltrate their positions and put a large catapult out of action. The Dura shield was painted a pinkish red on both sides and the front decorated

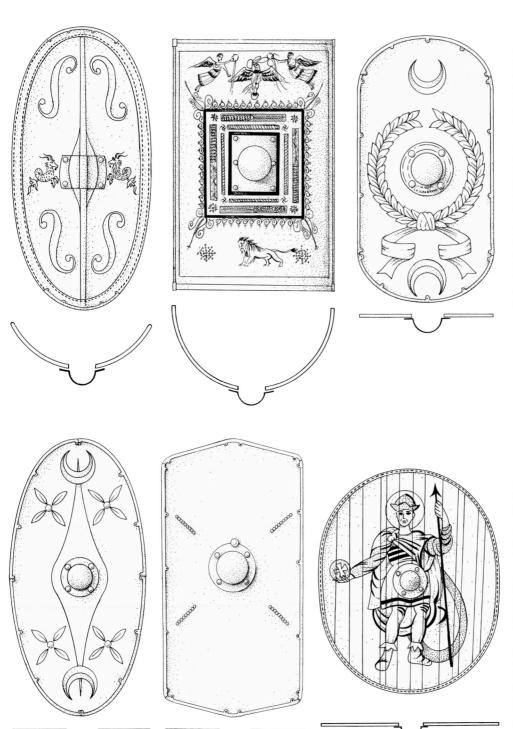

(Far left) A curved oval scutum *based on the Kasr el-Harit find in Egypt with a design taken from the Arch of Orange, southern France (in use from at least the 3rd century BC).*

(Centre left) A curved rectangular scutum *based on the example found at Dura Europus on the River Euphrates (1st–early 3rd century AD).*

(Left) A shield with straight sides and curved ends, based on a number of surviving shield covers. It is impossible to tell from these whether the shield was curved or flat (1st–2nd century AD).

(Far left) The dimensions of this flat oval shield are based on a shield cover excavated at Valkenburg in Holland. It has a design taken from an auxiliary's shield on Trajan's Column (1st–3rd centuries AD).

(Centre left) A flat shield based on an example found at Doncaster. Unlike most Roman shields it has a vertical handgrip (1st century AD).

(Left) An oval shield based on examples found at Dura Europus. On the original the detail of the figure's right hand is lost and this reconstruction is conjectural (3rd–4th centuries AD).

130

with a highly detailed geometric pattern, as well as the figures of a lion, eagle and twin victories. This was most probably the insignia of one of the legions in garrison. Such delicate detail can only have been subject to rapid wear, especially when the shield was employed in battle, and it is quite possible that on campaign more basic decoration would have been employed on replacements for damaged shields. Yet unit insignia were obviously important, and even the leather covers which protected shields on campaign sometimes included decoration. One mid-1st-century AD rectangular shield found in Holland belonging to a member of Cohors XV Voluntariorum civium Romanorum was decorated with two capricorns, the symbols of Augustus, who originally raised the unit. Even without heavy use, a single wooden and leather shield was unlikely to last a soldier for his entire 25 years service, unlike some metal gear, notably helmets which have sometimes shown signs of being owned by more than one soldier.

Other armour

Although various forms of muscled cuirass – most probably metal – are depicted as being worn by senior officers in Roman art, no example has survived from this period to confirm that this reflected actual practice and was not simply artistic convention. Similarly, it is now difficult to know whether or not the Romans employed any types of leather armour.

The Adamklissi metopes show that Roman legionaries in the late 1st or early 2nd centuries AD sometimes felt the need for greater protection than that offered by shield, helmet and cuirass. In all the scenes showing legionaries in combat these men are depicted as wearing greaves to protect their calves, and a segmented armguard or vambrace on their right arm. Many of their barbarian opponents carry two-handed, scythe-like *falces*, long weapons capable of reaching round the shield to strike at the right arm or lower leg, and the extra protection can be seen as a means of guarding against this specific threat. The armguard was constructed of articulated iron plates with leather harness underneath, in many respects similar to the segmented plate cuirass. Although plate armour is not shown on the Adamklissi metopes, where all legionaries wear scale or mail, an example of such a cuirass has been found associated with an armguard at Colonia Sarmizegethusa Ulpia, the capital of Roman Dacia. Yet finds from Newstead and more recently Carlisle in northern Britain have shown that this additional armour was not confined to the Danubian front but also employed in other areas. No example of Roman greaves clearly dated to this period has been found, but it is probable that, like earlier Roman examples, these were lined with leather and tied into place rather than clipping to the leg like those worn by Greek hoplites.

A detail from one of the metopes at Adamklissi showing a legionary using the boss of his scutum *to punch an enemy in the face and then stabbing him in the stomach with his* gladius. *This is the only clear depiction of a soldier using this well-attested fighting technique.*

Offensive weapons

The pilum: The *pilum* or throwing-spear was used by most legionaries until it gradually fell from use in the 3rd century AD, its design changing only in small details from the weapons in use under the Mid Republic. *Pilum* heads survive from a good number of sites, whilst several examples from Oberaden in Germany were excavated with parts of their wooden shaft remaining. There were two methods of attaching the long iron head to the wooden shaft.

Many of the legionaries on the Adamklissi metopes are shown carrying pila *with a circular object attached just behind the top of the staff. This is most probably a weight intended to increase its penetrative power when thrown.*

Some of the iron heads ended in a socket, the joint reinforced by an iron collet fitting over the top of the wooden shaft, but the majority had a wide rectangular tang which slid into a groove in the wood and was fastened into place by two rivets. One relief clearly shows a *pilum* with a butt-spike, but it is not known if this was always a feature of this weapon. Other sculptural evidence, most notably the Cancelleria relief showing praetorian guardsmen, and the Adamklissi metopes, show a ball-shaped object just below the wider top of the wooden shaft. This was most probably a weight, perhaps in lead, intended to increase the penetrative power of the *pilum* by focusing even more power behind its small head. One 3rd-century relief shows two of these weights. A *pilum*'s effective range was about 15 m (50 ft), but such modifications may well have reduced this. This weapon was intended first and foremost to kill or wound, punching through an enemy's shield and armour, but it required a high standard of discipline to refrain from using it until the enemy came within effective range. A single early tombstone shows a legionary carrying two *pila*, but, whilst it is possible that two were carried on campaign, it is extremely unlikely that a soldier took more than one into battle.

Spears and javelins: Legionaries may have sometimes employed other shafted weapons. The early 2nd-century AD Roman commander Arrian left an account of the formation of his army for an anticipated battle with the Alans, a nomadic people who relied predominantly on heavily armoured cavalry. His legionaries were formed up very deep to meet the enemy charge. The first four ranks carried *pila*, but the fifth to eighth ranks seem to have had the *lancea*, a type of javelin, and were ordered to throw these over the heads of their comrades once the enemy closed into contact. Ultimately the use of different types of throwing-spear can have required little re-training, certainly not in comparison to a modern infantryman being issued with a new rifle. Therefore it seems likely that legionaries were sometimes equipped with javelins other than the *pilum* if the particular situation required it. A series of 3rd-century legionary tombstones from Apamea in Syria suggest that Legio II Parthica had men skilled in a wide range of weapons, including light javelins (*lanceae*). Whether these specialists were always equipped in this way, or only when required, is impossible to say.

Spear and javelin heads are relatively common finds from Roman military sites. They vary consid-

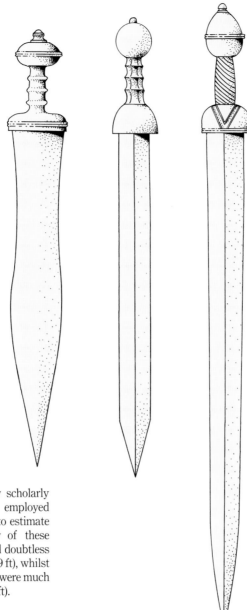

(Right) A scale drawing comparing the shapes of, on the left, a Mainz-type gladius, in the centre the Pompeii type, and on the right a longer spatha. Individual examples of each type vary to some degree in dimensions.

(Far right) The blade of a spatha found at Newstead in Scotland.

erably in size and shape, and the few scholarly attempts to classify them have rarely employed useful criteria. It is usually impossible to estimate the length of the shaft fitted to any of these weapons. Those used for fighting would doubtless have been long, perhaps just under 3 m (9 ft), whilst those solely designed for use as missiles were much shorter at a little more than a metre (3–4 ft).

The gladius: Although the evidence for Republican swords is limited, far more is known about the side-arms of the Imperial army. In the early 1st century AD the dominant type was the 'Mainz' pattern. This has a slightly tapering blade and an exceptionally long point. The length of blade on surviving examples varies from 400 mm (16 in) to 550 mm (22 in), and width from 54 to 74 mm (2.1–2.9 in) at the top to 48 to 60 mm (1.8–2.3 in) before the point. A shaped handgrip of bone was protected by a guard and pommel, usually of wood. The pommel also served as a counterweight and helped the balance of the weapon. Although especially suited to thrusting, with the long point – sometimes as much as 200 mm (7.87 in) – intended to penetrate armour, the Mainz-pattern sword was also an effective slashing weapon. Later in the 1st century AD, Mainz-pattern blades appear to have been largely supplanted by the 'Pompeii' type. This was a straight-bladed weapon with a much shorter point. Blade lengths vary between 420 and 500 mm (16.5–20 in) and widths between 42 and 45 mm (1.6–2.2 in). Even more than the Mainz pattern, the Pompeii-type *gladius* was a supremely well balanced and effective weapon for both cutting and thrusting. In the latter part of the 2nd century a similarly shaped pattern was introduced. The main difference was in the handle and fittings, for instead of the familiar pommel, the tang of the blade was extended into a ring of iron.

The *gladius* of whatever pattern was invariably worn on the right side, save by centurions, and perhaps other senior officers, who wore their swords on the left. Although awkward to modern eyes, experiments have repeatedly demonstrated that these swords can easily be drawn when slung on the right side, and that this avoids any entanglement with the shield. Analysis of several examples of Roman sword blades has shown that some were of very high quality, consisting of both low-carbon iron and carburized steel. The better weapons had been quenched to harden the metal and tempered. Other examples were less sophisticated, but in general the quality of the army's weaponry was good.

The pugio: The military dagger (*pugio*) varied in blade length from 250 to 350 mm (9–14 in) and provided a stout backup to the sword for both legionaries and auxiliaries. Their scabbards were often richly decorated, adding to the splendour of a man's weapons' belts. Daggers remained in use for most of the Principate, although they do appear to have become significantly less common in the 2nd century AD and are not shown on Trajan's Column. The dagger was worn on the opposite side to the sword – on the left for ordinary soldiers and one the right for centurions who wore their sword on the left.

Standards

The eagle (aquila): The eagle standard was an object of massive reverence. Given this importance, it is not surprising that no example has survived in the archaeological record and that we must rely largely upon sculptural evidence in reconstructing its appearance. Marius is said to have issued each legion with a silver eagle, but by the Principate the top of the standard appears to have been gold or gold plated. Decoration was usually fairly simple and the eagle's staff virtually bare, although a figure on the breastplate of the Prima Porta statue of Augustus does show a row of discs like those normally associated with *signa*.

The signum (pl. signa): The tradition of each century in a legion having its own standard (*signum*) appears to have continued throughout the Principate. Certainly, each century continued to have a standard-bearer (*signifer*) amongst its *principales*, and it is normally assumed that these men actually carried a standard. *Signa* appear to have been topped either by an ornamental spearhead or an upraised hand. Their shafts were heavily decorated with cross-pieces, wreaths, and from two to six large discs. The actual significance of any of these items is unknown, though it does seem probable that together they provided a system for identifying the particular century. The upraised hand may originally have been the symbol of the

maniple, for the word probably derived from the Latin for hand, *manus*, meaning a small group or handful of men.

The vexillum (pl. vexilla): A range of flags were carried by different units of the army. Traditionally a distinctive *vexillum* or flag, usually in red, marked out the commander's position in camp before a battle and on the battlefield. *Vexilla* also provided the main standard for detachments of troops serving away from their parent unit, so that in time such detachments became known as vexillations (*vexillationes*). Roman flags were suspended from a cross-bar to hang down in front of the main shaft. One example of such a banner has been found in Egypt and carries the figure of a Victory on a red background.

The imagines: Under the Principate each unit also included a series of images of the emperor and his close family which were mounted on poles and kept with the standards. These served as a reminder to the soldiers of their oath and loyalty. Mutinous troops, especially those incited to support their own commander in a bid for the throne, usually began by tearing down the *imagines*.

The draco: Auxiliary standards seem in general to have followed the patterns of those used by legionaries, but by the early 2nd century AD an additional type had been adopted by some cavalry units for use in parades and perhaps at other times. This was the dragon or *draco*, a bronze animal head with an open mouth and neck to which was attached a multi-coloured tube of material. When the standard-bearer moved quickly, the tube of material

(Left) Many legions had a particular symbol or symbols which often appear on sculpted stones or moulded on to tiles. Here we see the boar symbol of Legio XX Valeria Victrix.

A detail from a gravestone showing two standards, the square flag or vexillum and a heavily decorated century standard or signum. The standards of the praetorian cohorts were at times so heavy with ornaments that the Emperor Caligula gave his guardsmen permission to carry their signa on pack animals during a long march.

acted like a wind-sock, streaming behind the head and making a whistling sound. These standards seem to have been copied from some of Rome's opponents on the Danubian frontier, most notably the nomadic Sarmatians, and are depicted on Trajan's Column flying over the enemy armies.

Tools

On campaign a Roman legionary had to carry more than simply his armour weapons, personal belongings and food. Josephus, perhaps unconsciously echoing the old joke about Marius' mules, compared the legionary to a pack animal, saying that each man carried a saw, a basket, a pick and an axe, as well as a strap, a bill-hook and a chain. Whilst it is unlikely that every man was equipped with all of these items, it probably gives a fair impression of the range of tools available to a *contubernium* of eight men. As one modern commentator pointed out, the professional legionary was as much combat engineer as infantryman. Gnaeus Domitius Corbulo, one of the most famous generals of the 1st century AD, is even reported to have declared that 'battles were won with the pick-axe'. The Roman military pick-axe, or *dolabra*, was a well-designed implement, combining a cutting blade with a spike which could be used to break up the earth or undermine an enemy wall. Another type of tool blade is very similar in shape to a modern turf cutter, and is usually assumed to have performed a similar role, although its suitability for the task has been disputed. Controversy also surrounds the precise use of the so-called wooden 'palisade stakes'. Traditionally these were equated with the two stakes reportedly carried by each soldier and planted on top of an earth rampart to form a palisade. Recently, one scholar has suggested an alternative in which three of these stakes were tied together to form a self-standing barrier. Either interpretation is possible, but it must also be admitted that we may have wrongly identified these items in the first place. In addition to the tools and equipment required in some quantities, more specialized items were required for the men overseeing any project. Chief amongst these was the Roman surveying tool or *groma*, which consisted of an upright pole, mounting a cruciform piece with a lead weight hanging from the end of each section.

135

Auxiliary Equipment

It is in fact surprisingly rare that an excavated piece of military equipment can be incontestably associated with a particular unit or branch of the service, since only a tiny fraction of surviving finds carry such detailed identity markings. The distinctions in dress and equipment between legionaries and auxiliaries have as a result tended to be based primarily upon the depiction of soldiers on commemorative and funerary monuments. On Trajan's Column the clear distinction between the citizen legionaries and the native auxiliaries is maintained throughout. Legionaries wear the segmented cuirass and carry curved rectangular shields, whilst auxiliaries wear longer mail shirts, often wear breeches and have flat oval shields. Such a depiction is clearly stylized, and the contemporary Adamklissi metopes demonstrate that many legionaries in fact wore mail or scale armour. In spite of several attempts to argue that there were no distinctions in equipment between the two halves of the army, it does seem possible to state a few points. There is absolutely no evidence that auxiliaries ever wore *lorica segmentata*, used the *pilum* or, with the possible

A tombstone from Housesteads fort on Hadrian's Wall showing an auxiliary archer. He has an unusual pointed helmet, probably mail armour, a quiver over his shoulder and carries a short axe in addition to his re-curved composite bow. Apart from having an ordinary tunic instead of long robes, he is not too dissimilar from the eastern archers shown on Trajan's Column.

(Right) The tombstone of Maris, a horse archer, found at Mainz. Notice the servant standing behind him and holding a sheath of arrows. Servants appear on a number of cavalry tombstones.

exception of a handful of units called *scutata*, carried semi-cylindrical shields. Instead they appear to have carried spears or javelins, worn mail and probably scale, and had flat shields. The last may sometimes have been rectangular or hexagonal instead of oval. Scholars have frequently associated simpler, less well-made or decorated items – most notably helmets – as auxiliary equipment. Although this is plausible enough, it must be emphasized that it does not rest on any solid evidence.

The majority of auxiliary infantrymen wore a helmet and body armour, carried a shield and were equipped with one or more spears/javelins and a *gladius*. Although often described by modern commentators as light infantry who fought in a looser order than the legions, this view must be treated with caution. Apart from the shield, which may have been lighter than the *scutum* carried by legionaries, auxiliary equipment was of similar weight to that borne by their citizen counterparts. Our ancient sources do refer to light armed units who operated as skirmishers in open order, but the bulk of auxiliary infantry appear to have fought in much the same way as legionaries. Whether the actual light infantry were organized into separate units or were sub-units of ordinary cohorts is impossible to say. Nor is it clear precisely how these men were equipped. Slingers appear on Trajan's Column, but no unit of slingers (*funditores*) is known. At Lambaesis in North Africa Hadrian complimented the cavalry of a cohort on their prowess with slings, so it is more than possible that some units trained some or all of their men in the use of this weapon. Moulded lead sling bullets, sometimes with obscene messages on them, have been found at many sites, especially those associated with the civil wars of the Late Republic. Stone pebbles may well also have been used as ammunition.

Archers are depicted on Trajan's Column, some dressed in a caricature of eastern costume with long flowing robes and distinctive helmets. Many auxiliary units, both horse and foot, were formally designated as archers (*sagitarii*), although even here the evidence is a little unclear, since a few of these units appear to have carried other weapons whilst some units without this title employed bows. The Romans used a sophisticated recurved composite bow (i.e. made of more than one type of wood). Since wood rarely survives we have no example of such a weapon, but bone laths, which were fitted to the grip and 'ears' or ends of the bowstave, along with arrowheads, occur with some frequency at military sites. The vast majority of Roman archers employed what is known as the Mediterranean release, where the string is held in two fingers and drawn back to the chin. A leather bracer was worn on the inside of the left arm beneath the elbow to protect this from bruising as the released string whisked past. There is a little evidence to suggest that the alternative method, known as the Mongolian release, which used a thumb ring to grip the bowstring, was practised by some units in the 3rd century AD.

Cavalry Equipment

Helmets and armour

Cavalry helmets differ from those used by the infantry in several important respects. In the first place the soldier's ears were almost invariably covered by extensions from the cheek-pieces. This can only have impaired the wearer's hearing, and some helmets have small holes drilled in these cheek-pieces to counter this. In a whirling cavalry mêlée, when two squadrons interpenetrated each other, a horsemen could easily be attacked from the side or rear and so the extra protection to the face was clearly considered to be more important than some loss of hearing. The other most obvious difference to the patterns of helmet worn by Roman foot soldiers is the much deeper but comparatively narrow neckguards on cavalry helmets. A wide projecting neckguard could easily break a man's neck if he was to fall backwards from his horse. However, in many other respects, including methods of construction, Roman cavalry helmets mirror those of the infantry and, as we have seen, by the 3rd century the two styles drew even more closely together. Some types of decoration do appear unique to the mounted arm, for instance the sculpting of stylized hair on the helmet bowl. In a few examples, real animal or human hair was attached to the helmet instead of simply being depicted on it.

Auxiliary cavalrymen used flat shields in a similar variety of shapes to their infantry counterparts. The majority appear to have been oval in shape, but rectangular shields were used by some units, whilst others, including the cavalry which supported the praetorian guard, had hexagonal shields. A flat shield was found in a 1st-century AD Roman fort at Doncaster in Britain and was probably used by an auxiliary, and quite possibly a

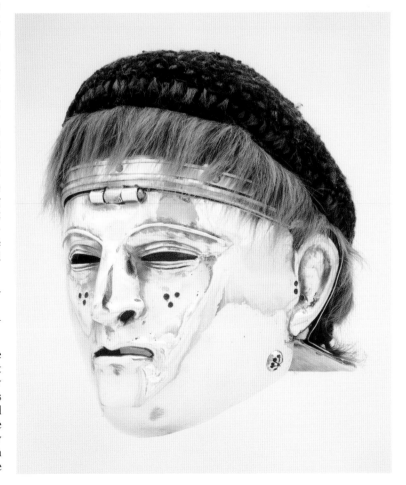

A cavalry 'parade helmet' from Nijmegen in Holland presenting a variation on the common style of having the top of the helmet shaped to represent hair. In this case real animal hair has been fixed to the helmet instead. This may have been a fashion most common amongst Batavian units.

(Left) The Bridgeness stone from the Antonine Wall portrays an auxiliary cavalryman in a pose reminiscent of many cavalry tombstones as he tramples over naked barbarians.

(Right) Two spatha blades found at Newstead in Scotland, giving a good idea of the longer, slimmer swords used by cavalrymen.

cavalryman. This example was large, measuring over 125 cm (4 ft) in length and 64 cm (2 ft) in width with straight sides and a curved top and bottom. Construction seems to have been very similar to the legionary shields discussed above, with three layers of plywood covered with thin leather, but unlike other Roman shields it had a vertical handgrip. A reconstruction proved almost as heavy as the Fayum shield, at 9 kg (20 lb), but was well balanced. The boss was slightly above the centre, which tended to make the shield's lower half angle back towards the legs, which may have been useful for a man on horseback. Oval shields of far simpler construction, made from a single layer of wooden strips glued together, were found at Dura and similar types may already have been in use by auxiliaries before the 3rd century.

Roman cavalrymen wore cuirasses of mail or scale armour. One relief from Belgium appears to show a combination of the shoulder sections of *lorica segmentata* with a mail shirt, but this is the only evidence for such a composite cuirass. In the 2nd century AD, Hadrian raised the first known *ala* of Roman cataphracts, Ala I Gallorum et Pannoniorum cataphracta, in which both horse and rider were heavily armoured. Amongst the armour found at Dura Europus was a set of scale horse armour.

The *spatha*

Roman cavalry employed a longer, slimmer sword known as the *spatha*, for a cavalryman required a weapon with a longer reach, especially if he was to strike at an opponent on foot. Blades range in length from *c.* 65 to 91.5 cm (26 to 36 in) with a width usually of under 4.4 cm (1.75 in). Pommel, guard and hand-grip were generally similar to *gladius* types. Like the *gladius*, these longer swords were usually also worn on the right side.

Spears and javelins

A range of shafted weapons were employed by Roman cavalrymen. The longest was the *contus*, a spear some 3.65 m (12 ft) in length and held in both hands by a shieldless rider. This appears to have been first adopted in the 2nd century AD and only ever equipped a small number of specialist *alae*. It was a weapon for shock action, and could not have been thrown with any great effect. Most cavalry carried a shorter, one-handed fighting spear, and usually several smaller javelins for throwing. A text

(Left) Another cavalry tombstone, from Gloucester, this time of a horseman from a cohors equitata and dating to the middle of the 1st century AD. The inscription reads 'Rufus Sita, cavalryman in Cohors VI Thracum, 40 years old and of 22 years' service, lies here. His heirs erected this in accordance with his will'.

(Right) Gaius Romanius Capito was a trooper in the Ala Noricorum. Notice once again a servant standing behind his master's horse and carrying extra spears or javelins, and also the decorated horse harness.

recording the inspection of the weapons of a cavalry *ala* in northern Britain in the late 1st century AD speaks of fighting spears (*lancias pugnatorias*) and the smaller javelins (*minores subarmales*). Each man was supposed to have one fighting spear and two *subarmales*, as well as a sword. This may have been the regulation equipment for this specific *ala*, for Josephus talks of Roman auxiliary cavalry with one long spear and three or more short throwing javelins carried in a quiver.

The saddle and horse harness

An idea frequently encountered in older books on ancient warfare is the belief that lack of stirrups prevented ancient cavalrymen from delivering any form of effective mounted charge and restricted them to tentative harassing action. This view was not reflected in our ancient sources, but these were ignored, for it was believed that without stirrups a horseman could not have had a stable seat. It is only in recent years that the reconstruction of the Roman saddle, pioneered by Peter Connolly, and its subsequent testing has finally demonstrated that this was simply untrue.

(Below) A drawing showing the construction and shape of the four-horned saddle employed by the Romans.

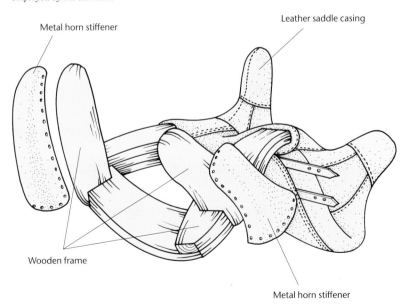

Metal horn stiffener

Leather saddle casing

Wooden frame

Metal horn stiffener

The four-horned saddle was employed by the Romans and also the Gauls, Parthians, Sassanid Persians and the Sarmatians, as well perhaps as other races. It is not known who invented it, although the Gauls must be prime candidates, and it is more than likely that the Romans copied the design from their enemies, as they did with so many other types of equipment. When the rider's weight is lowered onto this type of saddle, the four horns close around and grip his thighs. This provides considerable support, allowing him to throw or thrust a spear and wield a sword effectively, even leaning to one side and recover.

'Parade armour' and the cavalry games

Although the vast majority of Roman cavalrymen were not citizens, this arm of the *auxilia* enjoyed considerable prestige. Cavalry *alae*, most of all the small number of milliary *alae*, were expensive and prestigious, presenting an imposing sight on parade or in battle. Under the Principate the cavalry sports developed as spectacular public displays of the splendour and skill of the army's horsemen. For these events both horses and men were provided with highly ornate equipment. Most conspicuous in the archaeological record are the 'parade helmets'. Similar in basic shape to ordinary cavalry helmets, these were often silvered and always far more elaborately decorated and had a shaped face mask with eye holes permitting vision. Representations of hair were even more common and a significant number of surviving helmets have strong female characteristics, presumably intended to allow their wearers to represent Amazons. Arrian, the only source to describe these ceremonies in any detail, says that the helmets were normally topped by a streaming yellow crest, although there does not seem any obvious mounting for such a decoration on any surviving helmets. Horses wore leather-studded chamfrons (decorative and protective head-pieces), an example of which was found remarkably well-preserved at Vindolanda, with dome-shaped grills to protect their eyes but still permit vision. The horse's harness and saddle cloth, as well as the man's clothing, was brightly coloured and additional spectacle was added by the use of many standards, including the tube-like *dracones*.

Arrian appears to describe a standardized version of the games as set down by the Emperor Hadrian, but claims that much of the display had very ancient traditions. It began with a mixture of manoeuvring and charges, and this was followed by individual and group exercises. Divided into two sides, the cavalrymen lobbed blunt-headed spears at each other, aiming to strike the target's shield. Normal weapons were thrown at targets at various speeds and from different directions. During a straight charge across the display area a good soldier was capable of hurling

15 light javelins at the target, whilst a few of the very best managed 20. Though stylized, these exercises reflected many of the skills required in actual combat.

Helmets categorized by archaeologists as 'parade helmets' are common, scarcely less so than those thought to have been worn in battle. Although the cavalry games are well attested and were clearly an important phenomenon, we have perhaps been

(Below) A richly decorated leather chamfron (horse's head-piece) is reconstructed from an example found at Vindolanda dating to the late 1st or early 2nd century AD.

over-ready to ascribe any highly decorated piece of equipment to these sports. Roman military equipment often combined high levels of ornamentation with practical utility and it is at least possible that some helmets with face masks were worn in battle. Such a mask has been found amongst the equipment thought to have been lost by the Roman column during the Varian disaster in AD 9, suggesting that it was at least taken on campaign. An admittedly badly preserved tombstone from Germany appears to show a legionary *signifer* wearing a masked helmet, so such items may not have been restricted to the cavalry. The fixed features of a metal mask may have been very intimidating, hiding the fact that the wearer was simply an ordinary man. Perhaps under some circumstances this, and the added protection, were considered more important than unimpaired visibility.

These modern re-enactors give a good impression of the splendour of the Roman cavalry. The standard-bearer wears a helmet with a face mask, but in other respects the men's equipment is of the type worn in action. When taking part in parades or games Roman cavalrymen were often dressed even more elaborately.

Peacetime Duties

Distribution

It is very rare for our literary sources to go into much detail about the location of the units of the army at any fixed period. Even when they do so, these authors tended to be mainly concerned with the locations of the legions and are particularly vague about the garrisons provided by the *auxilia*. Any study of the army's deployment under the

(Right) The ruins of the city of Apamea in Syria give some idea of the grandeur of so many towns and cities within the Roman Empire at the height of its power. Ultimately all of this prosperity was only made possible by the effectiveness of the army in controlling and protecting the provinces.

Principate therefore rests heavily on the evidence provided by archaeology. A large number of military sites have been located and a reasonable number partially excavated, although it should be noted that some regions, notably Britain and Germany, have received far more attention, and are therefore much better known, than others. The size of a military base provides some indication of the type of unit for which it was originally intended. If we are fortunate, then the actual name of the unit may be recorded on inscriptions associated with the site, perhaps even in sub-literary material on writing tablets or papyrus. Where such evidence can be dated, it sometimes seems possible to trace the different units which came in turn to garrison the base. The movements of legions, given their sheer size, status and frequent appearance in the epigraphic record, are comparatively straightforward to trace, although even so there is often doubt about the circumstances in which a few of these

units disappeared. Auxiliary units are harder to track, but much useful information can be gleaned from the *diplomata* issued to discharged soldiers, since these readily datable documents usually list not only the man's own unit, but all the other cohorts and *alae* within the province demobilizing men in the same year. This information helps to build up a list of units garrisoning a province at a set period.

In general – and especially in Europe – the Roman army was spread around the frontier provinces. Deepest within the province were often the great fortresses of the legions usually lying on the most important route of communication, whilst auxiliary forts and smaller outposts were mainly dotted around the periphery.

In the eastern provinces a significant number of military garrisons were based in or near cities. The two-legion garrison of Egypt was concentrated for most of the Principate at Nikopolis just outside Alexandria, and significant detachments from the Syrian legions were often stationed at or near Antioch. After Rome, Alexandria and Antioch were by far the largest cities in the Empire. They were important political centres with turbulent populations, and it was not uncommon for the soldiers to be employed against rioters in these cities. Yet in general garrison life around such a great city was pleasant, for it gave the soldiers access to the many luxuries of urban life, hence the common literary theme that such comfortable conditions weakened military efficiency. It was not just legions which were stationed in cities. The garrison of Dura Europus in the 3rd century AD was housed mainly in a military compound within the city, although some troops may have been billeted in civilian housing. Until the rebellion of AD 66 the garrison of the small province of Judaea was predominantly stationed in the cities and towns. The cohort permanently stationed in Jerusalem appears to have been quartered in the three great towers built by Herod the Great near his palace (an area now known as the Citadel). When the equestrian governor visited the city, usually during festivals such as the Passover when the mood could become tense, he brought with him another cohort which took up residence in the fortress of Antonia adjacent to the Great Temple. When Pontius Pilate first visited Jerusalem in this way, an uproar was created because his escort had brought its standards, including the *imagines*, with them, thus bringing graven images into the Temple and offending Jewish law. After a period of rioting, Pilate backed down and had the standards publicly removed from the fortress and the city. Even in the western provinces there is growing evidence for garrisons being maintained in important towns, for instance the sizeable fort in Roman London. It is probably a mistake to see the internal areas of the provinces as wholly demilitarized.

(Left) The ruins of the fortified city of Dura Europus on the Euphrates. Excavations at this city have produced large quantities of military equipment as well as a great deal of other interesting material, including wall-paintings and many military texts on papyrus.

Garrison routine

Although we can locate the physical remains of many Roman military bases, it is much harder to deduce why the sites were chosen in the first place, how large the garrison was at any given time and what it was doing. Both forts and fortresses provided large amounts of accommodation, but it is only the rigid thinking of modern commentators which assumes that this must always have been occupied by soldiers of a particular unit type and size. A cooking pot of Ala I Thracum was found at the base of

Legio II Augusta at Caerleon, which may suggest the presence of auxiliary cavalry at the base. There are hints in the Vindolanda material of legionary personnel passing through the fort. Similarly, even though a unit may be attested on an inscription and then appear on another from the same site some decades later, this does not automatically mean that it remained in garrison there throughout the intervening period. Even if it had done so, this in turn does not rule out the possibility that the bulk of its manpower was actually serving elsewhere.

The strength report of Cohors I Tungrorum found amongst the Vindolanda tablets gave its total number of effectives as 752, including six centurions. No fewer than 456 soldiers, and five of the centurions, were absent from Vindolanda on detached duty. A large group of 337 men, probably commanded by two centurions, were no great distance away at Corbridge (Coria), but others were as far afield as London. Another, rather fuller strength roster was found in Egypt, although it refers to an auxiliary unit serving in Moesia on the Danube, probably in the year 105. Some fragments, especially numbers,

A badly eroded tombstone from Roman London depicting a soldier carrying writing tablets as an indication of his clerical job. The army provided most of the personnel who performed administrative functions on the staffs of provincial legates.

are missing or unclear, but it provides an indication of some of the many duties performed by the army. The cohort was part-mounted (*equitata*) although it does not say so, and was also known as *veterana*, probably to differentiate it from another, more recently raised Cohors I Hispanorum in the same province.

Much of the cohort's manpower was dispersed in penny packets inside and outside the province. Only

Strength Report

Strength Report (*pridianum*) of Cohors I Hispanorum Veterana quingenaria, commanded by Arruntianus, prefect. This is probably from AD 105, although we can't be certain.

Total of soldiers on 31 December 546
Including 6 centurions, 4 decurions; 119 cavalry; also including duplicarii, 3 sesquiplicarii, 1 infantry duplicarius, __ infantry sesquiplicarii.

Accessions after 1 January

__ Faustinus the Legate	2
_____	30
_____ the stragglers	__
Total accessions	50
Grand total	596

Including 6 centurions, 4 decurions; __ cavalry; also including 2 duplicarii, 3 sesquiplicarii, infantry duplicarius, __ _____.

From these are lost:

Posted to the fleet by order of Faustinus the Legate	__
____ by order of Iustus the Legate, including 1 cavalryman	__
Sent back to Herennius Saturninus	1+
Transferred to army of Pannonia	1+
Drowned	1+
Killed by robbers, 1 cavalryman	1
Killed	__
Total lost, among them	__
returned with the stragglers	1
NET	___,

among them 6 centurions, 4 decurions; 110+ cavalry; including 2 duplicarii, 3 sesquiplicarii, __ infantry duplicarii, 6 infantry sesquiplicarii

From these, absent

In Gaul to get clothing	__
Likewise to get grain	__
Across the River Erar (?) to get horses, among them __ cavalrymen	__
At Castra in garrison, among them 2 cavalrymen	__
In Dardania at the mines	__
Total absent outside the province, including __ cavalrymen	__

Inside the Province

Orderlies of Fabius Iustus the Legate, among them Carus, decurion	__
In the office of Latinianus, procurator of the Emperor	__
At Piroboridava in garrison	__
At Buridava in garrison	__
Across the Danube on an expedition, including __ sesquiplicarii, 23 cavalry, 2 infantry sesquiplicarii	__
Likewise across to defend the grain supply	__
Likewise scouting with the centurion A—uinus, including __ cavalrymen	__
At the grain ships, including 1 decurion	__
At headquarters with the clerks	__
To the Haemus Mountains to bring cattle	__
On guard over draft animals, including __ sesquiplicarii	__
Likewise on guard over ____	__
Total absent of both categories including 1 centurion, 3 decurions; __ cavalry; __; 2 infantry sesquiplicarii	__

one out of six centurions was serving away from the main body, compared to the five out of six at Vindolanda, but three out of the four decurions were elsewhere. There is a good deal of evidence to suggest that such patterns were common for army units under the Principate. In the early 2nd century, Pliny the Younger was sent as special Imperial legate to govern the province of Bithynia and Pontus (northern Asia Minor), and his correspondence with the Emperor Trajan during this period was subsequently published. The province was normally controlled by a senatorial proconsul and had a minimal military garrison. In spite of this, Pliny continually mentions small parties of soldiers performing a wide range of roles, from regulating traffic, to escorting officials and guarding prisons. Throughout Pliny mentions the Emperor's desire to have as few men as possible serving away from their units. Trajan's replies constantly re-state this ambition, whilst in nearly every case instructing Pliny to leave that particular detachment where it was. Roman emperors governed with the aid of only a very small civilian bureaucracy, and frequently called upon the army to perform many non-military tasks, simply because there was no one else available.

Soldiers as administrators

Republican governors appear to have had staffs numbering no more than a few dozen, but by the Principate the situation had improved, and the legate of an imperial province had far more assistance. His essentially military headquarters, known as the *praetorium* and usually commanded by a seconded centurion, and his horse and foot bodyguards, the *singulares* chosen from the pick of the auxiliary units, were backed by the administrative *officium*. This was directly supervised by clerks (*corniculari*) – the post which Julius Apollinaris had unsuccessfully sought soon after enlistment (p. 79) – and probably numbered several hundred men. All of its personnel was provided by the army and detached from parent units. Amongst the *officium* were *commentarienses*, who appear to have maintained the records of the province, secretaries (*exceptores* and *notarii*), book-keepers and archivists (*librarii* and *exacti*) and assistants (*adiutores*), as well as more senior men who ranked as *principales*, such as the *beneficiarii*, *frumentarii*, and *speculatores*. One of the principal tasks of the *officium* was the overseeing of the administration of the army within the province, but it could also be turned to any of the range of tasks likely to be encountered by the governor. All appointments to it were at the disposal of the legate, but it seems unlikely that every new governor dismissed all prior appointments to replace them with his own men. This probably meant that there was considerable administrative continuity in the military provinces.

Soldiers were very visible representatives of Roman power, and indeed in many rural areas probably the only agents of imperial government likely to be encountered. Officers in particular, whether the regional centurions or the equestrian commanders of auxiliary garrisons, seem commonly to have undertaken administrative work delegated from the provincial governor. Amongst the Dead Sea Scrolls – papyrus documents found in caves near Khirbet Qumran in Israel – was an archive of documents dating to the early 2nd century belonging to a local woman named Babatha. The archive includes a copy of a formal declaration made in December 127 detailing her property around the town of Maoza in Arabia. The original document was presented to Priscus, a cavalry commander – most probably a prefect of an *ala* – whose Latin receipt was translated into Greek to conform with the rest of the copy. The declaration was part of a census being carried out by the governor of the province, with Priscus acting as his representative in the area of Maoza. Another fragmentary papyrus contains the text of a similar declaration made to Priscus at Maoza by another person altogether, suggesting that this was not an isolated instance and that he was regularly involved in such administration.

Soldiers as builders

The Roman army, especially the legions, contained large numbers of craftsmen and specialists such as architects and engineers. Military bases, from the temporary camps constructed at the end of each march on campaign to the great stone forts and fortresses, were built by the soldiers themselves. Many inscriptions survive recording the original construction or restoration of defences or buildings in and around permanent bases. Usually such work appears to have been undertaken by the unit in garrison, although the situation is less clear with auxiliary forts. The non-citizen units were much smaller than the legions and thus contained fewer technicians. However, there is evidence for auxiliaries undertaking some building work, although perhaps it was common for these projects to be supervised by legionary engineers.

When very large projects were undertaken, manpower was drawn from a number of units. The construction of Hadrian's Wall required the participation of all three legions stationed in Britain, II Augusta, VI Victrix, and XX Valeria Victrix. Each legion was allocated a stretch of the wall to construct and in turn allocated sections to individual centuries. Centurial stones, marking the completion of a length of wall by one of these units, are

The Roman legionaries on Trajan's Column are frequently shown undertaking major construction projects, as in this scene where a group build a camp. On campaign soldiers were supposed to work while still wearing their body armour in case of sudden attack. In peacetime such precautions were unnecessary but the army found itself called upon to construct a very wide range of different structures, from amphitheatres to aqueducts and roads.

common finds. The division of building works between the normal sub-units of the army appears to have been a standard practice. Titus' army undertook the construction of lines of siege-works at the siege of Jerusalem in AD 70 in this way, and it was believed to foster healthy competition between units to complete their task faster and more effi-

ciently than everyone else. On Hadrian's Wall there are signs that each unit also interpreted the basic design slightly differently, for instance building milecastles and turrets to different patterns.

Road building was also commonly undertaken by the army. Such projects benefited the civilian community of the province, whilst providing the military with improved communications for moving men and material as required. As we have seen, most legions, and some auxiliary units, built amphitheatres outside their bases. However, there is also ample evidence for the army undertaking projects for the civilian community. The aqueduct still visible outside the colony of Caesarea Maritima on

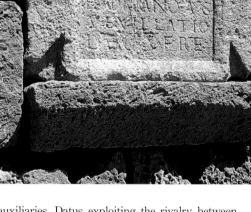

the coast of Judaea was restored by a vexillation of Legio X Fretensis, who left an inscription still *in situ* commemorating this. Other inscriptions record similar work on this aqueduct by other legions. In AD 75 vexillations from four legions and 20 auxiliary cohorts dug a 3-mile canal near Antioch along with bridges to cross it. As governor of Bithynia, Pliny wrote to Trajan proposing various engineering works, and mentioning others started by the local communities, but which had invariably failed or been abandoned. He asked Trajan repeatedly to instruct the governor of Lower Moesia, the nearest province with a legionary garrison, to send him an army engineer to supervise the project. In nearly every case Trajan refused, saying that there must be competent engineers and architects in Bithynia, but Pliny's requests testify to the widespread belief that the best engineers came from the army. An inscription from Lambaesis in North Africa seems to support the view. It reports the involvement of a veteran serving with Legio III Augusta, a certain Nonius Datus, with a project to bore a tunnel through a mountain to allow the flow of water to a town in the neighbouring province of Mauretania. Datus was requested to return to the site on several occasions by the local authorities, who each time sought permission from the legate of the legion, but does not seem to have stayed for any lengthy period, presumably because he had duties elsewhere. On one of his visits he took measurements of the two tunnels the workmen were excavating from opposite sides of the mountain, only to find that their sum was greater than its total width. Such mistakes caused serious problems. For at least some of the time the labour force was provided by sailors and

auxiliaries, Datus exploiting the rivalry between the two groups to speed the work.

Soldiers in industry

Claudius awarded triumphal honours – the highest reward a general from outside the imperial family was permitted to receive – to Curtius Rufus, who as governor of Upper Germany had set his troops to mining for silver in the territory of the Mattiaci tribe. Tacitus cynically commented that the labour had been massive and rewards insignificant, and says that the soldiers wrote to the Emperor requesting that he automatically grant each new governor this honour, so that they would stop trying to win it with such arduous but pointless exercises. This case was exceptional, and it was common in most provinces for the soldiers to be involved in a range of industrial and manufacturing activities. In western Britain, Legio II Augusta supervised the lead mines in the Mendip hills, as well probably as others nearer its base at Caerleon. The army ran quarries to provide the stone needed for its building projects. There were also military potteries, where not only cooking vessels needed by the troops were produced, but also the vast quantities of red clay tiles needed to roof fort buildings. Tiles in particular were often stamped with a unit's name, but their use does not appear to have been exclusive to military buildings, for they turn up on some civil sites. A few bear graffiti, and similar idle carvings on quarry walls, made by bored and weary soldiers.

Larger military sites often contained substantial workshops (*fabricae*). These were active in the production and maintenance of weapons and military equipment, but seem also to have made many of the other items required by the army. One of the Vindolanda tablets concerns the allocation of 343 men to the fort's workshops. Amongst the tasks mentioned in this fragmentary document are shoe-making, building a bath house, and uncertain tasks individually involving lead, wagons, the hospital, the kilns, probably digging clay, plastering, something to do with tents, and gathering rubble.

Soldiers as policemen

The provinces of the Roman Empire possessed no equivalent to a police force, although in some areas there were small numbers of local village constables with limited authority. Soldiers were agents of the imperial government, permitted to carry arms and employ violent force on command, and frequently found themselves on policing duties. The duty roster from Egypt mentioned earlier assigned men to patrols in Alexandria and to the enigmatic 'plain-clothes' duties. Along some of the roads in Egypt and other provinces at fairly regular intervals were small guard towers, which can have contained no more than a handful of soldiers. Clearly these were not intended to meet any large-scale military threat, but were to supervise traffic along the roads. Many legionary *beneficiarii* were assigned to way-stations (*stationes*) where they acted as local representatives of the governor and could be involved in a whole range of tasks, including making arrests and carrying out the punishments meted out by the courts. Even more important were the regional centurions, and other officers who found themselves dotted around the provinces, for they were by far the most powerful officials encountered by most provincial civilians.

Papyri from Egypt record many cases where provincials appealed to army officers, most often centurions, seeking redress for crimes committed against them. In 207 the woman Aurelia Tisais wrote to the centurion Aurelius Julius Marcellinus saying that her father and brother had disappeared on a hunting expedition and that she feared they were dead. If this were so, Aurelia wanted the officer to find those responsible and hold them to account. Thefts of various sort were common causes of such appeals, and we hear of clothing, grain and animals amongst other property being taken. Quite often the alleged thieves were named, and one letter lists six men, plus numerous accomplices and a soldier Titius whom the writer claimed had taken a large quantity of fish from one of his ponds. In this case, as in many others, the victim had been threatened or actually assaulted. In 193 the centurion Ammonius Paternus received an appeal from a certain Syros, aged 47, who identified himself as having a scar on his right knee. Since he was illiterate, the letter was written by another man. Syros accused several collectors of a tax levied on corn with having demanded more than their due, and having attacked and robbed his mother, who was left ill in bed as a result.

We do not know the outcome of most of these appeals, and whether or not any action was taken. The formulaic nature of so many of these documents suggests that seeking redress in this way was a common, and presumably effective, practice. One surviving letter was written by a centurion summoning a person accused in a dispute over the ownership of crops. If necessary, a centurion could despatch armed soldiers to bring an individual for judgment. Other documents record people effectively standing bail for the accused, guaranteeing to pay their fine if they failed to appear in court.

Soldiers as an occupying force

The Roman Empire brought peace and prosperity. Populations rose and economies boomed in many areas under Rome's rule. The benefits of the new regime were not shared evenly, and did not extend to some groups, but on the whole the majority of the Empire's population enjoyed a higher standard of living than before the arrival of Rome. Yet, in spite of such trends, Rome was a conquering power and ultimately her rule was based upon military supremacy. At times that rule had to be enforced, and the agent of this was the army. Major rebellions occurred in many provinces within a generation of their initial conquest. After this some regions appear to have accepted Roman rule, however grudgingly, but elsewhere sporadic and sometimes widespread outbreaks continued to occur. Strong military garrisons remained in Wales and northern Britain long after these had been occupied and the frontier moved some distance away. Mountainous or desert regions rarely became entirely settled and usually required a strong military presence. The violent elements inside the Empire were normally referred to as bandits and their attacks were more often directed against the settled population than the army as such. It is now very hard to say what

motivated such activity and to what extent these were political actions directed against Roman rule. Communities which had traditionally supplemented their incomes through banditry may have seen no reason to stop doing so with the arrival of Rome, but it is possible that in some areas resistance was provoked by the Roman presence.

Infinitely more is known about this sort of activity in and around the province of Judaea than any other part of the Empire. This material, derived from historians such as Josephus as well as the New Testament and the Talmudic literature, gives us an unrivalled view of Roman rule as seen from the perspective of the conquered population. However, we should be very cautious about assuming that similar activity went on in other provinces about which far less is known. The dictates of Jewish religion made it exceptionally difficult, perhaps impossible, for the Romans to absorb the Jews into the social system of the Empire. The situation was not helped by the general difficulty for the polytheistic Romans to understand the Jews, whose beliefs were considered so perverse as to be akin to atheism, and the repeated appointment as governors of Judaea of the most unsuitable individuals. Major rebellions erupted in the province under Nero and Hadrian, with another late in Trajan's reign amongst the large Jewish population in Egypt, but these were merely the highlights of fairly constant low-level banditry and rebellion.

The Roman response to resistance of any kind was usually brutal. In 4 BC, when disturbances followed the death of Herod the Great, the Syrian governor Varus arrested and crucified several thousand suspected rebels around Jerusalem. In spite of such brutal measures, banditry remained a constant problem and travel a dangerous prospect, a reality hinted at in the parable of the Good Samaritan and Josephus' casual comment that the rigorous religious sect called the Essenes only carried weapons when on a journey. Christ was executed on the orders of the prefect of the province, Pontius Pilate, the task being carried out by a party of soldiers led by a centurion. Barabbas, the man whom Pilate released instead of Jesus, is described in Mark's Gospel as a bandit (*leistis*) who had been imprisoned for leading a rebellion in Jerusalem. Josephus describes many other leaders who appeared and were suppressed by the Roman authorities. His attitude towards most is hostile, for they challenged the authority of the high priestly families to which the historian himself belonged. The Talmudic literature, which consists primarily of stories and teachings about various rabbis, makes relatively frequent reference to groups of men living outside the law. The attitude of these texts towards such rebels is much more ambivalent and sometimes positive. Archaeologists have discovered on a number of sites cave and tunnel complexes from which such bands of terrorists (or freedom fighters or bandits, depending on an observer's point of view) operated. In some cases military equipment, including helmets, have been found in these hides, perhaps representing the spoils of a raid.

Not all violence within the provinces was directed against Rome. In Judaea the Samaritans and Jews were not infrequently openly hostile both to each other and the Gentile communities within the region. Rioting between Jewish and Gentile communities periodically broke out in cities such as Alexandria and Caesarea. The rebellion in Egypt under Trajan became virtually a war between Jew and pagan, and many Egyptian communities raised volunteer units to fight with the Roman army.

Soldiers and civilian

When ordered to do so, Roman army units appear to have displayed no qualms about arresting and executing members of the civilian population, or burning down villages. Our sources also provide many instances of the brutal behaviour of individual soldiers. John the Baptist is said to have instructed soldiers to be 'content with their pay', rather than seizing what they wanted from civilians. He may well have been addressing troops from Herod's army but, since these units were modelled on the Roman pattern and subsequently taken into the regular *auxilia*, the distinction is minor. The brutal soldier was a familiar figure in Roman literature. The hero of Petronius' *Satyricon* is threatened and robbed one night by a legionary, whilst in Apuleius' *Golden Ass*, a soldier attempts to steal the ass and later, when he has been beaten up, his comrades seek revenge. Papyri from Egypt make it clear that such abuse of power occurred in reality. Soldiers were permitted under some circumstances to requisition animals and property, but were supposed to give receipts so that the owner could seek compensation. Clearly this did not always happen, and it could be difficult for a civilian to seek redress against a soldier. Private accounts survive from Egypt in which bribes paid to soldiers and other officials are listed along with other everyday expenses, which may suggest how commonplace such things were.

Much larger-scale contributions were often required officially by the state. Other Egyptian records survive recording the receipt of grain by soldiers on behalf of their units from individual landowners or communities. For instance in 185 the *duplicarius* Antonius Justinus of Ala Heracliana garrisoned at Coptos in Egypt was sent to collect grain by his commander, the prefect Valerius Frontinus. The provincial governor had declared that 20,000 *artabas* of barley were to be allocated to the unit from the year's harvest. Justinus took receipt of 100 *artabas* of this, which was the share of this grain tax required from the village of Terton Epa.

Roman troops could be the brutal enforcers of Roman power in the provinces. As bearers of weapons, individual soldiers sometimes abused their position to threaten civilians and extort money from them. The ancient world was often a cruel and violent place. However, this should not disguise the fact that many of the interactions between soldier and civilian were peaceful and beneficial to both sides. Soldiers could also be husbands and parents, customers of civilian traders, men who upheld the law, and provided the skills needed for the construction of valuable amenities.

A relief from the Adamklissi monument showing a soldier leading two chained barbarians. Roman soldiers were often called upon to enforce the decisions of the civil powers.

151

Frontiers

Large sections of the Roman army were concentrated near areas of political importance, such as the big cities of the east and, of course, Rome, for the praetorian guard and its supporting units steadily grew in size. Some regions within the Empire were never fully under control, with resistance movements or persistent banditry, and also required substantial military garrisons. However, the bulk of the army lay in the frontier provinces. Under the Principate these bases became steadily more permanent and substantial, so that eventually timber and thatch were replaced with stone and tile. Over the last century or so archaeologists have revealed many of the sites, and the distribution of the forts and fortresses seemed to indicate the priorities of the army in each frontier zone. Many units are attested at the same base for long periods, sometimes even for centuries. Alterations in the number and type of units stationed in a province and the location of each garrison have often been interpreted as reflecting changes in the military situation.

As we have seen, the presence of a unit's administrative headquarters and records at a site actually need not mean that the bulk of its manpower was there for all, or even most, of the time period, or tell us what it was doing. Many units were spread out over a wide area in a number of detachments, performing all sorts of tasks. A fort originally built to house a quingeniary auxiliary cohort was not so specialized in design that it could not be employed for a range of purposes. It might be garrisoned by a unit of the original type, though some or most of its personnel could be elsewhere at any time. Alternatively it might house several vexillations from several units of various types, including legionaries or irregulars. Save for short periods or at times of particular crisis, such a fort is unlikely to have housed substantially more men than the 'paper' strength of its original garrison without serious overcrowding. All this was even more true of the much larger legionary fortresses. For the entire legion to be physically present in its fortress at any one time can only have been an exceptionally rare occurrence, once these had ceased to be winter quarters where the unit rested in the months between

The Antonine Wall in Scotland was occupied for a much shorter time than the more famous Hadrian's Wall to its south. Nevertheless it was a substantial line of fortification as this picture of the wall and ditch at Rough Castle suggests.

A distance slab from Hutcheson Hill on the Antonine Wall marking the completion of a section of the line. In the centre Victory crowns the eagle standard of Legio XX Valeria Victrix. On either side kneel submissive captives with their hands tied behind their backs.

campaigning seasons. It made no sense to keep bodies of 5,000 or so men waiting idly at their base until needed to fight a large-scale war, when there were so many calls upon the army's manpower. Instead, legionaries were detached as administrators, builders, engineers, policemen, craftsmen, and to garrison outposts or to serve as entire cohorts or vexillations of other sizes for actual campaigning. Legions provided so many specialists of various sorts that the decision to move one from a province, rather than simply send a strong vexillation to wherever they were needed, was not taken lightly.

The Roman army was dynamic and busy, its manpower performing a great range of roles, both military and civil. Knowledge of the locations of forts and fortresses in a given period does not in itself tells us what the army of a province was doing on a day-to-day basis. Even so, whilst some troops were posted long distances away from their parent unit, the location of so many military bases in frontier zones does suggest that the main focus of the army's attention was often in these regions. Considerable expense had been invested in the construction of these bases, and even more in some of the massive frontier barriers such as Hadrian's Wall and the Antonine Wall in northern Britain. Our literary sources tell us little of activities on the Empire's frontiers, especially from the late 1st century AD onwards. We are therefore faced with the task of understanding how the frontiers functioned primarily from the archaeological evidence, the few fragments preserved in the literature and logical deduction.

Strategy and grand strategy

A surprisingly fierce scholarly debate continues to rage over the precise nature of the Roman Empire's frontiers. One view is to see Rome's overall aim as defensive. The army was stationed on the frontiers to counter the many external threats posed by neighbouring peoples, and so preserve the Roman Peace (*Pax Romana*) which allowed the settled and civilized provinces of the Empire to prosper. It is a view apparently supported by some ancient sources, for instance the Greek orator Aelius Aristides, who in the 2nd century AD compared the army to a wall running around and guarding the civilized (and of course Roman) world. As early as Augustus' reign, the geographer Strabo had argued that the Romans had already conquered the best parts of the earth and that further expansion was unlikely to be either worthwhile or profitable. After AD 14 Roman expansion was far less concerted and the conquest of new provinces comparatively rare, which appears to support the idea that emperors now thought more in terms of defence and consolidation than expansion. If defence was the army's primary role under the Principate, then it was a task which it performed exceptionally well in the 1st and 2nd centuries AD, but far less successfully in the 3rd century when the frontier was frequently penetrated by invaders. Scholars have attempted to reconstruct the system which underlay both the long period of effective defence and the factors which caused the subsequent failures. The sites along each stretch of frontier have been assessed under the assumption that a logical and, on the whole, efficient strategy lay behind them. At the wider level of the entire Empire – where we would talk of grand strategy since the entire resources of the state were marshalled for its long-term benefit – the emperor and his advisors carefully planned where and in what ways to commit their forces, balancing the needs of each region. In many ways this is to view the Roman Empire as a very 'modern' state, its main objective to defend its territory and possessions against aggressors, which is the ultimate objective of modern democracies. Rome's apparent success has been interpreted as providing lessons for the modern world.

The opposite argument tends to emphasize the 'primitive' qualities of the Empire, lacking as it did rapid communications and an extensive bureaucracy. The Roman world was substantially a world without maps, and the ancient view of geography was simplistic and crude, making detailed planning extremely difficult. As such, it is argued that emperors could not have implemented any grand strategy, even if they had been capable of devising one. Instead their decisions were almost invariably reactions to an event rather than part of a grand plan. At the lower strategic level on each frontier, the location of military bases was haphazard rather than the product of a system. Furthermore it is argued that there is little evidence for the existence of a concerted external threat in many areas. Both the Parthians, and the Sassanid Persians who succeeded them, rarely provoked a conflict with Rome and were too weak internally to seize and hold significant areas within her eastern provinces. Elsewhere the tribal peoples were too disunited to pose a serious military threat, except very rarely in the 4th century and slightly more often in the 5th century. It is also claimed that, far from adopting a defensive posture, Roman emperors until Late Antiquity still hoped for further expansion, and ultimately to fulfil the propaganda boast of limitless Empire/power (*imperium sine fine*). Rome remained aggressive, and in many areas the army was stationed in expectation of further conquest.

As yet no widely accepted consensus has emerged, but it is probably best to acknowledge that both interpretations have made some important points. The ancient sources suggest that there was no clear defensive or offensive ethos, but a range of opinions. More importantly they make it clear that the Romans were more concerned with power than the physical occupation of land, and dealt with political entities, states, kingdoms and tribes, rather than simply areas of territory. The Roman Empire extended as far as the Romans were able to make peoples do whatever they desired or, perhaps more accurately, deter them from doing anything which the Romans did not want them to do. The Roman ideology emphasized the need to maintain and protect Rome's power and reputation. Military defeat or perceived weakness damaged this and required vengeance. Roman campaigns were frequently aggressive – if only because the army was simply more effective whenever it adopted the offensive than when it tried passively to defend – but a successful war did not always require permanent occupation of new territory. Rome was far more powerful than any other nation with which she came into contact. The frontiers occupied by the Romans certainly were intended to oppose attacks from outside, but were not set as limits to Roman power. Rome could and did operate well in advance of these whenever she chose. The reality was that large sections of the Roman army remained based in the same regions on the edge of the Empire for long periods of time, and engaged in warfare with the peoples outside the province. Some central planning did occur, if only in such matters as how many units, and especially legions, were stationed in each province, but whether or not by modern standards this constituted grand strategy is questionable.

Frontier zones

The Romans did not really have a word equivalent to our 'frontier'. *Limes*, a Latin word which used to be understood in this sense, largely kept its real meaning of road. Roads were fundamental to any long-term military deployment, connecting individual army bases. Good, all-weather roads made possible rapid and efficient movement of troops and supplies. As stated earlier, Roman forts and fortresses were not primarily defensive structures in the sense that it was rare for their garrisons to fight from behind their walls. The army was usually better trained and disciplined, and had a more sophisticated command structure, than its opponents and was often also better equipped. This gave considerable advantages in open fighting, which could and did compensate for much smaller numbers. Therefore when attacked, Roman units left their fortifications at every opportunity to fight the enemy in the open. The road system facilitated the concentration of units to form a field force.

Several frontier zones were based around significant geographical features, if only because these had often determined pre-existing political geography. Much of the frontier in Africa was formed when the Roman province reached desert areas which were sparsely populated and difficult to cross. The Rhine and Danube in Europe, and Euphrates in Syria, formed important parts of the frontier system in each area. Rivers were patrolled by Roman vessels and transport of men and material by water was often more rapid than overland. They also presented barriers to an invader, especially since the army took care to guard any bridges. A large army would be delayed by a river, since it would need to carry with it, make or gather many boats to ferry itself across. Any delay gave the Romans more time to discover the incursion and gather a force to meet it. Only freak weather conditions, such as the occasional freezing of a river in winter, changed this. Yet these same rivers did not form significant obstacles to the Romans. They controlled the bridges and crossing places, and their navy was active on the water itself. A Roman army faced little inconvenience whenever it wished to advance suddenly and rapidly across a river line against the enemy. Frontier lines were essentially solid bases from which the army could launch an offensive or counter-offensive whenever it desired, not barriers to hinder movement in both directions.

Auxiliary forts tend to be arranged in a line on or near the road running along the fringe of the province. Positions of obvious importance, for instance mountain passes, water sources in desert areas, and river crossings, were usually protected by a fort. There was also a range of smaller military bases, from forts and fortlets for small vexillations to small turrets (*turres* and *burgi*) manned by no more than a handful of soldiers. The turrets were a feature along many Roman frontiers, as well as along important roads, and are depicted on Trajan's Column. In some cases they appear to have been simply observation posts, providing raised viewing platforms and also contributing to the army's visible presence to surrounding land. Such lines of towers may well have helped to suggest that the army was watching what occurred. In some cases the towers were part of a system for signalling

Small watchtowers were a common feature of many frontier systems and also within some provinces, for instance running along important roads. The garrisons of such stations consisted of only a handful of men, who were clearly not expected to deal with major attacks. In some cases such towers formed part of a system of beacons or other signalling devices to convey simple messages quickly. This reconstruction of such a tower from the German Limes *is based on excavation and the depiction of such outposts on Trajan's Column.*

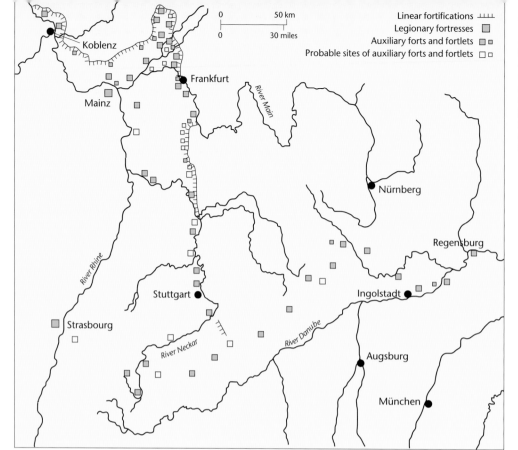

simple messages, using either fire signals or basic forms of semaphore. Observation from fixed points provided the army with some information, but far more could be derived from patrols. One reason for the high proportion of *cohortes equitatae* in relation to purely infantry units was that the small, balanced force of foot soldiers and cavalrymen were especially well suited to the patrolling and escort duties required of frontier garrisons. In desert areas some mixed cohorts acquired a small number of camel riders (*dromedarii*), who were especially suited for long-distance patrolling in the arid conditions. At least as important as anything that parties of soldiers themselves saw or heard was the diplomatic activity which went on well beyond the military zone. Frequent embassies to and from Parthia and later Persia are mentioned, but we also read of centurions sitting in on the gatherings of tribal chieftains in late 2nd-century Germany. Friendly leaders often received subsidies, and sometimes military advice or actual aid.

Linear boundaries

The most spectacular examples of Roman frontier systems were the great boundary walls and ditches constructed in northern Britain, Upper Germany, Raetia, and several places in the North African provinces. The use of sizeable linear obstacles was occasionally a feature of Roman campaigns. Caesar constructed such a line to block the passage across the Rhône of the migrating Helvetii in 58 BC, whilst in 71 BC Crassus had tried to hem Spartacus' slave army into the toe of Italy in a similar way. Sadly none of the more permanent frontier walls receive much attention in our sources. Most appear to date to the 2nd century AD. Yet even though the huge effort required to construct such structures may suggest a growing realisation that the army was unlikely to move forwards again, this is probably mistaken. Hadrian's Wall was virtually abandoned within a few decades of its building, when the army moved further north to construct and occupy the Antonine Wall. This in turn was swiftly abandoned, and the more southern line re-occupied. The army may then have moved north to re-occupy the Antonine Wall but, if so, this was soon permanently abandoned. Hadrian's Wall then continued in use for several centuries, although it is possible that this might have changed had the Emperor Septimius Severus not died before the completion of his operations against the Caledonians. Either the current Roman thinking on how best to deal with the military 'problem' in northern Britain, leading to different policies, or the situation itself had changed and required different solutions. The ditch and wall lines in Numidia may in turn have been solutions, or attempted solutions, to immediate local problems at specific points in time.

Hadrian's Wall

Rather than attempting to describe each of the different linear boundaries, it is probably best to concentrate on the best known and preserved of them all in a little more detail. Hadrian succeeded to the throne on the death of Trajan in 117, but the circumstances of his adoption as heir were somewhat suspicious and his position was initially insecure. Abandoning most of his predecessor's eastern conquests, Hadrian spent much of his reign touring the provinces, taking particular care to inspect the provincial armies and ensure their loyalty. It is possible that there was an outbreak of serious fighting in northern Britain at the beginning of his reign. The Emperor visited the island in 122 and ordered the construction of a great wall, according to his 4th-century biographer, to 'separate the barbarians from the Romans'. Although influenced by the line of the existing 'Stanegate Frontier', a line of forts and outposts running along an east–west road, Hadrian's Wall lay in general a little further north, running along the higher ground, especially in such sections as the craggy Whin Sill. Wherever possible, the wall ran along the crest of this and other ridges, stretching from one horizon to another. There is some evidence to suggest that the wall itself was originally whitewashed, which can only have increased its visible presence.

Hadrian's Wall was 80 Roman miles in length (73 modern miles or 117 km), extending from Bowness-on-Solway (Maia) in the west to Wallsend (Segedunum) in the east. Over half of the wall was built in stone, but the westernmost section of some 31 Roman miles was originally a turf-and-timber rampart. This section was later replaced in stone, usually on the same line, although in one or two places this was altered, allowing us to see short stretches of the original turf wall, for instance to the west of Birdoswald. This was just one of several major design changes made throughout the wall's life. At first the stone wall was planned to be 10 Roman feet wide (c. 3 m) and some stretches – known to archaeologists as the 'Broad Wall' – were completed to this width. Elsewhere, only the foundations were laid to this size and the actual wall was narrower at 8 or even 6 Roman feet (1.8 m). In at least one place the foundations of the 'Broad Wall' were abandoned altogether and a narrower wall built near the top of the crags. The stone wall always had a cobble stone foundation – as did some stretches of the turf wall – an inner core of rubble and outer faces of stone set in lime mortar. Its original height is unknown, nor is it certain whether or not it was simply a barrier wall as in Hadrian's German frontier system, or was topped with a walkway and battlements along which patrols could move.

The 'Broad Wall' marked the original plan, and it was at this stage that the buildings originally intended to form part of the system were marked

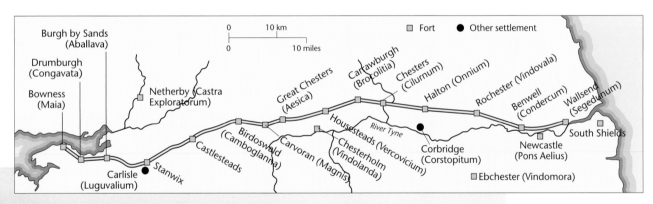

(Above) Hadrian's Wall is probably the most famous of all the fortifications built by the Roman army. It was built and developed over a long period of time, leading to numerous changes in its design. The function of the wall continues to be hotly debated.

(Left) The milecastles on Hadrian's Wall were small structures similar to the fortlets and outposts on other frontiers.

157

out and possibly constructed. Every Roman mile there was a small fortlet, known today as a milecastle and conventionally numbered from east to west. Between each milecastle were two small turrets. In several cases milecastles and turrets were clearly built with short sections of 'Broad Wall' either side, long before the main connecting wall was com-

pleted to the narrower gauge. Milecastles tend to average some 18 sq. m (60 sq. ft) internally, but as already mentioned, each of the three legions constructing the wall followed a slightly different design. The milecastles of Legio II Augusta tended to be wider than they were deep, the opposite of those built by the other two legions. All milecastles

had a gateway in their southern wall and another leading north. The latter was topped by a tower and this may also sometimes have been the case with the southern gateway. The survival of stone steps in the milecastle 48 at Poltross Burn demonstrates that the walls within a milecastle did have walkways, and suggests a height of about 4 m (13 ft).

(Above) The milecastle at Poltross Burn contains one of the few clear traces of stone steps in the installations along the wall. These make it clear that there was a walkway along the wall inside a castle, although this does not necessarily mean that there was a similar walkway and parapet along the wall itself.

A classic image of Hadrian's Wall rolling across the craggy landscape, in this case near Peel Gap to the west of Housesteads.

In the original design there were no forts actually on the line of the wall. This was changed before construction was complete and forts were added. At Housesteads this meant that the new wall of the fort was built over a demolished turret.

Milecastles in the turf wall were similar in basic design. Internal buildings seem to have been added after the original construction and tend to be fairly crude. As far as possible, positioning conformed to the original regular plan, with the result that some of these fortlets were in highly unsuitable locations. The northern gateways sometimes opened onto a slope or cliff, whilst the entire milecastle might be set into a steep valley which dramatically reduced visibility from the tower. The same rigid adherence to a plan marked the location of turrets. At Steel Rigg a third, extra tower was added, probably to permit observation into a wide area of dead ground left by the original design.

In the original design, the bulk of the garrisons for the frontier zone were to remain in the existing forts along the Stanegate, a mile or more to the south. However, within a few years this initial conception was altered and forts added to the line of

the wall itself. In several cases this involved the demolition of existing structures, for instance at Housesteads where the north wall was built on top of an at least partially completed turret. The forts on the wall added to the number of gateways giving the army access to the north. Eventually there were 15 forts actually on or very close to the wall, and other bases in advance of the line, behind it, and on both flanks. Some of the bases behind the wall had clear supporting functions. The military compound in the town of Corbridge appears to have been a depot with significant storage space and workshop facilities. South Shields (Arbeia) fort south of the mouth of the Tyne was at one stage a massive supply dump containing a large number of granaries. As usual, most forts were surrounded by large civilian *canabae*, and the impression given by inscriptions is of a very cosmopolitan community. The southernmost boundary of the military zone was marked by the *vallum* – a modern and somewhat inaccurate term which has nevertheless become conventional. The *vallum* was a broad, flat-bottomed ditch with a low mound running on either side of it. There were two formal crossing places, both controlled by the army.

The Cumbrian coast to the west contained what was effectively an extension of the system, with forts, milecastles and turrets, but no connecting wall. Most of these sites appear to have been abandoned long before the end of the 2nd century, presumably when the Romans' perception of the military situation had changed.

How did the wall work?

It is clearly mistaken to imagine vast hordes of Caledonian or later Pictish invaders hurling themselves at Hadrian's Wall as the Roman defenders manned the battlements to oppose them. Even if the wall did have a walkway, the whole structure was not intended as a fighting platform. It would have presented a large enemy army with a difficult, but not impassable barrier. The wall could be scaled with ladders, but this would be a slow way of getting a large number of men across and obviously not practical for horses. It would be better to capture a gateway, but further progress for animals would be impeded by the *vallum* unless one of the two crossing places could be taken. Any such delays only gave the Romans more time to assemble a field force and move to intercept the enemy. This was invariably the objective here as on the other frontiers, to bring the enemy to battle and defeat them swiftly and decisively. In most cases the mustering of a substantial tribal army should have been reported before it had a chance to make an attack. As on other frontiers, diplomatic activity will have kept the northern tribes under observation. The outpost forts also had an important role to play. Bewcastle appears to have been built around a long-established native shrine, and may have allowed the army to monitor religious gatherings amongst the tribesmen in that area.

The mustering of large armies would have been a rare occurrence. Raiding, often on a very small scale, is likely to have been far more common. A legal text does refer to the case of a woman condemned to penal servitude, but then captured from Roman north Britain in just such a foray. She was subsequently sold back into the province and bought by a centurion named Cocceius Firmus, quite possibly the same man who set up the altars in Scotland. The Vindolanda tablets pre-date Hadrian's Wall, but it is worth remembering the small number of wounded soldiers in the hospital, as well as a fragmentary text describing the fighting characteristics of the local 'little Britons' (*Britunculi*), which describes light horsemen. Whilst it cannot have been too difficult for a handful of men to sneak across the wall, they could only do so on foot, and returning with any bulky plunder would have been difficult. Such small-scale raids were extremely unlikely to be reported in our sources, and the distinction between these and violent crime was anyway indistinct.

Military activity was probably almost always on a very small scale, but it is a mistake to view this as utterly different and separate from larger-scale attacks. Many of the peoples of the ancient world, especially the warlike tribal societies, viewed raiding and warfare as normal parts of life. Where they were stronger than their neighbours, they did not need any greater provocation to attack them. Successful raids won men plunder and gave them prestige amongst their own people. A reputation for military might helped to deter those neighbours from attacking. Some tribes, especially amongst the Germans, took pride in the amount of land they could keep unoccupied around their borders, for this demonstrated their ferocity and frightened off potential enemies. To such peoples the Romans would have appeared no different from any other neighbours. If the Romans appeared to be weak then they would be raided. Each successful raid added to this perception of their vulnerability, and so encouraged more frequent and bigger raids. A small party crossing into the Empire and rustling cattle or taking a few captives did not seriously challenge Rome's authority. However, if this was allowed to happen frequently, then aggression against Rome would escalate. Unchecked, then this could lead to large-scale invasion.

Hadrian's Wall and the other frontier systems are best seen in this light. They helped to mark out Roman territory to any potential enemy, and contained large, impressive structures as demonstrations of Roman might. Linear boundaries in particular helped the army to regulate movements and trade across the area, and made it difficult, if never impossible, for hostile groups to raid successfully. Diplomatic activity and intelligence gathering monitored events beyond the frontier and ideally gave warning of future danger. Yet ultimately the security of the Empire rested more on Rome's reputation for military strength and this was best displayed when the army took the field. Roman frontiers were never intended to limit or restrict movements of the army, and always permitted punitive expeditions to attack the enemy whenever it was considered necessary. Every Roman victory added to the aura of overwhelming and irresistible force which was the greatest protection of the Empire. Any defeat, however small, dented this reputation. Left unavenged, then the frontier became liable to more attacks. It was no coincidence that an initial defeat in a frontier zone was often followed by more failures and a period of intensive large-scale campaigning to restore the impression of Roman might.

The Roman army, just like any other fighting force, existed to wage war. During the Principate, most soldiers spent the vast majority of their military service engaged in the peacetime routines of barracks life described in the previous chapter. Participation in active campaigning was an occasional interruption of normality, especially for troops stationed in the more settled provinces. On average the garrison of Egypt was only involved in a major campaign about once every 25 years, although many of the frontier areas experienced outbreaks of warfare far more often than this. Even when a unit did take part in operations against an enemy, most campaigns consisted of considerably more marching and labouring than actual combat. Sieges might last for months on end, but battles were rare and, with very few exceptions, decided within a single day. Most Roman soldiers probably spent only a tiny fraction of their military service on active service or actual fighting.

The Roman army's wars were fought for a range of different reasons and on very different scales. Almost always the Romans attacked, or, if the enemy had initiated the campaign, launched a counter-offensive as soon as possible. Some wars were won when the opposing field army was brought to battle and defeated, others when the enemy capital was taken by storm or siege, and still others by repeated ravaging of crops, herds and villages. The operations of the Roman army were characterized most by its flexibility, willingness to adapt, and the determination with which it persisted in any struggle. In battle the army's superior command structure, discipline, training and equipment gave it significant advantages over any contemporary opponent, and often allowed it to win decisive victories in the face of great numerical odds. The technical skill of the professional army also made it especially effective in siege warfare. Yet, if required, the legionaries and auxiliaries were equally adept at smaller-scale warfare, and were able to defeat enemies who traditionally fought by raid and ambush. At its best, the army of the Principate was the most sophisticated and effective fighting force until the modern era.

A battle scene from Trajan's Column showing a range of auxiliary and allied troops fighting against Dacian warriors. At the bottom left is an unarmoured slinger, beside him a bare-chested irregular, and in the top left corner a group of eastern archers.

IV   The Army at War

On Campaign

In the 3rd and 2nd centuries BC the Romans faced several opponents with regular armies which were better trained and disciplined, and sometimes better led, than the legions. Pyrrhus, the famous Greek commander hired by Tarentum to fight against Rome, defeated two Roman armies before finally succumbing in a third, hard-fought battle, whilst Hannibal's string of successes rested as much on the high quality of his army as his tactical genius. Fortunately for the Romans, their main clashes with Macedonia and the Seleucid Empire came at a time when the legions were of exceptionally high quality, a high proportion of both officers and men being veterans of the Second Punic War. The

legions produced by this generation were as confident and experienced as any professional soldiers, many having spent much of their adult life in the army, and this allowed them to exploit the greater tactical flexibility of the manipular system in comparison to the rigid Hellenistic pike-phalanx. In this period, and throughout the remainder of Rome's history, her armies also faced many opponents from the tribal peoples. Such armies were sometimes large, but, whilst the individual fighting skills of their warriors were often high, lacked discipline and tended to be clumsy in their movements. Against such armies the Mid Republican legions usually enjoyed a slight, though by no means decisive, advantage.

By the time that the Romans had converted their citizen militia into a professional army, most of the states with regular armies had already been defeated. From the 1st century BC onwards, most Roman wars were waged against tribes or kingdoms with unsophisticated military systems. Such forces often had only rudimentary supply systems, seriously limiting the time which they could spend in the field before having to disperse. Most lacked a clear command structure, and were capable of undertaking only the simplest strategy and tactics.

This meant that the professional Roman army was almost always markedly superior to its opponents. The Roman way of fighting had always tended to be very aggressive. In this period it became even more so, for Roman commanders could be fairly confident of victory even when heavily outnumbered or fighting in unfavourable circumstances. When boldness and confidence became rashness this could lead to disaster, but in most cases it produced spectacular success.

Types of war

Whenever the Romans fought a war, they fought to win, pursuing total victory with a ruthlessness and relentlessness that was unparalleled. However, the context of the campaign did much to determine the army's behaviour. For convenience we may divide Roman campaigns against foreign opponents into four basic types:

1. *Wars of conquest*: This was an attack upon a socio-political group such as a tribe, kingdom, city or league of cities, or state. Victory came when the Romans had reduced this entity, turning it into a directly ruled province or subordinate client state. How this victory was achieved varied from people to people. If the invaded state possessed a capital town/city with strong political or religious significance then its capture might well prompt a surrender. Similarly the defeat in open battle or battles of the enemy field army might trigger such a collapse. However, many tribal peoples

(Right) A monument, moved and restored at the end of the 1st century AD some 200 years after it was erected, commemorating the defeat of the Cimbri and Teutones by Marius in 101 BC. This conflict was to prove the last time for many centuries that Rome appeared to be fighting for her very existence against a foreign enemy.

(Opposite) In this sculpture from Rome defeated barbarians beg for mercy from the Emperor Marcus Aurelius. The proper end to any Roman war came when the enemy admitted defeat and surrendered, accepting whatever terms Rome chose to impose on them.

Warfare in the ancient world could often prove profitable. In addition to plunder taken from the enemy, captives could be sold into slavery. Julius Caesar is credited with having enslaved over a million people during his Gallic campaigns, at the end of which he was one of the richest men in the world. This relief from the principia *at Mainz shows barbarian captives chained by the hands and necks.*

surprise the Romans won a decisive victory, and all the tribes present at the battle swiftly capitulated. Contingents from some tribes had not joined the army in time and these peoples were defeated separately, Caesar besieging their main towns in turn.

2. *The suppression of rebellion*: This represented a war to suppress a people already within the Empire. Victory came when the rebels had been placed once again under Rome's dominion. At the beginning of a rebellion, the military initiative inevitably lay with the rebels. In its early stages a rising would be weak, for in general much of the population would not join until some initial successes suggested that the rebels had a reasonable chance of victory. At this stage, even Roman inaction allowed the rebels' confidence to grow, for this suggested weakness. Therefore the Roman response to rebellion was always to mount a display of force as soon as possible. Whatever troops were quickly available were mustered and sent immediately to attack the centre of the rebellion. Such forces were often numerically weak, under-trained and without proper logistic support. If they met strong opposition then this could frequently result in disaster. The Romans gambled that the rapid appearance of an army which appeared overwhelmingly confident of its success would overawe the rebels and stop the insurrection from gaining momentum. Where such initial responses failed, it was usually a case of waiting to muster a proper army and sending it to fight what was effectively a war of conquest.

The rebellion of Boudicca in AD 60 was suppressed by the Romans. Enraged by the mistreatment of their Queen and her daughters, the Iceni tribe (who occupied an area roughly equivalent to modern Norfolk) rebelled against Rome and, joined by other tribes, sacked in succession the colony of Camulodunum (Colchester), and the towns of Verulamium (St. Albans) and Londinium (London). The first Roman reaction was to despatch 200 ill-armed soldiers composed of men seconded from their unit to perform administrative and escort duties for imperial administrators. These were annihilated at Camulodunum. The second response was from a vexillation of Legio IX Hispana under the command of Petilius Cerialis, which boldly attacked the heartland of the rebellion, but this force was also defeated and, with the exception of the legate and some cavalry, massacred. Finally, the provincial legate, Suetonius Paulinus, returned from campaigning in north Wales and brought Boudicca's host to battle. The Britons were defeated and, throughout the autumn and winter, the Roman armed launched a series of brutal punitive actions against the rebellious tribes.

3. *Punitive expeditions*: This was an attack on a political group which was not intended to incorporate them into the Empire in any way. Instead the

lacked such an important centre and might not be able or willing to fight a massed battle. In this case the Romans had to adapt to fighting a lower level of campaign. Attacks could be made on individual settlements, however small, and less numerous local enemy forces brought to battle. In this case the enemy would be conquered after many much smaller reverses, rather than a single great defeat in battle or siege.

The conquest of the Belgic tribes in 57 BC is an example of one such war. Prompted by an attack on a Roman ally, Julius Caesar led his legions against the army of the Belgic tribes of northeastern Gaul. The two sides confronted each other across a narrow valley for some days, but neither proved willing to abandon their own strong position and attack the enemy at a disadvantage. The stalemate was broken when the Belgians' food supply ran out, and their army dispersed, harried by Roman pursuit. Caesar advanced and ravaged the territory of each tribe in turn. It took some time before the Belgians once again mustered their main army, which promptly attacked the Romans as they were building a camp near the River Sambre. Despite initial

object was to instil a fear of Rome's military might in the enemy. In some cases such expeditions were justified as revenge for attacks on the Empire. (In the earlier Republic the acquisition of plunder could be a primary aim, but this was very rare for most of the period.) Punitive columns moved rapidly, causing as much devastation to settlements and property as they could. In essence they were intended to show a people that they were vulnerable to appalling attack whenever the Romans chose to launch one. Sometimes such campaigns culminated in a pitched battle, often fought when the tribes attempted to block the Romans' path when the latter began to withdraw. Defeating an enemy army in this way could greatly add to Roman prestige. However, on other occasions the Roman force deliberately moved so quickly to avoid any confrontation. Punitive expeditions might inspire fear, but they were only ever a temporary solution and needed to be repeated fairly often. The memory of massacred people, burned villages and stolen herds was as likely to sow the seeds of future hatred of, and conflict with, Rome.

An example of punitive action occurred at Mount Amanus on the border between Cilicia and Syria in 51 BC. The proconsul of Cilicia, Marcus Tullius Cicero – more famous as an orator and author than a soldier – decided to punish the bandit tribes of the Amanus area and put together a force of two under-strength legions and some local allies. Dividing them into three columns, they suddenly attacked the tribes, capturing several of their villages. The Romans then spent 57 days besieging the tiny stronghold of Pindenissus, whose eventual surren-

der prompted the capitulation of another nearby fortified village. The operation was intended to show the tribes that the Romans were both capable of and willing to strike at their strongest places. However, when soon afterwards the Syrian governor launched a similar expedition in this region and suffered a defeat in a skirmish this impression of Roman might was greatly weakened.

4. *In response to raiding/invasion*: These were campaigns fought to intercept and defeat hostile forces which had broken into the Empire. As already mentioned, the Romans needed to stop or avenge each incursion into the provinces if it was not to encourage more attacks. The reaction was in many ways similar to that inspired by internal rebellion. The locally available Roman troops moved rapidly to engage the raiders as soon as they were reported. In most cases they were unable to prevent the bands from plundering, but the raiders' very success often made them vulnerable. Slowed down by booty, they were frequently caught as they retreated by swift-moving Roman columns and wiped out.

In AD 50 there was a raid by the Chatti on upper Germany. Several groups of Chattan warriors crossed into the Roman province and began to plunder the countryside. The provincial legate Publius Pomponius Secundus sent a small force of auxiliary infantry and cavalry ahead to cut off the raiders and to keep in contact with them while he mustered his main army. He divided this into two columns, one of which swiftly came across a band of tribesmen, most of whom were drunk, and killed or captured them. The other Roman force encoun-

The early 1st-century AD Arch of Orange, southern France, commemorated a victory won over Gallic tribes. This relief from the Arch shows legionaries and auxiliary cavalrymen fighting Gallic warriors. Roman convention meant that only enemy dead were shown in such battle scenes.

tered a more organized raiding party and defeated them in a pitched battle. Secundus then led his army on an invasion of the Chatti's own lands. The Germans declined his offers of battle and capitulated.

By their very nature wars of conquest and punitive expeditions were offensive operations. However, a striking feature of the Roman response to rebellion or raiding was the desire to seize the initiative and adopt the offensive as soon as possible. Roman strategy was always bold. This did not necessarily mean seeking a massed battle. At times, Roman commanders were not confident that they could win such an engagement. Instead they chose to harass the enemy with small-scale raids or to besiege his strongholds. As significant was the flexibility of the Roman system. The army had many advantages in siege warfare and large-scale battles. Even in Late Antiquity, the Roman army won the vast majority of the battles in which it engaged. However, when required, it could wage war at a lower level, the main army dividing into a number of columns. Such small forces could move quickly and fight by raid, surprise attack and ambush. It is certainly a mistake to claim that the professional Roman army was unsuited to fighting enemies who waged guerrilla warfare and avoided open battle. In time, the Romans were always able to adapt to the local situation. The sophisticated command structure, training and well-organized supply system gave them advantages in all levels of warfare.

Field forces and army size

The Mid Republican army had functioned best at the level of the two-legion consular force which, with *alae* and local auxiliaries, numbered some 20,000–30,000 men. This probably remained the optimum army size for the professional army, and very few field forces numbered more than 40,000. Significantly larger Roman armies had rather a poor record, and it is probable that these were difficult for a commander to control.

The composition of a force varied from period to period and region to region. Small forces, especially those engaged in local punitive expeditions or chasing barbarian raiders, might consist entirely of *auxilia*, and indeed a *cohors equitata* was in essence a miniature army with a balance of horse and foot. Usually, however, there was a legionary component, and these units, with their higher levels of command structure, grouped as they were in building blocks of *c.* 5,000, provided the heart of most armies. Under the Principate, three or four legions, perhaps augmented by vexillations from others, were the largest forces likely to take the field together in anything other than a major war led by an emperor in person. There does not appear to have been any fixed complement of auxiliaries to support a legion. Tacitus mentions eight cohorts of

Batavians, some apparently *cohortes equitatae*, which had been attached to Legio XIV Gemina during the Boudiccan Revolt and other campaigns in Britain. By contrast, Varus had only three *alae* and six cohorts with his three legions when these were destroyed in AD 9. The garrisons of the eastern provinces appear to have contained more units of

foot and mounted archers, and large numbers of such missile-armed troops were essential for facing the almost exclusively cavalry armies of the Parthians as well as nomadic tribes like the Alans. Also particularly common in the east, especially in the 1st century AD, were allied troops from the client kingdoms of the area.

Logistics in the field

Ensuring that his army was adequately supplied was a prime concern for any Roman commander. Under the Republic a system evolved for shipping large quantities of food and material from distant provinces to supply the troops in a war zone. Apart from the details of how this was administered,

A scene from Trajan's Column showing troops loading supplies onto a river barge. In keeping with the old adage that an army marches on its stomach, the Roman army derived great advantage over almost all its opponents from its highly organized system of supply. This allowed properly prepared Roman legions to operate under adverse conditions and surprise opponents.

much the same thing continued to occur under the Principate.

In the field, army commanders could carry necessary supplies with them, maintain supply lines to depots established in the rear, or attempt to forage for provisions from the land around. These methods were not mutually exclusive and Roman armies frequently employed a combination of them. Except in the worst desert conditions, at least some provisions could be foraged. Water was usually available, as was the firewood required to cook the army rations which were issued unprepared. Depending on the season, varying amounts of fodder for animals, and at harvest time considerable quantities of grain for human and animal consumption were available, whilst herds could be confiscated for meat. In winter there was little to be had, unless the storerooms of the native population could be found and seized. Foraging also had the disadvantage that it took time, and could lay the foragers open to ambush, but appears to have been practised on occasion throughout the period.

Small amounts of food could be carried in the soldiers' packs, but the bulk required transport by pack animals or in carts. The army placed great reliance on mules, but also employed other pack animals, whilst draught oxen were frequently employed to pull wagons. In peacetime only a small proportion of the animals needed to mobilize the army were kept, and the remainder were bought or requisitioned when needed, so that the choice of animal may have depended on what was available locally. All types of animal obviously needed to be fed, further adding to the army's total requirements. A basic equation determined how far any animal could travel before it would have consumed a weight of food equivalent to the amount it could carry. Mules were perhaps the most flexible, could move as fast as a marching infantryman and go virtually anywhere that he could go. Draught oxen had

A campaigning army normally included a good deal of wheeled transport. On the bottom right of this scene from Trajan's Column we see ox-carts carrying provisions in barrels. Over to the left is a light ballista *or scorpion mounted on a mule-drawn cart.*

campaigning army. During these years the Romans used various combinations of the three basic supply methods. Large supply dumps were established, often with the aid of allied communities. The army also carried a good deal of material, including not just food and equipment, but records and numbers of hostages, in its main baggage train. In the campaigning area, it was not uncommon for Caesar to establish the train under guard and then lead the remaining legions out for short expeditions. During this time they moved quickly, carrying the barest minimum of supplies, a state known to the Romans as *expedita*. For one or two weeks an *expedita* column was free to manoeuvre at some speed and through difficult terrain, providing that it returned to the main baggage train at the end of this time.

Operating in winter was difficult for any army, and virtually impossible for many of Rome's opponents. Given time to prepare, the Romans were able to operate for a limited period in spite of the season, granting them a massive advantage.

Marching camps

At the end of each day's march a Roman force spent probably two to three hours constructing a formally laid out camp protected by a rampart and ditch. This was a routine procedure which differed only in its details from that followed by the army from at least the 3rd century BC. Some modern commentators have seen this as an indication that the Roman army was a slow-moving, inflexible force, capable of waging only a form of trench warfare. This is undoubtedly a mistake, for this was really little more than the equivalent of 'digging-in' for a modern infantryman. The time and effort required to build a marching camp did not significantly slow the rate of march of a Roman column, which was determined to a far greater extent by the speed and endurance of its pack train. The camp offered security from surprise attacks – there is no record of one having been successfully stormed unless the Roman army had already been defeated in the open field.

The only detailed description of the layout of a temporary camp in this period is provided by the probably 2nd-century AD work normally attributed to Hyginus. This describes the area allocated to each type of unit in a highly varied field army, consisting of praetorian guard and guard cavalry, whole legions as well as vexillations, auxiliary units, detachments from the fleet and various allies. Only limited space is set aside for the baggage train, and this may be the reason why Hyginus' camp seems comparatively small for the number of troops, especially when compared to the size of surviving marching camps. Marching camps are rarely excavated in an extensive way, since if the army only stopped there for a night or two, it is unlikely that they would have left much trace. The siege

considerable pulling power and could usually be fed by grazing, but were very slow, and ideally needed roads or tracks of a reasonable standard. A large army, even one gathering some of its requirements through foraging, inevitably had a huge baggage train if it did not wish to be tied to supply lines and so carried the bulk of its supplies with it. Equally inevitably, such a large number of animals made its column exceptional big and so slowed the rate of march. Maintaining a clear supply line back to dumps of material still involved convoys of pack or draught animals going back and forth between this and the main army. These were vulnerable to attack, especially if the enemy was as mobile as some of Rome's opponents, most notably the Parthians and Persians. Therefore the need to provide guards for the supply line took manpower away from the main force.

Caesar's campaigns in Gaul provide by far the most detailed account of the supply system of a

(Above) During the siege of Masada the soldiers had the time to build low stone huts using their tents as roofs. Traces of these temporary structures are visible today and can be seen in this view of Camp F. Part of this camp was employed by a smaller number of troops after the fall of the fortress and their smaller camp is in the top left corner. The huts built by these troops appear even to have had a storage room for equipment similar to the pairs of rooms occupied in a permanent barrack block.

camps at Masada and elsewhere give more of an idea of the actual layout of short-term camps. These were occupied for several months, so that the soldiers built themselves low-walled huts, using the tent as a roof. Traces of these remain, and suggest that, as with more permanent bases, the layout of temporary camps varied slightly, whilst being to a recognizable pattern.

Camps of various periods were frequently built on virtually the same site. Sometimes this may simply have been because the factors which originally made the location a good choice for a temporary camp were still obvious in later campaigns. However, it also emphasizes the Roman tendency to think in terms of routes to a place.

'A desolation called peace': winning and losing

Most wars in this period (and indeed throughout history) ended when one of the opposing sides lost the will to fight on and conceded defeat. Rarely was it possible for a side to destroy the opposition's ability to fight on. Roman strategy was devoted to putting sufficient pressure upon their opponents to trigger this collapse of will. This might involve

(Right) Each contubernium *of eight soldiers lived in a leather tent like this reconstructed example. The mule which carried the tent was tethered to the ground behind it.*

Roman forces targeting the enemy's field army, its major city or cities, or attacking its villages, burning crops and seizing farm animals. When fighting against an enemy led by a charismatic leader, the Romans' main objective became to kill or capture that individual, for without his presence resistance usually collapsed.

Devastation (*vastatio*) was a frequent object of punitive expeditions. The area affected was usually comparatively small, including the area covered by

the column's march and some relatively short distance either side. The experience was undoubtedly appalling for the communities within this zone, but others even a comparatively short distance away suffered no direct harm. In spite of this, the ability of the Romans to strike suddenly, wherever they chose, and with dreadful force, instilled a sense of their own vulnerability on the inhabitants of a much broader region. The Roman army's methods were often brutal. Apart from the devastation of

property and agriculture, enemy peoples faced massacre, massed crucifixion and enslavement. After the surrender of the Gallic town of Uxellodunum in 51 BC, Julius Caesar gave orders for the defenders' hands to be cut off as a warning to others, and during the siege of Jerusalem in AD 70, the legionaries crucified prisoners within sight of the walls. Atrocities were considered acceptable by the Romans as long as they achieved some practical end and were not done simply for the sake of cruelty.

The Roman method of waging war was highly aggressive. The initiative was seized as soon as possible and maintained, continued pressure being put upon the enemy until his will to continue collapsed. Even when faced with serious reverses in the field and an apparently hopeless military position, the Romans were unwilling to admit the possibility that they might lose. Roman commanders who presided over defeats sometimes faced criticism, but the worst thing that any leader could do was not to lose, but to admit that he and Rome had lost. Any negotiations or treaties ending a war had to make clear Rome's outright victory. The utter refusal to concede defeat – a Roman characteristic which persisted until well into Late Antiquity – made it very difficult for Rome to lose a war. In the end, persistence and continued aggression almost always brought Rome victory. Sometimes that victory reduced a people to the position of subject allies or saw their incorporation into the Empire. Less often it saw the enemy's destruction as a political entity. At other times Rome's victory was more a question of retrieving honour and pride lost in earlier defeats.

(Above) A scene from Trajan's Column showing Roman auxiliaries setting fire to a Dacian town, abandoned by its defenders who retreat while looking back to see the destruction. Behind them is a line of Dacian fortifications, the parapets decorated with a row of severed heads mounted on poles. Over on the right a column of legionaries marches through difficult terrain. One man is shown fording a river, holding above his head his helmet, armour and equipment in his shield.

Battle

The use of violent force to subdue an enemy is the ultimate function of any army, and the most concentrated expression of this purpose was the clash in open battle of massed armies. The accounts of the Roman army's campaigns provided by our literary sources are dominated by descriptions of pitched battle. Although comparatively rare events, battles were spectacular, intensely dramatic, and often decisive. When an opponent possessed a substantial field army, its defeat in battle would often prompt capitulation. The wealth of evidence, as well as their intrinsic importance, make a detailed examination of battles worthwhile.

Moving into contact

Roman field armies rarely numbered more than 40,000 men, and were more commonly half that size or smaller, as we have seen. Enemy armies may on occasions have been significantly larger, although the figures given by our ancient sources are inevitably unreliable on this point. Rarely would the Romans have had precise information concerning the size and composition of their opponents, and in many cases the enemy leaders themselves may have had only the roughest idea of the number of troops under their command. Apart from this, there is always the danger that enemy numbers were exaggerated to increase the glory of Rome's eventual triumph.

Moving several tens of thousands of soldiers, along with their mounts, pack and draught animals, servants and camp followers, across the countryside was no simple task. The professional army placed great emphasis on preserving march discipline, and also on sending out scouts to reconnoitre the route which the column was going to take. When Vespasian led his army into Galilee in AD 67, Josephus tells us that they marched in the following order:

1 Auxiliary light infantry and archers sent ahead to trigger any ambushes and to examine any cover, notably woodland, in case it concealed the enemy.
2 A contingent of legionaries [or close order auxiliaries] and heavy cavalry.
3 Ten men from each century, carrying their own kit and equipment for marking out the camp.
4 A party of men carrying tools, tasked with straightening the road and clearing any obstructions. [In Hyginus' Manual, this role was allocated to a detachment of sailors.]
5 The army commander's baggage and his staff, escorted by cavalry.
6 The commander himself, his personal bodyguard and a picked force of horse and foot.
7 The cavalry of the legions.
8 The siege train.
9 The legates of the legions, and the prefects and tribunes escorted by picked troops.
10 Each legion in turn, led by its eagle and other standards, the men marching six abreast.
11 The allies and auxiliaries.
12 A rearguard of both light and heavy infantry and cavalry.

Vespasian did not expect to encounter an enemy field army, but even so took precautions to meet any sudden attack. When there was a greater likelihood of encountering a numerous enemy force, the Roman column might march ready to deploy directly into battle order, or, if the direction of enemy attack was uncertain, in hollow square.

Great care was taken to gather as much information about the enemy location, strength and intentions as possible – a marked change from the old Mid Republican militia, which had tended to blunder into ambush or contact with remarkable frequency. Roman generals often went out in person to reconnoitre, and supervised the interrogation of captives.

The Battle of the Sambre, 57 BC

'After addressing Legio X, Caesar hurried to the right wing, where he saw his men hard pressed, and the standards of Legio XII clustered in one place and the soldiers so crowded together that it impeded their fighting. All the centurions in the fourth cohort had fallen, the *signifer* was dead and his standard captured; in the remaining cohorts nearly every centurion was either dead or wounded, including the *primus pilus* Sextus Julius Baculus, an exceptionally brave man, who was exhausted by his many serious wounds and could no longer stand; the other soldiers were tired and some in the rear, giving up the fight, were withdrawing out of missile range; the enemy were edging closer up the slope in front and pressing hard on both flanks. He saw that the situation was critical and that there was no other reserve available, took a shield from a man in the rear ranks – he had come without his own – advanced into the front line and called on the centurions by name, encouraged the soldiers, and ordered the line to advance and the units to extend, so that they could employ their swords more easily. His arrival brought hope to the soldiers and refreshed their spirits, every man wanting to do his best in the sight of his general even in such a desperate situation. The enemy's advance was delayed for a while'.

Caesar, *Bellum Gallicum* 2. 25.

Caesar's account of the battle of the Sambre, 57 BC.

When and where to fight

When a Roman army came into contact with an enemy force, it usually pitched camp, part of the army forming up to cover the men digging entrenchments. From the 3rd to 1st centuries BC, it was then very common to remain within a few miles of the enemy for days or even weeks before actually joining battle. On many of these days one or both sides would march out of camp and form up ready to fight, so that sometimes they were as little as a quarter of a mile apart, only to stare at each other for a few hours, and then return to camp. How far forward from its own camp and towards the enemy line an army was willing to go demonstrated its confidence. Morale has always played a critical role in deciding the outcome of combat, but this was especially true in the ancient world where much of the fighting was hand-to-hand. Generals attempted to build up their men's morale before risking an actual clash with the enemy. Skirmishes and single combats might be fought, especially by the cavalry and light infantry, and the outcome of these was felt to demonstrate the relative courage and prowess of the rival sides. The battles in this period were very formal affairs, the subtle manoeuvrings of the rival armies having an almost ritualized feel to them. The good commander chose the ground on which he would fight a battle, seeking terrain which favoured his own forces more than the enemy. Then he also took great care in deciding when to push his men forward that little bit further so that the enemy would either have to fight, or retreat and demonstrate their lack of confidence.

There were long delays before many of Julius Caesar's battles, against both foreign and Roman opponents. After suffering a reverse, Caesar also frequently formed his men up in an exceptionally strong position and offered battle, knowing that the enemy would not risk fighting at such a disadvantage. Thus he was able to assure his men that the enemy were still frightened of them.

None of our sources for the Principate mention such long delays before a battle. Instead many of the army's battles occurred when the enemy were encountered on the march or, at the most, after halting and building a camp for the night. This may well be a reflection of a changing military situation when most campaigns were fought against less politically united opponents. Much of the fighting on Rome's frontiers was on a smaller scale than the wars of earlier periods. Few enemies could muster armies which required large concentrations of Roman troops to be sent against them. However, much of the fighting occurred in areas where the terrain was difficult, and good roads rare. Supplying an army operating in such conditions and simply finding the enemy were major problems. The Roman army was so confident of its superiority over its opponents that it could afford to risk battle under circumstances that were less than ideal.

The battle line

The manipular legion of the Mid Republic had essentially one battle formation, and variations on this were extremely rare. Only a few, highly imaginative and gifted commanders, such as Scipio Africanus, at the head of very experienced armies were able to use anything other than the standard three lines (*triplex acies*), with the legions in the centre, *alae* on either side and cavalry on the wings. The Marian reform changed this, and the greater flexibility of the legion based upon the cohort rather than the maniple resulted in far more variation.

In most large-scale actions the terrain was fairly open. There were some exceptions to this rule, and at times Roman armies fought effectively through forests and marsh if that was the only place where they could bring the enemy to battle. Forming up on a ridge or hill gave an army an advantage, though carried with it the danger that the enemy would decline to attack at all. Terrain features were often used to protect an army's rear or flanks, especially if the enemy was significantly more

One of the sculpted reliefs from the principia *in the fortress at Mainz shows two legionaries in fighting positions. The man in front crouches down to gain the maximum protection from his rectangular* scutum. *His* gladius *is held ready to deliver an under-arm thrust to his opponent. Behind him another legionary has his* pilum *still resting against his shoulder, and holds his* scutum *high to protect the other man. It is unclear whether this figure accurately represents the role of the second rank of a line during a combat, or whether he represents in a less literal sense the support given to the fighting-line by the men and cohorts behind.*

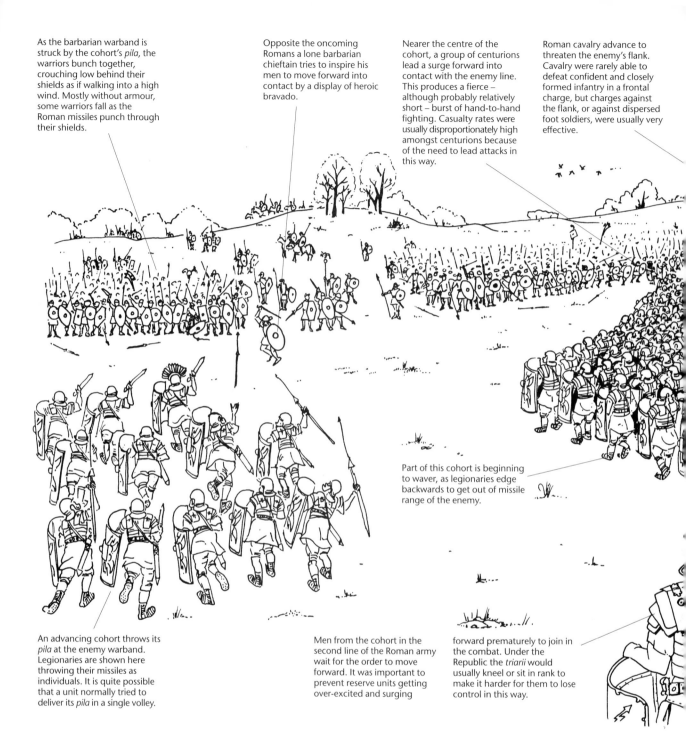

As the barbarian warband is struck by the cohort's *pila*, the warriors bunch together, crouching low behind their shields as if walking into a high wind. Mostly without armour, some warriors fall as the Roman missiles punch through their shields.

Opposite the oncoming Romans a lone barbarian chieftain tries to inspire his men to move forward into contact by a display of heroic bravado.

Nearer the centre of the cohort, a group of centurions lead a surge forward into contact with the enemy line. This produces a fierce – although probably relatively short – burst of hand-to-hand fighting. Casualty rates were usually disproportionately high amongst centurions because of the need to lead attacks in this way.

Roman cavalry advance to threaten the enemy's flank. Cavalry were rarely able to defeat confident and closely formed infantry in a frontal charge, but charges against the flank, or against dispersed foot soldiers, were usually very effective.

Part of this cohort is beginning to waver, as legionaries edge backwards to get out of missile range of the enemy.

An advancing cohort throws its *pila* at the enemy warband. Legionaries are shown here throwing their missiles as individuals. It is quite possible that a unit normally tried to deliver its *pila* in a single volley.

Men from the cohort in the second line of the Roman army wait for the order to move forward. It was important to prevent reserve units getting over-excited and surging

forward prematurely to join in the combat. Under the Republic the *triarii* would usually kneel or sit in rank to make it harder for them to lose control in this way.

It is extremely difficult for us to imagine what a battle in the Roman period was like. This picture attempts to reconstruct a section of a battle in an encounter between the Romans and a 'barbarian' army.

mobile or numerous. In Britain in AD 60 Suetonius Paulinus fought against Boudicca's huge rebel army in a narrowing ravine, with his flanks and rear protected by the high ground and thick woodland. In Cappadocia in the early 2nd century AD, Arrian planned to anchor his flanks on high ground to prevent the mobile Alan horsemen from threatening them. Where nature failed to offer such features, the army could make its own, as for instance at Chaeronea in 86 BC when Sulla dug a

series of ramparts and ditches to guard the flanks of his heavily outnumbered legions against Mithridates of Pontus.

The details of the army's formation depended on its composition and the local tactical situation. Usually, as in earlier periods, the cavalry was divided between the flanks of the line, sometimes with an additional force kept in reserve. However, if the enemy was overwhelmingly superior in horsemen then the Roman cavalry was either closely

The royal commander in battle

Before a battle a Roman general summoned a council (*consilium*). Although often translated as council of war, this was not a forum for debate, but a gathering in which orders were issued and explained to the senior officers of the army. Legionary legates and tribunes certainly attended the *consilium*, and it is probable that auxiliary prefects and senior legionary centurions were also present. Issues covered included the army's formation and tactics, and the orders necessary to put these into effect. The officers present would then in turn go to brief their own subordinates in similar sessions. Moving an army into position, and making sure that each unit reached the right place at the right time and knew what it was supposed to do, was a major task, requiring close supervision from all the officers of the army, including the general.

Another important function of the *consilium* was to allocate commanders to each section of the battle line. Normally, each legion had its legate who automatically controlled the 10 cohorts. Legionary vexillations also usually had an acting commander, often one of the tribunes. Auxiliary *alae* and cohorts were independent units and had no higher command structure. Sometimes individual units were attached to a legion, but usually they were temporarily brigaded together and placed under the command of an officer, who was most often one of

The commander of a Roman army was expected to be very active before, during and after a battle, but was not normally expected to fight. A general was there to direct and inspire his men. Other senior officers performed a similar function in the sector of the line placed under their charge. In most cases generals would control a battle on horseback, making it easier for them to see what was going on and move from one crisis point to the next.

supported by strong detachments of infantry or placed behind a dense infantry line. The entire army could form a huge square if faced with a very mobile opponent. Sometimes the auxiliary infantry was stationed on either side of a centre formed by the legions, but it could also form the first line and be supported by the citizen troops. The cohort legion most often deployed in three lines, but there were many variations, and sometimes entire legions were stationed in reserve.

their prefects. In the largest armies, it was sometimes felt necessary to impose a higher level of command over the *c.* 5,000-man blocks formed by the legions. Caesar routinely divided his army up into a right wing, centre and left wing, each under the control of one of his senior *legati*, and this appears to have been standard practice.

All of these subordinate commanders were directly or indirectly responsible to the general. There was no fixed position which a Roman general was expected to occupy during a battle. In a few exceptional cases Roman commanders chose to lead one of the front-line units, fighting hand-to-hand with it after the manner of Hellenistic leaders such as Alexander the Great. Such heroic leadership could inspire the army, but a general wielding his sword in close combat had little sense of what was going on throughout the rest of the battlefield and was in no position to issue orders. This was a major disadvantage, because the Roman system of deploying in more than one line meant that a high proportion of the army began the battle in reserve. Slightly more Roman generals adopted the opposite style of command, establishing themselves well behind the army, preferably on higher ground which offered good visibility. From there they were able to observe the battle as a whole and react to the changing situation, issuing fresh orders by messengers. Remaining in one place also meant that reports sent by his subordinates could reach him

easily. Yet such a distant commander was unlikely to inspire his soldiers, and may not always have been able to judge how the fighting was going until it was too late to do anything about it.

The vast majority of Roman generals adopted a style of command which was a compromise between these two extremes, keeping close behind the fighting line, whilst not actually getting involved in the mêlée. From there, the general was far more able to judge how the fighting was going for the nearest units, since he was able to see if unwounded men were beginning to slip away from the rear of the line, and listen to the noise and observe how confident each side appeared to be. This allowed him to judge whether or not to commit troops from the reserve line, either to reinforce success or prevent an impending breakthrough. Reinforcements from the reserve lines were either summoned by messenger or the commander himself could ride over to them and lead them up into position. If he felt it necessary he could choose to lead such a unit or one already in the fighting line in a charge, actually fighting for a short time before resuming his role directing the battle. A general who kept close to the fighting was also able to encourage his men by cheering them on. He also acted as a witness to their behaviour, a witness who had the power to reward courage and punish cowardice. The Roman army was lavish in issuing

A Roman general was supposed to act as a judge of his men's behaviour, praising and rewarding the brave and punishing the cowardly. In this scene from Trajan's Column auxiliary soldiers present the Emperor with the severed heads of Dacian warriors. Rome had suppressed headhunting within the provinces, but it seems to have continued to flourish amongst certain auxiliary units.

decorations to courageous individuals, but acts of bravery needed to be noticed if they were to be commended. Roman soldiers were thought to fight much better when they believed that their commander was watching.

The general was not tied to one particular part of the battlefield, but able to move around. He needed to anticipate where each crisis or critical point would occur and move to that spot in time to meet it. All along the line, the officers in charge of each sector were doing much the same things as the commander-in-chief. The Roman style of command was highly effective, but also dangerous. Generals were conspicuous figures, marked out by their red cloaks, and often even more spectacular costume. Moving around only just behind the fighting line they risked being hit by missiles. There was also the danger that individual enemies would single them out in an effort to win glory by killing the enemy commander.

Unit formations and tactics

We do not have a manual describing the drills and tactics of the professional Roman army in detail, although to some extent Arrian's *Tactica* covers some aspects of cavalry tactics. Polybius appears to say that a Roman legionary occupied 1.8 m (6 ft) of frontage and 1.8 m of depth in formation. In contrast Vegetius, writing much later but employing earlier sources, says that the frontage per man was 0.9 m

(3 ft) and the depth 2.1 m (7 ft). A depth of 1.8–2.1 m (6–7 ft) was probably essential to allow a soldier to throw his *pilum* without striking the man behind him. A frontage of 1.8 m seems exceedingly wide, and it is more probable that 0.9 m (3 ft) was the standard frontage, which was certainly the case for other close-order infantrymen in the ancient world.

Our sources occasionally provide some detail concerning the formations adopted by Roman troops. At Pharsalus in 48 BC Pompey deployed his infantry 10 ranks deep, because they were both more numerous and of poorer quality than Caesar's men. Josephus says that the Romans marched six abreast and mentions both infantry and cavalry deployed in lines three deep. This would appear to suggest a drill system based on multiples of three. Arrian's infantry marched four abreast, and deployed in battle eight deep, which would then suggest a system based on multiples of four, the number usually found in Hellenistic manuals. Perhaps the Roman army as a whole had adopted a new system of drill, but it may also be that such things varied in detail from legion to legion and period to period.

Formation was in part dictated by practical factors. The wider a line was, the more likely it was to encounter obstacles as it moved. Unless it proceeded slowly, constantly halting to reform, it would rapidly break up and fall into disorder.

A painting showing the formation which Arrian, legate of Cappadocia, in modern Turkey, during Hadrian's reign, ordered his legionaries to adopt before an anticipated encounter with the Alans. The latter were a Sarmatian people, whose main strength consisted of heavily armoured cataphract cavalry. In order to resist their attack, Arrian's legionaries – elements of XII Fulminata and XV Apollinaris – deployed in eight ranks, backed by a ninth rank of archers and a tenth of horse archers. Ranks five to eight in the legions were armed with the lighter lancea *javelin, rather than the* pilum. *While the front ranks packed tightly together, those behind deluged the Alans with missiles.*

deploy a line of archers behind a legionary or auxiliary cohort, so that the bowmen could shoot over their heads. This was done during the Jewish Rebellion in AD 66–73 when a three-rank formation of heavy infantry was backed by a single rank of archers. In Cappadocia in AD 135 Arrian's eight ranks of legionaries had a ninth rank of foot archers and tenth rank of horse archers shooting over their heads, as well as artillery positioned on high ground. Clearly, archers standing behind formed infantry cannot have seen and thus aimed at their targets. They were shooting blind, hoping to drop large numbers of arrows into a beaten zone enclosing the attacking enemy.

Slingers, some javelinmen, and sometimes archers, operated in open order, skirmishing with the enemy. This allowed them to single out a target and aim, whilst the space also made it easier to dodge and avoid incoming missiles. According to Vegetius, archers trained by shooting at a post 180 m (590 ft) away. The effective range of a bow or sling in battle is rather harder to estimate, since a great deal depended on the skill of the man employ-

Therefore a narrower, deeper formation could move and manoeuvre more quickly. However, only troops in the front, and to some extent second, rank of a formation could use their weapons in combat. The role of men in the ranks behind this was primarily psychological. To the enemy they made the formation look more impressive and frightening. Their physical presence also made it very difficult for the men in front of them to run away. Higher-quality troops tended to form up in shallow formations, perhaps three or four deep, whilst less experienced or confident units deployed six, eight, or 10 deep.

Missile combat

Most Roman soldiers carried some form of missile weapon, whether it was a *pilum* or lighter throwing-spear. A smaller number carried longer-range weapons such as the bow or sling. Archers could be employed in close formation, although it does not seem to have been possible for them to defend their own frontage simply by firepower, and we read on several occasions of archers being swept away by an enemy charge. A more effective tactic was to

ing the weapon. Skirmishers rarely proved decisive in the battles of the period covered by this book. At best they could defeat their counterparts and begin to harass the main line, but many skirmish combats appear to have gone on for a considerable time without achieving much. Ancient missiles all moved at a comparatively low velocity. Arrows and javelins, though not sling bullets, were readily visible in the air and so could be dodged. Casualties in skirmish combats appear generally to have been few as a result.

When missiles were directed at a body of troops in close order, there was far less opportunity for them to avoid the projectiles and greater reliance was placed on shield and armour to stop these. Arrows would normally be stopped by a shield, except at very close range, but modern tests suggest that they would readily penetrate mail, though not segmented, armour at battlefield ranges. Fatal injuries would be rare, but wounds to the exposed limbs fairly common.

Artillery (see p. 188) was comparatively rare on the battlefield, because of its poor mobility. Its advantages were far longer range, greater accuracy and far more penetrative power than other missile weapons. When a Roman field army deployed artillery, especially against barbarian opponents, they were able to single out and pick off conspicuous enemies at ranges far beyond the opposition's ability to respond. Artillery probably would kill relatively few enemies, but its power was such that it would do so in a spectacular way, which could have a deep effect on enemy morale.

Hand-to-hand combat

Armies might begin a battle deployed as close as a quarter of a mile apart. After a period of skirmishing which could last some time but rarely achieved a decisive result, one or both of the opposing armies would advance and the major clash begin. It was very rare for Roman infantry to remain stationary and await an attack, although this was sometimes necessary when facing large numbers of enemy cavalry. Caesar believed that it was a mistake for infantry to meet a charge at the halt, since advancing troops were more confident. → p.184

Although artillery was mainly used in sieges, the Romans sometimes employed light ballistae or scorpions in battle. Some of these engines, known as carroballistae, were mounted on carts drawn by mules. These engines fired bolts with massive force capable of penetrating shield or armour with great ease.

The Battle of Pharsalus
9 August 48 BC

During 49 BC civil war had broken out between Caius Julius Caesar and his rivals in the Senate, led by Pompey the Great. Caesar had rapidly overrun Italy and then defeated the Pompeian armies in Spain whilst his opponents massed their main strength in Macedonia. After an initial check at Dyrrachium, Caesar confronted Pompey near the small town of Pharsalus.

The forces

1 The Caesareans: about eight understrength legions totalling 22,000 men supported by 1,000 cavalry.
2 The Pompeians: 11 strong legions totalling 45,000 men and 7,000 cavalry.

The fighting

Caesar had rested his left flank on the River Enipeus, so Pompey resolved to use his vastly superior cavalry to turn his opponent's right flank. Taking one cohort from the third line of each of his legions, Caesar formed a fourth line, angled back behind his own cavalry on the right. The Pompeian cavalry led by Labienus attacked and drove back the Caesarean horse, but in the process lost much of their order. Unexpectedly counter-attacked by the fourth line, the milling mass of cavalry was stampeded to the rear. In the meantime Caesar's infantry had advanced to engage the main enemy line. The Pompeians did not move forward to meet them, so Caesar's men checked

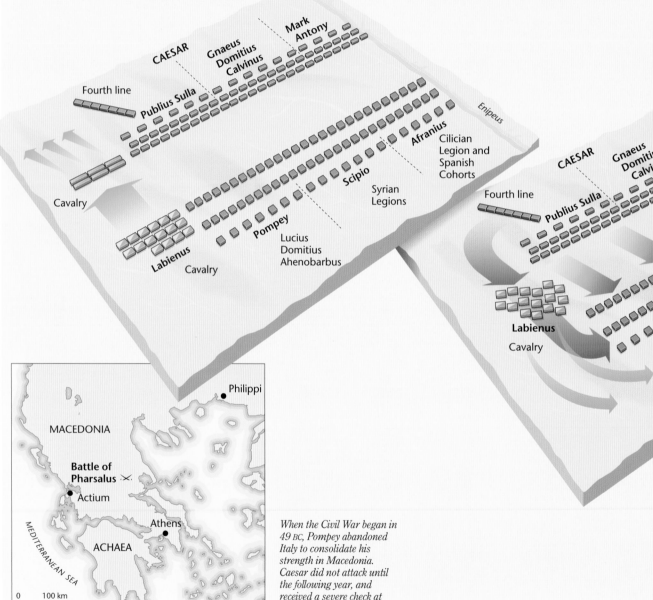

When the Civil War began in 49 BC, Pompey abandoned Italy to consolidate his strength in Macedonia. Caesar did not attack until the following year, and received a severe check at Dyrrachium, before winning a decisive victory at Pharsalus.

their charge and reformed before advancing into contact. A hard fight developed. Eventually Caesar ordered his third line to reinforce the fighting line and sent the fourth line against the exposed left flank of the enemy foot. Pompey's army collapsed into rout.

Casualties

1 Caesarean: 30 centurions and about 200 legionaries.
2 Pompeian: allegedly 15,000 killed and 24,000 taken prisoner. Nine eagles and 180 *signa* standards were captured.

Results

Pompey's main hope was destroyed. He fled to Egypt and was murdered there. The war might have ended at this point had not Caesar then spent half a year involving himself with Egypt's dynastic struggles and carrying on an affair with Queen Cleopatra.

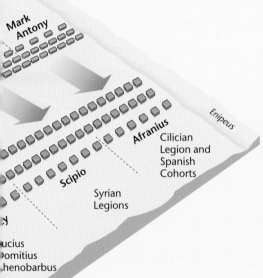

Julius Caesar was widely acknowledged by the Romans themselves as probably the greatest, and certainly the most successful, commander they ever produced. He also wrote commentaries on his campaigns (Gallic Wars) which provide the most detailed account of the legions on campaign.

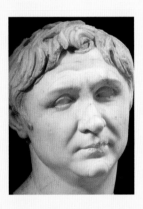

Six years older than Caesar, Pompey the Great had won wars in Africa, Sicily, Italy, Spain and throughout the east, but had not seen active service for over a decade before the Civil War. In spite of some initial successes, he was decisively defeated at Pharsalus.

Caesar's legions

Caesar's cavalry

Pompey's legions

Pompey's cavalry

JULIUS CAESAR (*c.* 100–44 BC)

Caesar was widely held to be the greatest of all Roman commanders. He was a member of a noble family which had enjoyed only minor political success in recent generations and, in spite of involvement in several public controversies, his early career was largely conventional. He then formed a secret political alliance with Pompey and Crassus, which allowed him to gain the consulship in 59 and brought him a five – later extended to 10 – year command in Gaul during which his successes brought him fabulous wealth and massive prestige.

However, Crassus had been killed by the Parthians in 53 and a breakdown of relations between Caesar and Pompey culminated in the Civil War which began in 49. Caesar overran Italy in a matter of weeks, and then out-manoeuvered Pompey's commanders in Spain and forced their surrender just a few months later following the main confrontation at Pharsalus. The pursuit led Caesar to Egypt where he found Pompey murdered. He spent several months in Alexandria, conducting a highly public affair with Queen Cleopatra and defeating her rivals in an internal dynastic struggle. This delay in returning to Rome allowed the Civil War to fester on, and required Caesar to fight further campaigns in Africa in 46 and Spain in 45. Although victorious in war, Caesar was unable to win the peace, and he was murdered on 15 March 44 by a senatorial conspiracy.

POMPEY THE GREAT (106–48 BC)

One of the most successful Roman generals, Pompey's career was highly unorthodox. He did not enter the Senate until 70 BC, despite having already held a long succession of military commands as a private citizen. He served in the Social War (90–88) under his father Pompeius Strabo, and supported Sulla in the Civil War. Following Sulla's victory in Italy Pompey was sent to re-take Sicily and Africa and was given the title 'the Great' (Magnus). In 76 he was sent to Spain to fight against Sertorius, but victory proved elusive until Sertorius was murdered by one of his own subordinates. In 71 Pompey returned to Rome and won the consulship for the following year.

In 67 Pompey was given massive power and resources to co-ordinate a campaign against the fleets of pirates marauding through the Mediterranean. A highly talented organizer, Pompey completed the war within a single year and then went on to finish a major conflict against King Mithridates VI of Pontus. During the course of his operations in the eastern Mediterranean, he was the first Roman to besiege and capture Jerusalem. Pompey did not serve in the field again until the civil war with Caesar in 49, when divided councils in the Pompeian camp eased Caesar's victory. After his main army was smashed at Pharsalus, Pompey fled to Egypt, where he was murdered on the orders of the young Egyptian king who hoped in this way to win favour with Caesar.

The Battle of Thapsus, 46 BC

'Caesar was doubtful, resisting their eagerness and enthusiasm, yelling out that he did not approve of fighting by a reckless onslaught, and holding back the line again and again, when suddenly on the right wing a *tubicen*, without orders from Caesar, but encouraged by the soldiers, began to sound his instrument. This was repeated by all the cohorts, the line began to advance against the enemy, although the centurions placed themselves in front and vainly tried to restrain the soldiers by force and stop them attacking without orders from the general.

When Caesar perceived that it was impossible to restrain the soldiers' roused spirits, he gave the watchword 'Good Luck' (*Felicitas*), spurred his horse at the enemy front ranks.'

The African War, 82–83.

Account by one of Caesar's officers of the start of the battle of Thapsus, 46 BC

During the advance, each side hoped to intimidate the enemy before they came into contact. Individual appearance – plumes which added to a man's height, highly polished armour and bright painted shields – hinted at the prowess of each soldier. The impression created by the group was also vital. Large, deep formations were frightening, but even more important was the confidence with which they came on, the degree to which their ranks kept in good order, and the noise they made. A unit's battle cry expressed its confidence, to the extent that German tribesmen believed that they could predict the outcome of a fight simply by listening to the *baritus* shout raised by the rival warbands. Many of Rome's opponents added to the shout raised by the warriors with drums or trumpets or, in some cases, crowds of women screaming encouragement from behind the lines. This great barrage of noise was terrifying, but it also spread confusion, and tended to hasten the loss of order and control that was inevitable under the pressure of combat.

The old militia army had similarly been very noisy as it advanced, the legionaries yelling and banging weapons against shields. The professional army adopted a different approach, advancing slowly to maintain as good a formation as possible and maintaining absolute silence. *Optiones* paced behind the line to prevent anyone from straggling or speaking. When the enemy were close, perhaps as close as 10–15 m (30–50 ft), a legionary cohort threw its *pila* and only then raised a shout, sounded their *cornu* trumpets, and charged at a run. These tactics were only made possible by the army's exceptionally high standards of discipline. It took massive self control to keep advancing at a steady walk whilst a mass of screaming enemies came running towards you. Human instinct urged each man to do something to cope with his fear, whether by running forward to get the inevitable clash over with or by throwing a weapon, even if the enemy was still out of effective range. Simply because such tactics were difficult to emulate, probably impossible for most of Rome's enemies, the eerie silence of a Roman attack was far more intimidating than a noisy advance.

Just before contact a Roman unit delivered two massive shocks to the enemy – the physical shock of a volley of *pila*, and the shock to their morale of a hitherto silent and slow-moving enemy suddenly launching into a screaming charge. Sometimes this was enough to shatter the enemy's confidence and rout them before contact or after only the briefest of combats. Less often it was the Romans who panicked and fled, overawed by the opposition's frightening appearance. If neither happened then the two sides met and fought hand-to-hand.

This type of fighting has been rare in recent centuries and is especially hard for a modern audience to imagine accurately. Hollywood images suggest a frenzied mass of individual combats, each one ending in death for one of the participants, with the two armies inter-penetrating each other and no trace of units remaining. Such fighting does not fit with the descriptions in the ancient sources and could not possibly have lasted for the two to three hours which were considered the typical length of a battle in this period without far higher casualties than are recorded. Real combat appears to have been much more tentative, and occurred in short bursts, after which the two lines separated and, standing a short distance apart, hurled abuse or missiles at each other until one side had built up enough enthusiasm to close once more. In the actual fighting the objective was to cut an enemy down and then step into his place, breaking into their formation. Once the opposing side felt that there were enemies amongst them they would become nervous and very soon degenerate into flight. This was obviously extremely dangerous, and a man forcing his way into the enemy formation stood a good chance of being killed by the enemies in the second rank. Few men would be killed in the actual fighting, but once a unit collapsed, the men turning their backs to the enemy and running, then casualties amongst the losing side would be huge as the pursuing victors were able to strike freely.

Close combat was highly stressful and at any time a unit could collapse. Men knew that this was

the point when they were most likely to be killed and that this fate would surely befall anyone who did not realize what was happening and did not run quickly enough. Soldiers in the rear ranks of a formation, especially a deep formation, could see little of what was going on, but had to judge the progress of the combat largely from what they could hear and the sense of whether or not the unit was going forward. As a combat went on, nervousness amongst these men in the rear caused a unit to waver. Soldiers would begin to edge backwards, and if many started to do this then the *optiones* might not be able to restrain all of them. Routs usually began at the rear of a unit. Winning a close combat was a question of both endurance and aggression. A unit needed the endurance to stay in the fighting line for as long as was necessary, but simply outlasting the enemy was an uncertain path to victory. Aggression was necessary to make the men in the front rank go forward to renew the combat time after time as they became more physically and emotionally exhausted. The Roman army's discipline and harsh system of punishment, combined with emphasis on unit spirit, was intended to give the men the stamina to stay in combat. The high quality of its leaders, and the encouragement and reward given to bold individu-

als, provided the men who could urge the line forward time after time. At a higher level, the emphasis on reserves was critical. The Romans' multiple line formation provided fresh troops to feed into the fighting line, renewing its forward impetus.

The Romans had significant advantages in battle and were likely to win far more often than they lost. Yet, by its very nature, hand-to-hand combat was especially uncertain and there was always an element of doubt. Roman commanders riding behind the line had to judge very carefully when to commit reserves. Too early and these fresh troops might achieve nothing whilst quickly becoming as tired as the men already in the fighting line. Too late and the first line might collapse altogether, and perhaps the panic would spread to the rest of the army. Victorious armies usually suffered comparatively light casualties, which might be as much as 5 per cent, but were usually far less. Defeated armies suffered many times these losses. Roman doctrine emphasized the value of an aggressive pursuit, led by the cavalry, with the simple objective of slaughtering as many of the fleeing enemy as possible. In this way the defeat was to be made so appalling that the enemy would be forced to capitulate or, at the very least, dread future confrontation with Roman forces.

(Far left) A metope from Adamklissi showing a legionary using his pilum *as a spear, stabbing downwards to kill a barbarian warrior. It was quite common for tribal armies to be accompanied by the warriors' wives and children riding in wagons.*

(Left) In another scene from Adamklissi a legionary wearing scale armour wields his gladius *under-arm. His opponents, one of whom has his hair drawn into the Suebian knot style, are armed with curved two-handed swords or falces. To counter the long reach of these weapons the legionaries at Adamklissi wear greaves and articulated armguards on their sword arms.*

(Right) Several of the Adamklissi metopes, including this one, show Roman cavalrymen charging into battle. Each of the horsemen wears mail armour and carries a hexagonal shield. Curiously none appear to have helmets.

185

Siege

Many Roman campaigns involved siege operations. Sometimes this involved attacking enemy forts or military strongholds, but more often than not it was a case of attacking fortified villages, towns and cities. Such places might possess sufficient political importance to warrant their capture in any case, and when they were strongly defended by nature or artifice their loss was an even greater blow to enemy pride. Where the enemy field army could not be forced into a decisive battle the capture of one fortified place after another weakened the prestige of their leaders, so that either their support base collapsed, or they were forced to risk a battle. In other circumstances, the defeat of the enemy field army in open battle was followed up by a drive on, and the capture of, his capital or main cities. Such concerted pressure was frequently sufficient to force his capitulation.

Sieges were therefore often important components of a war, serving either to win a victory, to complete one, or to force the enemy to alter his strategy and fight on Rome's terms. As with battles they could vary tremendously in scale. Wealthier, and more politically centralized peoples were more likely to possess large fortified towns, but a less united opponent could well possess large numbers of small strongholds. In 51 BC Cicero spent 57 days besieging the walled village of Pindenissus during his punitive expedition against the warlike tribes of Mount Amanus of eastern Cilicia (southern Turkey). The siege of a substantial town or city often took even longer and its outcome was uncertain. To conduct the siege the Romans needed to remain in the same place for months on end, which inevitably created serious supply problems. Sources of food and fodder from the area around a city would quickly be exhausted, even if the defenders had not already removed or destroyed everything. Other important supplies could also run short, and Josephus tells us that in AD 70 the Roman besiegers of Jerusalem stripped the surrounding land for miles around completely bare of trees as they gathered timber for construction and firewood. A besieging army had to devote effort to protecting its supply lines, especially if the enemy possessed a field army.

Fortifications

The defences surrounding Roman army bases in the 1st and 2nd centuries AD were relatively modest. This was not through any lack of engineering skill, but a reflection of their function as barracks rather than strongholds. Roman military doctrine was to leave their defences and fight the enemy in the open wherever possible. On those occasions when a fort or fortress was attacked, their simple ramparts, towers and ditches proved formidable enough to enemies lacking knowledge of siegecraft, as long as

a sufficient number of defenders were present. Excavation at several army bases, notably in Britain, has revealed a layer of burnt material amongst the occupation levels. It is largely a question of academic fashion whether this is interpreted as a sign of deliberate destruction when the army decided to abandon the site or the result of enemy attack.

Hellenistic styles of fortification already existed in much of the eastern Mediterranean and tended to be employed throughout the area until well into the Roman period. Client kings such as Herod the Great in Judaea constructed massive lines of fortifications around important cities such as Jerusalem, where the steep terrain added to their strength. Herod also constructed luxurious places of refuge such as Herodium, Machaerus and especially Masada, where a naturally strong position was made apparently impregnable. In the larger projects the walls were solid and composed of very large blocks of dressed stone.

A Hellenistic influence was also apparent in some of the hilltop towns (*oppida*) of Transalpine Gaul, such as Entremont where evidence has been found of a successful Roman siege in the late 2nd century BC. However, in the main the strongholds of northern Europe were constructed according to local patterns. Caesar described the strength of the native *murus Gallicus*, a type of stone wall given greater resilience by a box framework of wooden beams. The fortifications built by the Kingdom of Dacia suggest a range of influences, ranging from Greek to Gallic and Roman. Walls of essentially

Trajan's wars in Dacia (AD 101–02, 105–06) were dominated by sieges. Dacian strongholds like this one at Blidaru combined Hellenistic, Roman and native methods of fortification with the natural strength of the Carpathians.

(Above) The fortress at Masada that came under siege in AD 73 (see p. 190).

Hellenistic pattern, consisting of two facing walls and a loose rubble core, were strengthened by long wooden beams joining the two facing walls. In Britain native stone fortifications were rare, and most strongholds had earth and timber defences. The grandest were the great multi-banked hillforts of the Durotriges in the South West, where ditches and walls were arranged to permit the defenders to make maximum use of the sling. This was especially true of the approaches to their gateways, where a complex system of ramparts and ditches created a winding path along which it was easy for any attacker to lose his way, and where he would be constantly exposed to missiles against his unshielded side.

Methods of attack

There were essentially three ways of capturing an enemy stronghold:

1 *Through starvation:* This involved the blockade of the stronghold, preventing men or supplies from leaving or entering. In time it was hoped that the defenders would consume all their provisions, or run out of an essential such as water, and be faced with a choice between surrender or death. Sometimes such desperate situations led to extremely brutal behaviour. During the siege of Alesia in central Gaul in 52 BC (p. 192), Vercingetorix, the Gallic rebel leader, expelled all the civilians from the town so that the remaining food would only have to meet the needs of his warriors. Caesar refused to let the refugees through his siege lines, so that these unfortunates were left to starve to death within sight of the two armies. There were often rumours of cannibalism amongst garrisons running out of food, for instance at Numantia in Spain in 134 BC (p. 32). Starving a garrison into submission required time, especially if the defenders had prepared for the attack or possessed a port and so could bring in supplies by sea. Some cities were able to survive for years on end. The warehouses and cisterns cut into the rock at Masada (p. 190) to gather water from the very occasional rainfall of the area were capable of supporting its garrison almost indefinitely. Maintaining a sufficiently close blockade required a large number of troops to remain around the stronghold for a very long time.

2 *By stealth:* Some fortifications could be taken by a surprise attack. If a small force was able to approach by stealth and get into a town, it could then seize control of key positions, most notably a gateway, and admit the main body. Yet this was risky, for if the defenders became aware of their presence then the small force could easily be annihilated. At Amida in Mesopotamia in AD 359, a captured civilian led a group of 70 Persians by a secret entrance into the city. The Persians occupied a tower and were able to support a major assault from outside, but when this failed they were destroyed. Such attacks were most likely to be successful if the besiegers possessed detailed information about the defences and defenders, or were assisted by traitors within the walls. Rarely could this be guaranteed, and surprise attacks required a good deal of luck. Capsa in Numidia was taken when a Ligurian auxiliary hunting for snails discovered a way up the cliffs behind the town and was able to lead a party of legionaries up there. The Romans were ready to seize any opportunity for a surprise attack, but did not rely on this method.

3 *By storm:* The final method of capturing a stronghold was by direct attack, sending men over, through or under the wall to overwhelm the defenders. This was by far the most costly method, for in an assault all the advantages lay with the defender and it was likely that casualties would be high. Penetrating the main line of fortifications was by no means certain, and even if the army managed to break in, there remained the possibility that the defenders would rally and drive them out. Street fighting was comparatively rare in the ancient world, but when it did occur displayed all the brutality of more modern periods. So traumatic was a failed assault that it was usually impossible to make another attempt for days or even weeks. A large city like Jerusalem, divided into several districts and quarters each protected by its own perimeter wall, required the attackers to storm successive walls. Attacking a city directly was difficult and required not simply considerable engineering skill, but a good deal of raw courage and savagery. This was the most common method employed by the professional army.

Artillery

The Roman army occasionally made use of light artillery on the battlefield. Some, known as *carroballistae*, were mounted upon small mule-drawn carts to improve their mobility. However, the chief use of artillery came in the attack and defence of fortifications.

Roman torsion artillery consisted of two basic types – single and double armed. The single armed, a pattern which would remain essentially unchanged throughout the Middle Ages, was rare before the 4th century AD. It had a single upright throwing arm and could lob or shoot a stone with considerable force. The Romans called it the *onager*, or wild ass, because of the engine's powerful kick. Ammianus describes an occasion when a misfiring *onager* killed one of its crewmen in a gruesome manner. It was aimed by pointing the entire

Re-enactors demonstrating a reconstruction of a two-armed engine or ballista. *A machine of this sort could fire bolts, but was more normally employed to shoot stone balls.* Ballistae *could be much larger than this but retained the same basic design.*

(Below left) A reconstruction of a light ballista of the type normally employed as an anti-personnel weapon. The bolt fired by such an engine could travel with great accuracy further and with greater force than the arrow of any archer.

(Below) A reconstruction of a single-armed engine showing the very different shape of such weapons. Known as the onager, *or 'wild ass', from its violent kick, catapults of essentially the same design would remain common throughout the Middle Ages.*

machine at the target and was reasonably accurate. Far more common for most of the period were the more sophisticated two-armed engines or *ballistae*. These look something like a crossbow, although working on different principles, for the force was not derived from the tension in the arms, but, like the *onager*, the tightness of the coils of sinew rope holding them. *Ballistae* varied considerably in size, some being small enough to be man portable whilst others were massive, and could fire either bolts or stones with great accuracy and force. The lightest *ballistae* were often referred to as 'scorpions' (*scorpiones*).

Although powerful, even the largest torsion engines were incapable of breaching a well-built and substantial stone or earth wall. They could knock down thinner parapets, or temporary structures added on or around permanent fortifications → *p.192*

The Siege of Masada

AD 73

In AD 66 the province of Judaea rebelled against Roman rule. One extremist faction of political assassins – known as the *Sicarii* from the curved flick-knife they used – infiltrated and captured the fortress of Masada, built by Herod the Great as a luxurious place of refuge. In spite of initial successes, the Jewish rebellion was stamped out in several years of heavy fighting culminating in the storming of Jerusalem in AD 70. Only a few strongholds continued to hold out, and the last of these to resist was Masada. In AD 73 the governor of Judaea, Flavius Silva, led an army against the fortress.

The forces

1 The Romans: Legio X Fretensis and an unknown number of auxiliary units. Both the legion and auxiliaries were probably significantly under strength after years of campaigning and may have together mustered little more than 5,000 men.
2 The *Sicarii* (often, though mistakenly, referred to as Zealots): about 960 people including a significant proportion of non-combatants such as the elderly, women and children. The defenders were led by Eleazar Ben Yair, who came from a family with a tradition of militant resistance.

The fighting

Masada is situated on a steep-sided, rocky hill, accessible only by a winding and difficult pathway on the eastern side. It was amply provided with storerooms – there was also space for some cultivation of crops on the summit – and had deep cisterns cut in the rock to gather and hold water from the rare rainstorms of this area. There was therefore sufficient food and water to supply the garrison for several years and the Romans realized that they could not hope to starve the enemy into submission. Since a direct attack up the eastern path was also unlikely to

Defenders led
by **Eleazar
Ben Yair**

The Western
Palace

MASADA

Camp C

Line of circum-
vallation with
towers and fortlets

Camp D

(Left) The main centre of the Jewish rebellion had been Jerusalem, but a few strongholds like Masada on the west bank of the Dead Sea continued to resist after its fall.

(Right) Camp F may have housed as much as half of Legio X Fretensis. It is built on a steep slope near the foot of the ramp.

Map detail:
0 — 50 km
0 — 50 miles

MEDITERRANEAN SEA

● Caesarea Maritima

JUDAEA

Jerusalem ●

DEAD SEA

Engedi ●

Siege of Masada ⚔

succeed, Silva ordered his men to begin the construction of a massive siege ramp against the sheer western side of the hill. To prevent any escape, and also as a stark reminder that they were now surrounded, the Romans built a line of circumvallation around the hill, strengthening it with six fortlets and a number of towers. Two larger camps were built behind the line. When the ramp was completed, a siege tower carrying a battering ram ascended it and battered a breach in the fortress's wall. Before the final assault could go in on the next day, the *Sicarii* killed their families and committed suicide.

Results

The Jewish Rebellion was over, and the Roman army had delivered a stark warning to their other provincial subjects of the relentless punishment which awaited any rebels. A small Roman garrison was stationed at Masada for some time after the siege.

(Below) The massive siege ramp built by the Romans at Masada was originally even higher, for the top was crowned by a section constructed from timber.

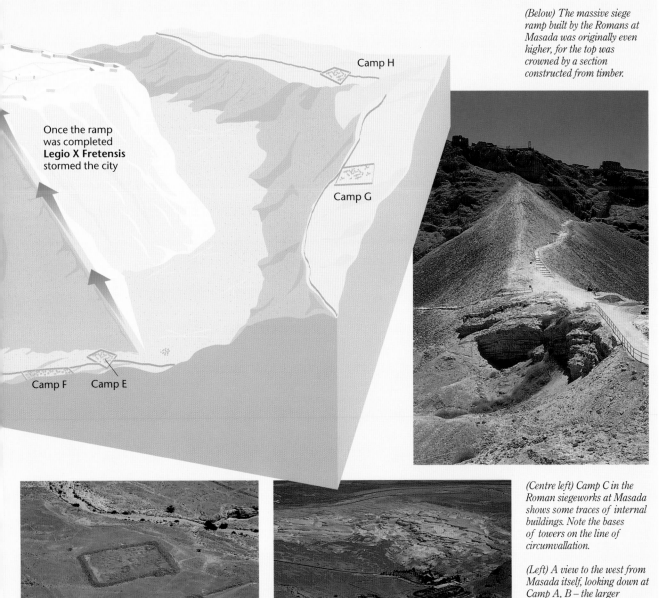

Camp H

Once the ramp was completed **Legio X Fretensis** stormed the city

Camp G

Camp F   Camp E

(Centre left) Camp C in the Roman siegeworks at Masada shows some traces of internal buildings. Note the bases of towers on the line of circumvallation.

(Left) A view to the west from Masada itself, looking down at Camp A, B – the larger structure in the centre of a size comparable to F – and C. Note the line of circumvallation.

191

'One of the men standing on the wall beside Josephus had his head carried away by a stone, and his skull was shot, as from a sling, to a distance of three furlongs; and a woman with child was struck on the belly just as she was leaving her house at daybreak, and the babe in her womb was flung half a furlong away. So mighty was the force of these stone-throwers. More alarming even than the engines was their whirring drone, more frightful than the missiles was the crash.'

Josephus, *The Jewish War* 3. 245–6 (Loeb translation).

Josephus' description of the terrible power of missiles hurled by the Roman catapults at the siege of Jotapata in AD 67.

to increase their height or strengthen them in some other way. However, their primary role was as anti-personnel weapons. The attacker used his artillery in an attempt to drive the defenders from the walls and so prevent them, and especially their own artillery if they possessed any, from hindering the progress of his siegeworks or attacks by battering rams and siege-towers. Artillery missiles possessed such momentum that armour or other protective gear was of little value. The impact of a stone from a *ballista* on a human body was especially appalling. Josephus tells the story of a man being decapitated and his head flung hundreds of yards from the body. Even more gruesome is his tale of the pregnant woman hit by a stone which tore her apart and threw the unborn child some distance away. At Jerusalem in AD 70 the rebels began keeping a careful watch for incoming missiles and calling out 'baby coming' as a warning. Observing this the Romans, who had probably been carving ammunition from the local light-coloured stone, began to paint the projectiles a darker shade. This made them far less visible as they approached and once again increased the rebels' losses to artillery fire.

According to Vegetius, each century of a legion was supposed to have been equipped with a mobile scorpion (or *carroballista*), whilst every cohort possessed a larger *ballista*. Whether or not there was a fixed complement of artillery for a legion, it is probable that the number taken on campaign varied according to the local need. Artillerymen were drawn from the ranks of the cohorts rather than forming a separate unit. The size of engine and skill of their crews produced by each legion probably varied, and Josephus tells us that amongst the army suppressing the Jewish Rebellion those of Legio X Fretensis were thought to be the best. There is no direct evidence for auxiliary troops ever using artillery, but it remains possible that at times some units did.

Surrounding the enemy

In 52 BC, Caesar pursued the army of Vercingetorix throughout most of central Gaul before finally cornering it outside the hill-top town of Alesia. During the previous few months he had successfully besieged and stormed the strongly fortified town of Avaricum and failed to take Gergovia in a surprise attack. The Gallic army was large, making a direct attack on its camp and the town of Alesia itself highly risky. Instead Caesar surrounded the hill with a circuit wall 10 Roman miles long (known as a line of circumvallation), incorporating eight camps for his troops and 23 forts to strengthen the position. Towers were built along the line of the main earth and timber rampart at 119-m (130-yard) intervals to provide observation points and platforms for throwing or shooting missiles. The wall itself was some 12 Roman feet high (just under 4 m), had sharpened stakes sticking out from it to hinder anyone trying

to climb over, and was protected by two ditches, the inner one filled with water. In front of the ditches were rows of stakes and a checkerboard pattern of individual stakes concealed in round pits, a trap which the soldiers nicknamed 'lilies' because of their shape. Caesar was aware that Vercingetorix had sent messengers to gather forces from all of the Gallic tribes to march to his relief. Therefore, once the line of circumvallation was complete, Caesar set his men to building another line of fortifications, this time facing outwards (and therefore known as a line of contravallation), extending 14 Roman miles. Thus, whilst Caesar blockaded Vercingetorix inside Alesia, his own army was effectively under siege from the much larger Gallic force attempting to come to the rebel leader's aid. Fighting was fierce as the Romans struggled simultaneously to prevent the Alesia garrison from breaking out and the relieving army from breaking in. At times it looked as if the defences would be breached, but Caesar and his officers led an aggressive defence, rushing reinforcements to threatened sectors and at times leading counterattacks against the enemy flanks outside the Roman lines. When food finally ran out, Vercingetorix was forced to surrender.

Caesar's army made use of extensive lines of fortifications at other times, most notably at Dyrrachium in 48 BC during the civil war. There Caesar's army attempted to blockade Pompey's more numerous forces, who in turn responded by building their own line of fortifications to prevent this. In this case it was Caesar who was eventually forced to abandon his aim and withdraw. Lines of circumvallation were used at other times in situations which were more clearly those of siege rather than part of the complex manoeuvrings of field armies. In 134 BC Scipio Aemilianus surrounded the Celtiberian town of Numantia, in Spain, with a wall strengthened by forts, traces of which have been found by archaeologists. Interestingly enough, he did this because he preferred to avoid battle with the Numantines and preferred to use his greatly superior numbers to impose a blockade.

Lines of circumvallation were not restricted to blockade, but were often used as part of a direct assault. At Jerusalem in AD 70, the Romans suffered some initial reverses when they tried to take the second of the three walls surrounding the city. Great siege ramps built up against the fortress of Antonia in 17 days of hard labour had just been destroyed by fire or undermining. At this point, Titus ordered his men to construct a dry stone rampart surrounding the city. This huge task was completed in just three days, the units competing with each other to finish their section first. After this the Romans returned to preparations for an assault on Antonia and over the next weeks captured the remaining parts of the city piece by piece. The line of circumvallation served the practical purpose of hindering any attempts by the defend-

A view of the reconstruction of Caesar's lines of circumvallation at Alesia. Wherever possible at least one of the ditches was filled with water. Light ballistae *or* scorpions *were mounted in the towers to shoot down on any attackers.*

ers to break out. In addition it was also a strong visual statement of the Romans' intent. The defenders had taken refuge behind a wall for their own protection. Now the Romans had encircled them with another wall to make certain of their destruction. The point was even more clear at Masada, where the most complete remains of a Roman siege can be seen on the ground today. At the beginning of the siege in AD 73 Legio X Fretensis completely surrounded the hilltop fortress with a wall strengthened by five forts and a number of towers. In many sections the wall ran along the top of the cliff on the

opposite side of ·the valley, against which it was inconceivable that the rebels would try to break out. The wall was a constant reminder of the defenders' isolation and hopeless position. They were trapped, and every day the siege ramp which the Romans were constructing against the hillside grew a little bit higher. The psychological pressure on the besieged was massive. At Machaerus, and probably also Narbata, where traces of Roman siege lines have also been found dating to the Jewish Rebellion, this grew too much and prompted surrender before the Romans launched their final assault.

At Alesia the Romans dug pits, fixed a sharpened stake in the centre, and then covered them over with vegetation. Caesar tells us that the legionaries with their macabre sense of humour nicknamed these traps 'lilies' (lilia) from their circular shape. The technique was often used to protect other army bases as is shown by this complex of lilies from Rough Castle in Scotland.

Breaking into a fortress

Since artillery was rarely capable of breaching a strong wall, other means had to be employed. Some walls could be undermined by men using picks and crowbars, as long as these were able to reach and work at the foot of a defended wall. It was in situations like this, far more than open battle, that the famous Roman *testudo* or tortoise formation was most often employed, with a roof of overlapping shields protecting the legionaries from enemy missiles. During one siege in the civil war of AD 69, the defenders grew so desperate at their inability to break the combined strength of the *testudo* with ordinary arrows and stones that they actually pushed over the wall one of their own great catapults. This smashed the interlocking shields and inflicted heavy loss, but also took with it much of the rampart and opened a breach into the town.

Although an essentially simple concept, the battering ram remained one of the most effective methods of knocking a hole through a wall. Save in the simplest of fortifications, gateways were usually avoided since, although wood could be burned, the chief ingenuity of the defenders' engineers had usually been exercised to protect these spots. The army constructed massive rams mounted either in a wheeled shed or mobile tower, and consisting of a long beam, bound round with thick ropes to stop it from splitting, with an iron tip, usually shaped like the head of a butting ram. Both

(Above) A scene from Trajan's Column showing a group of legionaries adopting the famous testudo *or tortoise formation. With their shields lifted to form an overlapping roof above their head, the soldiers were well protected from most missiles. This formation was often used to approach and undermine a wall with crowbars.*

(Right) Re-enactors from the Ermine Street Guard form testudo *during a display in the amphitheatre at Caerleon. The historian Livy claimed that the* testudo *had first been developed as a spectacular entertainment performed at festivals in Rome.*

rams and towers usually required the construction of huge ramps from earth, timber and rubble, to allow them to cross the defensive ditches and moats and reach the wall itself.

Throughout the siege the defender would hope to hinder the progress of this work. Sallies were made to prevent the besiegers' working-parties from performing their task, and to demolish or burn what they had already completed. Roman rams and towers were protected from fire by a covering of hides or iron plates. Once the rams reached a wall then it was only a matter of time before breaches were made. Therefore renewed efforts would be made to burn these engines. At Jotapata in Galilee in AD 67 the rebels managed to drop a large boulder and snap the head off one of the Roman rams. Another method was to lower sacks of straw over the wall and swing them onto the spot where the ram was expected to strike, deadening the force. Sieges were often contests between the ingenuity and determination of the attacker and defender.

An alternative to breaching a wall by battering ram was to dig a mine beneath it and fill it with combustible material. The props supporting the mine could then be fired, collapsing the tunnel and bringing the wall down with it. To guard against this the defenders dug counter-mines, judging the route of enemy tunnels from sound and vibration. These could be used either to undermine the attacker's ramps and other works, or to connect with the

enemy tunnels and allow an attack upon their miners. Dura Europus' Roman garrison was besieged by the Persians in the 3rd century AD. Archaeologists discovered a Persian mine and a Roman counter-mine joining on to it. Inside were the bodies of Roman defenders and Persian attackers, killed in a gloomy skirmish or when the entire complex collapsed, undermining a section of the town's wall and one tower. Tunnelling often carried risks for both sides. At Jerusalem the rebels managed by mining to destroy Roman ramps approaching the fortress of Antonia, but were dismayed when hours later the same tunnelling also caused the fortress to collapse and opened a route into the Great Temple.

The only other alternative to breaching or undermining a wall was to climb over it. At its simplest this meant an attack by escalade, the assaulting troops putting ladders up against the wall and climbing them. This required careful judgment, for it was important to ensure that the ladders were long enough to allow them to reach the parapet. Soldiers climbing ladders were horribly exposed to missiles of all types, and the ladders could be overturned or broken. Even if the men managed to fight their way onto the wall they could easily be overwhelmed, for it took time for more men to climb and reinforce them. For the same reason it was very difficult to retreat, and the leaders of such an attempt

A scene from Trajan's Column showing legionaries and auxiliaries attempting to storm the Dacian capital of Sarmizegethusa by escalade. On the extreme right an auxiliary soldier climbs a ladder and strikes at the enemy while holding a severed head in his left hand. Also notice the ladder-carrying party on the left.

The town of Gamala in the Golan Heights was besieged by the Romans in AD 67. A breech in the wall is visible just to the left of centre in this picture and stones and arrow heads from Roman artillery were excavated on this site. Although the first assault failed when the attackers lost momentum in the maze of narrow alleyways threading through the town, a second attack proved more successful. As at Masada, many of the defenders chose to commit suicide rather than face capture.

were almost invariably killed if it failed. A more effective method was offered by siege towers which could lower a drawbridge onto the rampart and permit men to approach the wall in cover and climb onto it in larger numbers. Even so the fighting could be vicious as the defenders met the men crossing the bridges.

The assault and sack

Whichever method the attackers employed to assault a stronghold, the actual storming was an extremely difficult and dangerous operation. Technology could make a breach or assist a soldier to climb a wall, and perhaps help to suppress the defenders, but ultimately the storming party had to climb sword in hand up into the town. Casualties were often heavy, especially amongst the boldest men who led the way, and the chance of failure was high. If the main line of defences were crossed and troops entered the town then it was easy to become

lost in the maze of narrow streets composing many ancient settlements. In AD 67, attacking the hillside town of Gamala on the Golan Heights, the Roman troops had trouble making progress through the alleys, most of which were just wide enough to permit passage of a donkey with panniers. The legionaries climbed onto the roofs of houses and began pushing up the slope, by scrambling from one building to the next. However, the weight of men packed onto the houses caused roofs and buildings to collapse. As the attack lost momentum, the defenders rallied and counterattacked, chasing the Romans back out of the town. At Jerusalem in AD 70 the Romans struggled for weeks to capture the Great Temple even after they had managed to cross its outer wall and gain a lodgement. The siege of a large settlement defended by a determined opponent was a slow, gruelling business, which wore down the soldiers' morale, as one attack was followed by another.

When an army finally did capture a stronghold, its occupants, civilians as well as active defenders, were subjected to a brutal sack. Polybius claimed that the Romans deliberately caused as much destruction as possible, slaughtering and dismembering animals as well as people, to deter other communities from resisting Roman demands to surrender. Convention developed into a law that the defenders were allowed to surrender on favourable terms if they did so before a Roman ram touched their wall, but that otherwise they could expect little mercy. Male inhabitants were usually slaughtered, women raped, though only in exceptional circumstances killed in the initial orgy of destruction. After that, as tempers cooled and the desire for profit took over, prisoners would be taken for sale as slaves, though at times any considered to have a low market value, such as the very old, were still massacred. Looting was widespread. In theory it was organized and the army pooled all its plunder for a fair distribution, but the practice may not always have been so neat. Josephus tells us that after the capture of Jerusalem in AD 70 the price of gold was devalued throughout the eastern provinces as the soldiers returned to their bases and started disposing of their plunder. Amidst the burnt levels of aristocratic houses destroyed in the sack of Jerusalem an arm was found. At Maiden Castle in Dorset the skulls of the defenders, including several already seriously wounded, were repeatedly hacked by the Roman attackers. Even more gruesome evidence of the horror of a Roman sack was found in Valentia in Spain, and probably dates to the capture of the town during the civil war in 78 BC. Skeletons were found showing signs not just of wounds received in the fighting, but of torture. One individual appeared to have been singled out for special attention, having his arms tied behind his back and a *pilum* thrust up his rectum. Perhaps a civil war created stronger passions and produced such atrocities, but it is important to remember that the ancient world was often an extremely brutal and unpleasant place.

Roman siegecraft

Sieges figure heavily in the propaganda of ancient cultures from Egypt and Assyria onwards as amongst the proudest achievements of 'Great Kings'. In part this was because attacking fortified places was always extremely difficult and the balance of advantage normally lay with the defender. For the professional Roman army, almost alone amongst the fighting forces of the ancient world, the balance for a time changed. Engineering skill, combined with the army's characteristic determination and aggression, and a frequent willingness on the part of its commanders to accept the casualties inherent in direct assault, gave the Romans the capacity to capture any fortified place. More often than not they succeeded, even against such apparently impregnable fortresses as Masada. The army's great proficiency in siege warfare gave it a marked advantage over all its opponents.

The philosopher-Emperor Marcus Aurelius commemorated his Danubian campaigns in a column that was at once more stylized and in many ways more brutal than Trajan's Column. In this scene we see Roman troops burning a native settlement. On the far right an auxiliary infantryman prepares to behead a kneeling German captive. The price of fighting against Rome was always high.

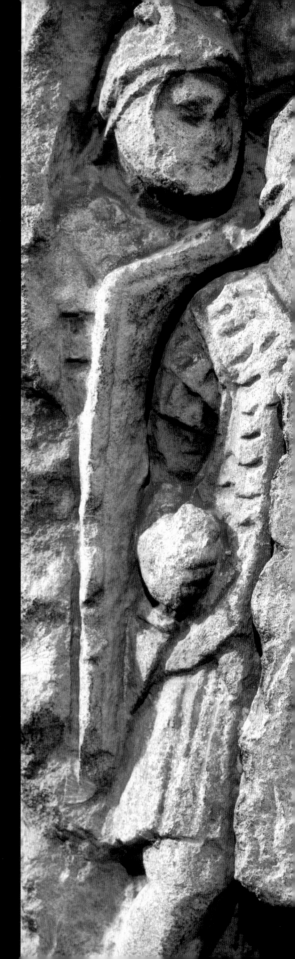

During the 3rd and 4th centuries AD the Roman Empire was all too frequently disturbed by outbreaks of civil war and external invasions.
Periods of peace and stability were few and far between. The army
continued to display high levels of military efficiency, but over time
its strength was eroded fighting against fellow Romans. Yet the
Roman Empire was big, and the threats facing it uncoordinated and
weak, and it did not quickly collapse. The army changed to deal with
the new circumstances. The defence of fortified positions became
more important, whilst pitched battles occurred less frequently than
in earlier periods. The army emphasized speed of movement and surprise, striking unexpectedly at enemies who ideally were unprepared
for such an assault.

In some respects the Late Roman army remained very much like its
predecessor under the Principate. The names of many units and the
titles of many officers changed, but most functioned in much the
same way as they had in earlier periods. However, all ranks were now
essentially career soldiers and the old tradition of the senior posts
being held by senators following a mixed military and civilian career
was abandoned. Emperors based their power directly on the control of
troops and needed to maintain this if they were not to be deposed by
the army's senior officers.

Eventually the distinction between legions and *auxilia* became very
slight, and far more important was the division between field army
units (*comitatenses*) and static frontier troops (*limitanei*). The legions
dwindled in size, probably to no more than 1,000 men, less than a
quarter of their strength in earlier centuries. Cavalry units figure
prominently in the accounts of the late army, but in fact there does not
seem to have been a significantly higher proportion of horsemen than
in earlier times. Very large armies were fielded in civil wars, which frequently went to the side with the most troops, and for major
expeditions against the Persians, but otherwise most campaigns were
waged by comparatively small forces. This trend would continue into
the 5th century and set the pattern for medieval European warfare.

*This 3rd-century relief from Gaul depicts a formation of soldiers in a uniform very
similar to that worn under the Principate. Each man wears an imperial helmet and
mail armour, and carries a rectangular* scutum.

V   The Army of Late Antiquity

Changes in the Late Roman Army

(Above) One of the few depictions of another nation triumphing over the Romans, this Persian relief shows the Sassanid King Sharpur I with a captured Roman kneeling before him. Sharpur defeated and killed the Emperor Gordian in AD 244 and Valerian in 260.

(Left) The Tetrarchic system was created by Diocletian at the end of the 3rd century AD by which the Empire was divided into an eastern and western section, each controlled by a senior emperor or Augustus, assisted by a junior Caesar. The ideal relationship between these four men was symbolized by this group of statues.

Problems and changes

Augustus rose to power through bloodshed and civil war, but the regime he established gave Rome the internal peace and stability which the Late Republic had lacked. Nero was the last of Augustus' extended family to rule, and following his suicide in AD 68, the Empire was wracked by civil war for over a year, until Vespasian, the fourth man to occupy the throne in just over 12 months, was able to create a stable regime. From AD 69 to 192, Rome enjoyed a period of prolonged peace, prosperity, and political stability, when attempts to usurp the throne were rare and gathered little momentum and most emperors died natural deaths. In 192 Commodus, the deranged son of the philosopher-Emperor Marcus Aurelius, was strangled in a household conspiracy involving the commander of his praetorian guard. His successor, Pertinax, lasted a mere three months before he was lynched by the praetorians, having failed to pay them the full donative which he had offered to gain power. The commanders of the guard then auctioned the throne off to the highest bidder from the walls of their barracks in Rome. The purchaser had little time to enjoy power, since the largest provincial garrisons in the Empire, Britain, Upper Pannonia and Syria, each rallied behind their respective governors in bids for supreme power. It was not until 197 that Septimius Severus had defeated all his rivals and became undisputed Emperor.

In 211 Severus died at York, having spent the last few years of his life campaigning against the Caledonian tribes of what is now Scotland. He bequeathed power jointly to his two sons, but within a few months the younger of the two, Geta, had been murdered by his older brother Caracalla. In 217 Caracalla was about to embark on a major eastern war, when he was stabbed to death by one of his cavalry bodyguards. The praetorian prefect, Macrinus, seized power, but was defeated and killed by a rival claimant before the year was out. The 3rd century witnessed a cycle of civil wars which rivalled, and eventually out-stripped the chaotic last decades of the Republic. Usurpations were common, but it was considerably easier to reach supreme power than to hold on to it. Many emperors lasted for no more than a few months, and reigns of more than a decade were rare periods of stability. The vast majority of emperors met violent ends, usually through assassination, but sometimes in battle fighting against Roman rivals or foreign enemies. In 251 the Emperor Decius and his son and heir were both cut down when their army was defeated by a force of Goths. The Sassanid Persians defeated a number of Roman expeditions, and in 260 captured and executed the Emperor Valerian. Disorder within the Empire encouraged attacks on almost all the frontiers, with barbarian raids driving deep into the provinces.

Yet in the main the Empire endured this long period of chaos, and territorial losses, such as the province of Dacia and much of Mesopotamia, were comparatively slight. However, there were growing signs of political fragmentation. In the second half of the 3rd century there was for more than a decade an independent Gallic Empire with its capital at Trier, whilst Queen Zenobia of Palmyra united for a while many of the eastern provinces into a kingdom for her infant son. At various times in the past, emperors had chosen to rule jointly with a colleague, or sometimes been forced to acknowledge, at least temporarily, another man's right to rule part of the Empire. In the late 3rd century, the principle of having more than one man in charge of the Empire became formally accepted. Diocletian (284–305) took this a stage further when he established the Tetrarchic system, where the Empire was divided into an eastern and western part. In each region a senior Augustus ruled with the aid of a junior Caesar. The system in its purest form did not long survive Diocletian's retirement, but in various modified forms it endured for over a century. Strong rulers like Diocletian and Constantine did bring periods of stability, but it is only in comparison with the 3rd century that the 4th appears as a time of strong government, freedom from civil war, and greater success over foreign enemies. Usurpations remained common, and in a sense the Tetrarchic system encouraged such attempts, for it was now possible for a man to advance to imperial power in stages.

The division of imperial power between several emperors was reflected in a fragmentation of authority at all levels. Provinces became more numerous, but much smaller in size, so that by the late 4th century each province from the Principate was divided into four or more smaller regions. Within these civil and military power was separated and there were no leaders equivalent to the old provincial governors. Much of the military activity in the later Empire occurred on a much smaller scale than had been the case in the past, with even emperors involving themselves in minor local campaigns.

It was within this context of weakening central authority, frequent outbreaks of civil war, and serious problems in many frontier areas that the army of Late Antiquity was forged. As society and the political system changed, so did the army, and by the 4th century many of its institutions were profoundly different from earlier periods. Not everything changed, and there was probably more continuity than is at first suggested by the many new ranks and unit types, whilst in other areas the shift was more one of emphasis than fundamental change. Many aspects of daily routine and military ritual would still have been recognizable to soldiers from the Principate. The army's strategic thinking continued to be dominated by the offensive, punitive expeditions which were mounted in much the same way in the 4th century AD as in the 1st. There were some tactical innovations, but in battle the later army continued to prove itself superior to its foreign opponents, winning far more battles than it lost, although it probably engaged in this type of fighting less readily than in the past. Similarly the basic methods of siege warfare remained the same, although it became more common for the Romans to be the defenders rather than the besiegers.

Much remained the same. This chapter will concentrate on some of the chief differences between the later army and its better-documented predecessor, the army of the early Empire.

Commanders: the rise of the equestrian officer

The intimate link between political and military leadership had been at the core of the Roman system since at least the early Republic. Senators, following a career which brought them in turn civil and military responsibilities, provided the army with its commanders, and wise emperors portrayed themselves as the most prominent member of the Senate. In Late Antiquity this all changed, and senators gradually ceased to have a military role. In the

Legio II Parthica, one of three new legions raised by Septimius Severus (AD 197–208) for his eastern campaigns, was stationed in Apamea in Syria for some time. This tombstone is one of several found in the city depicting legionaries from this unit. In this case it marked the grave of Aurelius Mucianus, who was an instructor in the use of throwing-spears (discens lanciarius). *He holds a bundle of lanceae in his right hand and – like the soldiers on other tombstones of II Parthica – carries an oval, almost circular shield. His sword is worn on the left. Several of the other Apamea tombstones commemorate specialists with other weapons, such as the bow, not normally associated with legionaries. It is unclear if this reflects a general shift in the equipment carried by the legions or II Parthica in particular, or whether a unit as large as a legion often contained a wide range of weapons specialists.*

An iron helmet found in Holland sheathed in silver and decorated with semi-precious stones. Such an expensive piece of equipment seems most likely to have been worn by an officer. It would have offered good protection, but restricted the hearing of the wearer.

2nd century some emperors, most notably Marcus Aurelius, began to promote equestrian officers to command first legions and then whole armies. Usually these men were first enrolled in the senatorial order before being given such senior posts, but in the 3rd century this practice was largely dropped. An equestrian prefect replaced the senatorial *legatus* as the commander of a legion, and in time equestrians were appointed to command armies and govern provinces. Most of these men were career officers, spending far longer with the army than had senators following the traditional political career. They were probably more experienced than their senatorial predecessors, though it is much harder to judge whether they were on average any more competent. At first it must have seemed to emperors that equestrian officers posed less of a potential threat to them, for they lacked the political connections of senators. Yet at a time when the emperor was required to spend much of his reign on campaign with the army, such factors became of less significance. An officer who could secure the support of the other senior commanders in the army could readily arrange the murder of the current ruler and seize power himself. The latter part of the 3rd century was dominated by a group of equestrian officers from the Danubian provinces who made emperors from amongst their own number, and in some cases broke them as readily.

The traditional rank structure of the army appears to have been altered at all levels during the 3rd and 4th centuries. Unit commanders had a range of titles, which do not always appear readily to conform to a fixed pattern. The rank of *praepositus* at first meant an officer temporarily placed in command of another unit, but swiftly became a permanent title. Many prefects and tribunes appear in our sources, often as unit commanders, but all three titles seem to have embraced a very broad range of responsibilities. Some tribunes and prefects were sometimes also referred to as *praepositi*. At a lower level were the ranks of *primicerius* and the junior (as well as intriguingly named) senator. Within a unit there might be *ducenarii*, who according to Vegetius commanded 200 men, and beneath them *centenarii*, presumably commanders of 100 or century sized sub-units, and so perhaps equivalent to the old centurions. Apart from their titles, even less is known about the various more junior ranks attested in the later army.

Field armies and static forces

Alongside the changes which reduced the large provinces of the Principate to the more numerous but much smaller regional military commands of the 4th century, came another fundamental division between army units. These were now either *comitatenses*, allocated to one of the field armies, or *limitanei*, assigned to garrison a particular area, usually on the frontiers. The *comitatenses* were at the immediate disposal of one of the emperors or his senior subordinates. The *limitanei* were commanded by the *dux* assigned to that region. The development of this system cannot now be traced with any certainty. In some respects it was foreshadowed by earlier developments, such as Septimius Severus' creation of a force based around the foot and horse guards and Legio II Parthica – in total equivalent to a strong provincial army – just outside Rome at the end of the 2nd century, or Gallienus' formation of a powerful army, including especially strong cavalry forces, at Milan in the middle of the 3rd century. Important stages in the process appear to have occurred in the reigns of Diocletian and Constantine, although the details remain obscure. Our best evidence is provided by the *Notitia Dignitatum*, which lists imperial posts and military commands at the very end of the 4th century. This was the system in its fully developed form and attempts to reconstruct earlier versions remain to a fair extent conjectural. In the *Notitia* the Eastern Empire mustered five field armies, two associated with the imperial court, whilst the West had seven, three of which were comparatively small.

The *comitatenses* have sometimes been seen as mobile strategic reserves, which were able to move to each trouble spot as required. Most were certainly stationed well within the provinces, in marked contrast to the deployment of the army of the Principate which was primarily spread around the Empire's perimeter. The old system meant that if an enemy was able to penetrate the frontier zone, it took considerable time to shift forces from other frontiers to defeat them. This in turn weakened those frontiers and could lead to new problems there. There is a measure of truth in this interpretation, but the mobility of the *comitatenses* should not be exaggerated. Ultimately, one of these armies could move no faster than a marching infantryman or, which in many ways was even more of a restriction, the speed of its baggage train. The field armies moved no quicker than other armies, but they did have the advantage of not being tied to a particular region. Under the Principate the legions in particular performed so many administrative roles that their removal from the area to fight elsewhere caused major problems. This had led to the frequent use of legionary vexillations rather than entire units. Moving a field army caused no such administrative dislocation, but the extent to which these troops provided a strategic reserve for the entire Empire is highly questionable. What is certain is that they provided a powerful military force to protect the emperor from the internal threat of usurpers. Civil wars remained common throughout the late Empire, so that the army's structure was to a great extent intended to guard against threats of this nature.

In the past the *limitanei* were often depicted as local militias of part-time farmer-soldiers, in a sense closer to the legionaries of the Mid Republic than to the later professional soldiers of the Principate. This idea is clearly mistaken. The *limitanei* were regular units of trained troops, who differed only in status from the *comitatenses*. The *limitanei* undertook the day-to-day patrolling and garrison duty on most frontiers, as well as some areas with problems of internal disorder. In general they seem to have performed their duties well. Although their numbers were inadequate to stop a major raid or invasion on their own, the *limitanei* appear to have coped with much smaller-scale warfare. On occasions units of *limitanei* were attached to the field armies and operated effectively. In some cases this attachment became permanent, and the units were rated as *pseudocomitatenses*.

Units in the late Roman army

A range of different units appear in the *Notitia Dignitatum*, with legions, auxiliary *alae* and cohorts alongside less familiar types. The cavalry of the field armies were now formed into units called *vexillationes*. A few units were given the apparently honorific title of *comites* (or companions). Additional cavalry were provided by the imperial guard regiments or *scholae*, which at some periods often served with the field armies, although they were not formally part of them. Infantry consisted of legions or *auxilia palatina*. The latter seem to have been a creation of Constantine. They are sometimes seen

(Right) This late 4th-century AD depiction of a standard-bearer shows a man whose appearance differs in many ways from soldiers in the earlier Roman army. His shield is large and almost circular, while his sword is worn on the left.

(Below) The Notitia Dignitatum *comprises an order of battle for the Roman army at the very end of the 4th century. Military bases and their garrisons are listed, and the insignia of each unit shown. Although it seems probable that the shield patterns are simplified forms of the original, this still represents one of the best sources for military insignia in any period.*

The Field Armies as Listed in the Notitia Dignitatum

The East

Emperor
and 7 *scholae*

Master of Soldiers of Praesentalis I
5 *vexillatio palatina*
7 *vexillatio comitatenses*
6 *legio palatina*
18 *auxilia palatina*
Total: 36 units

Master of Soldiers of Praesentalis II
6 *vexillatio palatina*
6 *vexillatio comitatenses*
6 *legio palatina*
17 *auxilia palatina*
1 *pseudocomitatenses*
Total: 36 units

Master of Soldiers of Orientis
10 *vexillatio comitatenses*
2 *auxilia palatina*
9 *legio comitatenses*
10 *pseudocomitatenses*
Total: 31 units

Master of Soldiers of Thracum
3 *vexillatio palatina*
4 *vexillatio comitatenses*
21 *legio comitatenses*
Total: 28 units

Master of Soldiers of Illyricum
2 *vexillatio comitatenses*
1 *legio palatina*
6 *auxilia palatina*
8 *legio comitatenses*
9 *pseudocomitatenses*
Total: 26 units

The West

Emperor

Master of Infantry

Army in Italy:
5 *vexillatio palatina*
1 *vexillatio comitatenses*
8 *legio palatina*
22 *auxilia palatina*
5 *legio comitatenses*
2 *pseudocomitatenses*
Total: 44 units

Master of Cavalry

Army in Gaul:
4 *vexillatio palatina*
8 *vexillatio comitatenses*
1 *legio palatina*
15 *auxilia palatina*
9 *legio comitatenses*
21 *pseudocomitatenses*
Total: 58 units

Count of Illyricum
13 *auxilia palatina*
5 *legio comitatenses*
4 *pseudocomitatenses*
Total: 22 units

Count of Africa
19 *vexillatio comitatenses*
3 *legio palatina*
1 *auxilia palatina*
8 *legio comitatenses*
Total: 31 units

Count of Tingitania
2 *vexillatio comitatenses*
2 *auxilia palatina*
1 *pseudocomitatenses*
Total: 5 units

Count of Britain
4 *vexillatio comitatenses*
1 *legio comitatenses*
Total: 5 units

Count of Spain
11 *auxilia palatina*
5 *legio comitatenses*
Total: 16 units

Key

scholae:	imperial guard cavalry regiments
vexillatio palatina:	elite field army cavalry regiments
vexillatio comitatenses:	field army cavalry regiments
legio palatina:	elite field army legions
auxilia palatina:	elite field army auxiliary regiments
legio comitatenses:	field army legion
pseudocomitatenses:	formerly border troops, now part of field army

as a distinct break with the past, marking an important stage in a perceived overreliance on German recruits from outside the Empire, but in fact they shared many features in common with the auxiliary cohorts of the Principate. There does appear to have been little difference between legionary and auxiliary infantry by this time in equipment or tactics. The best *vexillationes* and legions were called *palatina* rather than *comitatenses* and enjoyed a higher status. Another distinction which had more to do with precedence than any practical difference was between two identically named units of which one was known as *seniores* and the other as *iuniores*. Quite a few cavalry and infantry units in the *comitatenses* were paired with another of the same type to form a brigade. We do not know whether such units had a permanent commander, but it does appear to have been rare to split them up. All types of unit quite often appear in our sources under the vague label of *numeri*, and this is also the term normally used for the foreign units or *foederati*. Initially recruited from a single ethnic group, and often specializing in a particular fighting technique, over time these tended to draw manpower from any available source and become assimilated into and indistinguishable from the regular army.

The *limitanei* included an even wider variety of unit types. There were old-fashioned auxiliary cohorts and *alae*, legions, often divided into several detachments, as well as cavalry *vexillationes* and *cunei* and other units with less specific titles, including *numeri*. There is no trace of a brigade structure linking separate units, although some of the legions had several cohorts. Both *comitatenses* and *limitanei* included naval squadrons where appropriate. For the first time in Rome's history, there were now also specialist artillery units, although it is likely that many ordinary units continued to employ catapults, especially in the defence of forts or cities.

The majority of infantry units, whether legions, *auxilia palatina* or *limitanei,* normally fought in close order. A single statement in Vegetius has often been used to suggest that body armour was rare, but this belief is certainly mistaken. Most infantrymen wore a helmet, cuirass of mail or scale and carried a long oval shield. The longer *spatha* sword had by now superseded the *gladius* in all units. A variation on the *pilum*, the *spiculum*, was sometimes used, but various throwing- or thrusting-spears were far more common. A man might in addition to

A re-enactor from a group formed by English Heritage representing a horse-archer in the late Roman army. By the 6th century many of the best Roman cavalrymen were skilled archers, even if at other times they willingly fought at close quarters.

his fighting spear carry a number of short javelins and/or weighted throwing darts. The latter, known as *plumbatae* or *mattiobarbuli*, had a range of somewhere between 30 and 65 m (100–200 ft) – the effective range probably near the lower end of the scale. Vegetius tells us that some late 3rd-century legionaries carried five of these darts clipped into the backs of their shields. A number of units – both foot and horse – are listed in the *Notitia Dignitatum* as archers (*saggitarii*), but it seems likely that a proportion of men in many other units were also trained and equipped with bows.

Some cavalry units were even more heavily armoured than the infantry. In units of *cataphracti* and *clibanarii* the rider and often the horse were heavily armoured. The distinction between the two terms is now obscure. The name *clibanarius* was derived from the word for an iron bread oven, and may have reflected not just the armoured soldier's appearance, but the discomfort of wearing such gear, especially in hot weather. There were far more units of cataphracts and *clibanarii* in the eastern than western armies, reflecting the need to defeat the large numbers of equally heavily armoured Persian cavalry. The vast majority of these special units were in the field armies. The bulk of the remaining units of Roman cavalry, whether they were called *scutarii*, *promoti* or *stablesiani*, were primarily, but not exclusively, trained for shock action, in much the same manner as the vast majority of *alae* under the Principate. Horse archers, and a few other units, such as the *Mauri* and *Dalmatae*, appear to have been primarily light cavalry. There is a persistent myth that cavalry became far more important in the later army, an idea often connected with the emphasis on the mobility of field armies. In

(Left) These re-enactors from Cohors V Gallorum – one of the only groups attempting to recreate the Roman army of the 3rd century AD – look very different from the classic image of the legionary in lorica segmentata *and imperial Gallic helmet. Instead these men wear boots, trousers, long-sleeved tunics, scale armour – and in one case a coif. They also carry their swords on the left, wield spears and have oval shields. Yet although the style of equipment, and in some respects the methods of fighting, had changed, the Roman infantryman was still better protected and more disciplined than the vast majority of his opponents.*

Unit size

The evidence for the size, and still more the internal organization, of all these unit types is exceedingly poor. In general our sources give the impression that most units were comparatively small, and that certainly there was no longer any equivalent to the *c.* 5,000-man legions of earlier periods. When the legions were reduced in size is difficult to say. Vegetius believed that under Diocletian at least some legions still consisted of as many as 6,000 men. Why the change occurred is equally obscure, though it may simply have happened as units were split into detachments which over time became effectively independent. Most modern commentators suggest that a legion in a field army numbered some 1,000–1,200 men in the 4th century. *Auxilia palatina* may have been of a similar size, or possibly round the 500–600 mark. Cavalry *vexillationes* perhaps were theoretically 600 strong, and the *scholae*, in the 6th century at least, consisted of 500 men. These are estimates of 'paper strength' and the meagre evidence would seem to suggest that actual units tended on average to have about two thirds of their full complement at any time. Unit sizes amongst the *limitanei* are even more poorly recorded, and we do not know whether legions were of similar size to their counterparts in the field army.

Most modern reconstructions are based upon the assumption that there was a system of standard sizes for each type of unit and that this was, on the whole, adhered to. We cannot know whether or not this was in fact the case.

Forts and fortifications

Far more effort was put into the construction of fortifications in Late Antiquity. Existing military bases were strengthened and many new forts built, often on sites chosen primarily for defensive reasons. Walls were higher and thicker, and sometimes included platforms for artillery. Towers, sometimes square or fan shaped, but most often round, were built so that they projected in front of the walls, allowing the defenders to lay down enfilading fire against any attackers. Gateways were in general narrower, but better defended. Ditches tended to be wider, and flat-bottomed rather than the v-shaped cross section of earlier periods. The same trends were also pronounced in the curtain walls built from the 3rd century onwards to protect many of the towns and cities in the provinces. In a number of cases it seems unlikely that the community actually faced a direct threat, but the urge to fortify may well reflect the uncertainty of the times,

as well perhaps as competition between cities for status.

Whilst the defences of army bases were often far more formidable than had been the case in the past, the sites themselves were considerably smaller. Many legionary bases, such as Chester and Caerleon in Britain, were largely abandoned by the 3rd century and no new installations of a comparable size built. Instead of the traditional playing-card shape, forts were often square. Some existing forts continued to be used but were dramatically reduced in size. These trends may be an indication of the generally smaller size of army units in this period.

Stronger fortifications reflected the much greater importance of forts and fortified settlements in the warfare of Late Antiquity. Direct attack on a military base was now a real possibility, and the army was no longer quite so confident about advancing to destroy the enemy in the open. It was not always possible to dominate the enemy beyond the fron-

(Opposite above) The fort at Qasr Bsheir in Jordan was constructed in the reign of Diocletian. In many respects it typifies the army's forts in the late 3rd and 4th centuries AD, being smaller in size, but better fortified than the bases of the Principate. Corner towers project beyond the walls in contrast to earlier fortifications, and would allow the defenders to enfilade any attacker.

(Right) The walls of the late 3rd-century Roman fort at Porchester on Britain's south coast were later incorporated into the defences of a Norman castle. Notice again that the towers – in this case round rather than square – project beyond the curtain wall. The substantial fortifications protecting bases of the army in this period suggest that serious attack was considered to be far more likely than in earlier times.

tiers and so deter raiding, and as we have seen in the earlier periods, it was impossible at the best of times to intercept every incoming raid. Vegetius recommended that Roman forces should retreat to their strongholds in the face of invasion, having first gathered up local food supplies. Barbarian peoples had little knowledge of siegecraft and under most circumstances would be unable to capture a fortified place. They might starve a town or city into surrender, but this required them to keep a strong force concentrated outside its walls for months on end. This normally proved impossible or gave sufficient time for a Roman force to march to the city's relief. When shortage of food or lack of interest persuaded attackers to withdraw, they became vulnerable to Roman counterattack. In this way raids could be endured and the damage they inflicted kept to a minimum. Ideally, in time, an emperor would concentrate sufficient forces to mount a major punitive expedition, striking against the tribes in their own homelands.

Soldiers and Warfare in Late Antiquity

Recruitment

By the 4th century soldiers served 20 years, apart from in some of the less prestigious units amongst the *limitanei*, where men were expected to serve for 24 years. Some men were volunteers, but conscription appears to have been far more common than in earlier periods. Under the Principate soldiers were not legally permitted to marry, but the army informally ignored the rule, let soldiers raise families and often recruited their sons born 'in the camp'. Severus' decision to remove this legal ban led eventually to legislation forcing all sons born to soldiers during or after service to enlist in the army, making soldiering an hereditary career. Conscripts were also levied from the Empire on an annual basis, each community being obliged to provide a set quota of men. The assessment appears to have been based on land ownership, and tended to fall especially heavily on rural communities. Certain categories of men, chiefly those employed in imperial service, were exempt from this obligation, whilst men following unsuitable professions, and, in all but the most exceptional circumstances, slaves were barred from military service. In some years the emperor chose not to raise this particular levy, so that it is difficult to know how frequent it was. It also appears to have been fairly common for governors to permit the communities to pay a conscription tax in money instead of recruits, a system which was clearly open to corruption. Some officials levied the tax, and then used a small proportion of it to find sufficient volunteers – often inevitably of low quality – to provide the original quota of recruits. Attempts were made to prevent such abuses, but a constant trend in Roman law was aimed at preventing those eligible for conscription from avoiding military service. Cases of self-mutilation to avoid military service – a common method was to cut off the thumbs – occur sporadically throughout Roman history, but this may have been more of a problem as conscription became widespread. Constantine passed a law obliging soldiers' sons who disfigured themselves in this way to undertake civil service in their communities, but measures became harsher as time went on, with Valentinian ordering such men to be burnt alive in 386. By the end of the century a different approach was adopted, and in 381 Theodosius stated that mutilated recruits were still liable to conscription and that two such men would count as one normal conscript.

Desertion had long been a problem in the Roman army, probably inevitably given the long terms of service and often harsh conditions. References to deserters appear frequently in the sources for the later period, but it is difficult to say whether or not this had become more common.

Barbarization? Recruits from outside the Empire

Significant numbers of recruits were drawn from communities of barbarian tribes settled with imperial approval within the Empire. Often the treaty granting them land required them to supply a set number of recruits on a regular basis. These were known as *laeti* or *gentiles*, but did not usually serve in distinct units and were treated much like other conscripts. Many men from outside the Empire were also drawn into the Roman army. At the end of a conflict prisoners of war were often conscripted into the army, though usually they were posted some distance away from their place of origin. A defeated people might also provide a number of warriors as part of the peace settlement imposed by Rome. Some individuals also chose to travel to the Empire and volunteer.

The recruitment of barbarians appears to have been fairly routine, and in principle was nothing new, for the *auxilia* of the Principate had also included men from outside the directly governed provinces. Yet we have no reliable statistics to establish the scale of barbarian recruitment in Late Antiquity. In the past it has often been seen as a sign of a desperate shortage of recruits, and perhaps additionally of the low quality of many conscripts from the provinces. Steadily, the Roman army became barbarized, as more and more of its officers and men were drawn from the uncivilized peoples, and in particular the Germanic tribes. These men had little reason to feel political or cultural loyalty to Rome. The problem became worse with the growing use of *foederati*, units in which barbarians served under their own tribal leaders rather than Roman officers. The Roman army is supposed to have decayed until it was little more than a mass of mercenary warbands led by barbarian chieftains. This is sometimes held to have been a major factor in the collapse of the western Empire.

As early as AD 69, Tacitus had depicted an army from the Rhine provinces, both legionaries and auxiliaries, as uncouth barbarians, shocked by the splendour and size of Rome. Similar rhetorical exaggeration may well have influenced the few late sources which criticize the spread of barbarians within the army. In the main our sources for the period do not appear to have seen this as a problem. Barbarian recruits were in general as loyal and efficient as any others, even when fighting against their own people. Occasionally barbarian soldiers turned traitor, but so in this period did some Romans. By the late 4th century many senior officers were of

208

barbarian descent, yet most of these men appear to have been culturally assimilated into the Roman military aristocracy. The belief that 'barbarisation' of the army contributed to the fall of Rome has now been largely discredited.

Soldiers and civilians

By the 4th century the real value of the soldier's pay was very modest, and needed to be supplemented by many payments in kind, including clothing as well as rations and fodder for animals, plus occasional imperial donatives. Most clothing and equipment was issued by the state, and provided either through levies on the provinces or produced in the imperial factories listed in the *Notitia Dignitatum*. The *comitatenses* in general had no fixed camps and for much of the time were billeted on the civilian population of towns and cities within the provinces. This was exceedingly unpopular – as it had been on the rare occasions it was employed in earlier periods – and there were frequent complaints from civilians accusing soldiers of taking more than was their legal right and of using violence.

→ p.212

Constantine's Soldiers, AD 312

In Late Antiquity, Roman troops were engaged in civil wars almost as often as they fought foreign enemies. As his army marched on Rome to defeat his rival Maxentius, Constantine claimed to have seen a vision of the cross in the sky, and following a dream, publicly became a Christian. Whether this conversion was political or genuine – or perhaps a mixture of both – is hard to say. However, his subsequent overwhelming victory at the Milvian Bridge seems to have confirmed him in his beliefs. Before the battle he had ordered his men to paint the Christian symbol of the Greek letters Chi and Rho on their shields. In this scene we see a senior officer inspecting the results.

Pilum: Versions of the *pilum* still appear to have been in use at this period, although more conventionally shaped spears and javelins had probably become more common.

Helmet: This man's helmet is based upon a highly ornate example found in Holland and dating to the 4th century. In the original the iron is covered in a thin layer of silver. Notice the nasal guard, a feature which begins to appear in this period.

Cloak: This fringed cloak is evidently an expensive item, of the type affordable only by an officer. It is fastened at the right shoulder by a 'crossbow-style' brooch.

Trousers: Both civilian and military fashion had changed by the 4th century and trousers had become part of normal dress. Although in earlier years such a garment had been seen as characteristically barbarian, there is no good reason to see this change as an indication of the barbarization of the army.

Helmet: This man wears an Intercisa-type helmet, its bowl formed from two separate plates joined in the centre. Such helmets were cheaper and easier to make than earlier versions, but still offered fairly good protection.

Shield and darts: From the 3rd century AD some soldiers carried weighted darts (*plumbatae* or *mattiobarbuli*). Shields were designed so that several of these missiles could be clipped into place behind them.

Tunic: From the 3rd century AD a new style of long-sleeved tunic came into common usage amongst both soldiers and civilians. These often appear to have been decorated with borders and patches. Each of the tunics worn by these men is based upon surviving textiles from Roman Egypt. It seems probable that the solid lozenges, squares and circles seen decorating tunics in wall-paintings and mosaics were in fact far more intricately detailed.

Sword: By the 4th century infantry and cavalrymen alike were usually equipped with a long-bladed *spatha* sword. In most cases this was worn on the left side.

Shield: Most troops by this period also carried oval shields, which could be flat or slightly concave.

Boots: Even by the 2nd century AD the old-fashioned *caligae* appear to have fallen from favour, at least amongst soldiers in the northern provinces. Over time, the army – and indeed most civilians – began to wear various styles of enclosed shoes and boots.

The Battle of Strasbourg

AD 357

A confederation of Alamannic tribes had temporarily united under the leadership of two kings, Chnodomar and his nephew Serapio, and launched a plundering invasion of the Roman provinces along the Rhine. Julian the Apostate, the Caesar in the west, marched to confront them and, under pressure from his enthusiastic troops, attacked the barbarians near Argentoratum.

The forces

1 The Romans: 13,000 men including several legions and units of *auxilia palatina*.
2 The Alamanni: according to our Roman sources 35,000 men.

The fighting

Before the battle began, Chnodomar and his chieftains dismounted to fight on foot, showing their warriors that they would share their fate. The Germans concealed some men in broken ground on their right, but the Romans were suspicious and held back their left wing. On the Roman right their cavalry, including a unit of cataphracts, were routed and fled behind the two lines of Roman infantry, where they were rallied by Julian. The Alamanni launched a heavy onslaught at the first Roman line. Led by a group of chieftains they smashed through the Roman centre, but were stopped by the Primani, a legion stationed in the second line. Gradually, as the Romans committed more and more of their second line, the

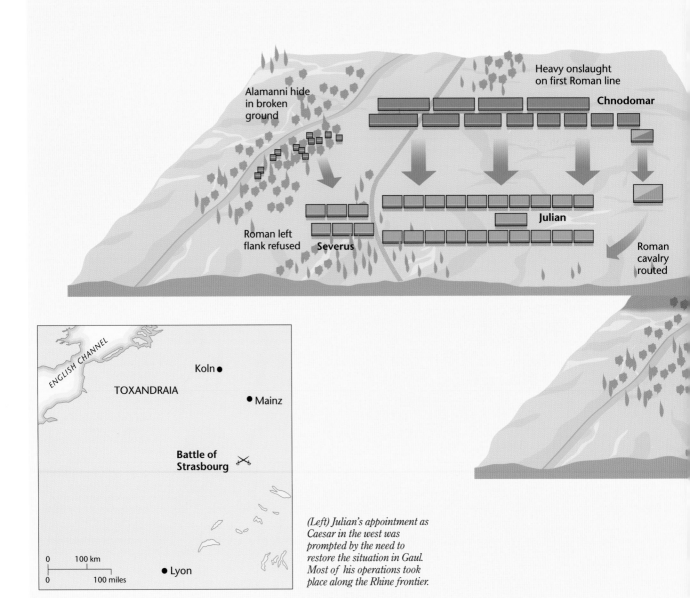

Alamanni hide in broken ground

Heavy onslaught on first Roman line

Chnodomar

Roman left flank refused

Severus

Julian

Roman cavalry routed

ENGLISH CHANNEL

Koln ●

TOXANDRAIA

● Mainz

Battle of Strasbourg ✗

0   100 km
0   100 miles

● Lyon

(Left) Julian's appointment as Caesar in the west was prompted by the need to restore the situation in Gaul. Most of his operations took place along the Rhine frontier.

Germans were driven back and eventually collapsed in rout.

Casualties

1 Roman: 4 officers and 243 men killed.
2 Alamanni: our Roman sources claim that some 6,000 were killed. Chnodomar was captured.

Results

The victory helped to deter other raids on this section of the Roman frontier for a while. However, this would only prove effective for as long as the tribes outside the Empire believed that the Romans were strong enough to mete out similar retribution to any new raid.

JULIAN (AD 322–63)

The son of Constantine the Great's half brother, Julian survived the brutal Civil War that swiftly followed the former's death in 337, but spent most of his early life as a well-cared-for prisoner. In 355 he was appointed Caesar of the western provinces by the Augustus (or Senior Emperor) Constantius II. During the next few years he campaigned with some success along the Rhine frontier. In 360 Julian's troops proclaimed him Augustus in opposition to Constantius, but the latter died of natural causes in the next year. As ruler of the entire Empire, Julian attempted to reverse Constantine's decision to establish Christianity as the main religion of the Roman world. For this reason he is known as Julian the Apostate. However, the cult of his own devising, based around worship of the sun god, failed to become established.

In 363 Julian massed a huge army of some 70,000 men for an invasion of Persia. Although he penetrated deep into the enemy's heartland, he was unable to force them into a decisive battle and his troops began to run out of supplies. In a confused night skirmish Julian was struck by a javelin and mortally wounded. The subsequent retreat of the Roman army was disastrous and Julian's successor granted considerable concessions to the Persians to gain peace.

(Above) A statue of Julian the Apostate, now in the Louvre. Julian had no prior military experience before he was appointed Caesar and never developed the ability to understand his soldiers' moods.

German infantry

German cavalry

Roman infantry

Roman cavalry

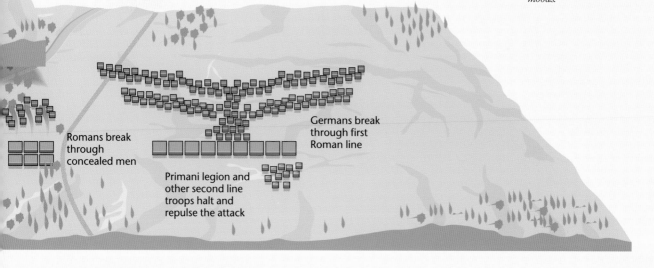

Romans break through concealed men

Germans break through first Roman line

Primani legion and other second line troops halt and repulse the attack

(Right) A medallion celebrating Constantius' recovery of Britain from the rule of a usurper in 297. Constantius would later campaign extensively in northern Britain and died at York, where he was succeeded by his son, Constantine the Great.

The *limitanei* in general lived in forts. Some earlier forts, notably Housesteads and Great Chesters on Hadrian's Wall, have revealed traces of extensive alterations in the design of barrack blocks near the end of the 3rd century. A single range of paired *contubernium* rooms was replaced by a row of some half-dozen individual sheds, each with their own external walls and roofs and separated by narrow alleyways. At Housesteads the individual sheds vary in size from around 8–10 m (26–33 ft) by 3.6–5.15 m (12–17 ft). These are known as chalet-barracks. There were invariably fewer of these buildings than there were *contubernium* rooms in the earlier, communal barrack block. Most chalets seem to have had hearths. One interpretation was to see these as homes occupied by one or two soldiers and their families, providing an indication of the diminishing size of army units in the Late Empire. There is no direct evidence to support this, and the discovery of similar chalet-barracks from the early 3rd century, before the supposed reduction of unit strength occurred, makes it extremely dubious. More probably the different design was a simpler and lower-maintenance alternative to rebuilding ageing barrack blocks to the original design.

The new religion: Christianity and the Roman army

Roman soldiers frequently acted as the agents of the state in the persecution of the early church. However, it is important to remember that in the 1st and 2nd centuries the suppression of the Christian cult was sporadic and not directed by central authority. Roman emperors did not in the main view the new religion as a serious problem, and most persecutions were prompted by periodic outbursts of hostility and suspicion in the local communities. This changed in 251, when Decius ordered an Empire-wide suppression of the cult. Other emperors, notably Diocletian, ordered similarly broad persecutions, but by this time the religion was too well established to be eradicated.

The attitude of early Christians to military service varied. The Book of Acts records the conversion of Cornelius, a centurion of a Cohors Italica, by St Peter. There is also a little evidence for Christians serving as soldiers, even within the praetorian guard by the 3rd century. However as late as 295, when summoned for military service as part of the annual levy, one Maximilianus could declare, 'I cannot serve in the army; I cannot do evil; I am a Christian.' His refusal subsequently led to his martyrdom.

In 312 Constantine destroyed the army of his rival Maxentius at the battle of the Milvian Bridge outside Rome. He claimed to have received a vision of the cross, and as a result had ordered his men to paint the symbol of Christ, the Greek letters chi-rho, on their shields. The next year Constantine and the Eastern Emperor, Licinius, proclaimed freedom of worship for Christians throughout the Empire. Throughout his reign Constantine actively, but not exclusively, promoted the new religion, although it was not until near the end of his life that he was baptized. The impact of the adoption of Christianity on the Roman army was in many ways slight, the ceremonies of the new religion replacing those of the old in army ritual and ceremony. By the mid-5th century each unit in the eastern army had a chaplain, and these may have been introduced both there and in the west much earlier. The new faith did not significantly change Roman methods of war-making.

Warfare in Late Antiquity

The problems faced by the later Roman army varied from frontier to frontier. In the east the Sassanid Persians, who had supplanted the Parthians in the early 3rd century, were large and powerful neighbours. On a few occasions Sassanid armies drove deep into Rome's eastern provinces, at times even threatening Antioch. More often the Romans invaded Persia, the expeditions following much the same route down the Euphrates as had those of earlier emperors, such as Trajan, Lucius Verus and Septimius Severus. Neither side was ever able to turn temporary successes into permanent occupation. In the main the Romans and Persians concentrated their efforts on controlling the regions bordering their Empires. Pitched battles were rare, and raiding the most common military activity. This was often carried out by allies drawn from the local, nomadic peoples. Strongholds assumed a critical importance in these campaigns, since these provided bases from which raiders or interception forces could operate. Only the side which controlled these fortified towns could hope to dominate the surrounding area. Besieging such a stronghold took a great deal of time and effort, and ran the real risk of failure, which would seriously diminish a leader's prestige. At times, the attackers' skill and determination proved inadequate, but more sieges were ended when a field army came to the defenders' relief. A good proportion of the battles which were fought occurred in these circumstances.

On other frontiers, the problem posed by tribal peoples remained much the same as it had under the Principate. There does not seem any good reason to suppose that the tribal confederations which periodically appeared were any greater than the ones which had at times faced earlier Roman armies. Certainly at a strategic and tactical level, the military practices of the barbarian tribes had remained essentially unchanged. The *limitanei* were there to deal with small-scale attacks. Larger incursions, made by several hundred or more warriors, could not be stopped, and so it became a question of seeking refuge in forts or fortified towns and either

waiting for relief or to harass the enemy when the latter decided to leave. Battles were rare on these frontiers as well as in the east. The Roman objective was to move quickly and strike suddenly. Whenever possible, barbarian raiders were ambushed or taken by surprise, so that their defeat was made as certain as possible and Roman casualties were kept to a minimum. The acknowledgment that many attacks could not be stopped before they reached the settled parts of the provinces was in some respects a change from the earlier period, but in essence most of the principles of frontier warfare remained the same. If the Romans were perceived to be weak then they would be attacked. Frontier defence was still primarily based on creating a façade of overwhelming power which deterred raids in the first place. This was done through a combination of diplomacy, emphasis on inflicting heavy losses on

The Arch of Septimius Severus, Rome, commemorated his victories in Parthia and was decorated with reliefs showing these campaigns. Unfortunately most are very badly eroded and it is difficult to make out much of the detail of soldiers' equipment.

The Arch of Constantine, Rome, openly celebrated his defeat of Roman rivals and was probably the first public monument to show dead and defeated Romans. In this scene Constantine's soldiers – some of them perhaps auxilia palatina – attack a fortification. Note the large oval shields, spears and javelins.

raiders, even if this was done as they withdrew, and aggressive expeditions into the tribal heartlands to instil fear of Rome's military might. On the whole the army performed this task well until the beginning of the 5th century. Yet bouts of civil war weakened the army, even if only temporarily, increasing the chance of minor defeats on the frontiers. Every such defeat, however small, diminished respect for Roman military might, if it was not speedily avenged.

Battles were rare events in wars against foreign opponents in all areas, although the likelihood that they would produce a decisive result ensured that many civil wars were decided by such an encounter. Whilst the smaller units of Late Antiquity were especially well suited to the small-scale mobile warfare being waged on most frontiers, they also operated effectively as part of larger armies in massed encounters. As in earlier periods, the army

The late 3rd-century AD Arch of Galerius in Thessalonike, Greece, commemorated his successful war against the Sassanid Persians and contains a number of reliefs depicting soldiers. Most wear scale armour, spangenhelms and carry oval shields.

continued to form in more than one line, keeping at least half of the available forces in reserve. Roman generals still controlled a battle in the traditional manner, encouraging and inspiring the men from close behind the fighting line and managing the commitment of reserve units. In most respects unit tactics were similar to earlier periods, although Roman close-order infantry do appear to have been a little less aggressive. Ammianus speaks of Roman legionaries charging at a dash, in spite of the inevitable loss of order, to close the distance and sweep away Persian archers quickly, but in most other battles they tended to remain on the defensive. Forming a dense line, Roman infantry would bombard the enemy with javelins, darts, perhaps a heavier throwing-spear, and often arrows fired by archers in the rear rank. We also read of them employing the *barritus*, a war-cry of Germanic origin, which began with a low murmuring, the men holding their shields close to their faces to create an echoing effect, and rose to a crescendo. These tactics were in contrast to the slow, silent advance, *pilum* volley at point blank range, and screaming charge of the professional legionaries in earlier periods, although in many ways they were more similar to the behaviour of the older, militia army.

Conclusion: The army and the end of the western Empire

By the end of the 5th century the western Roman Empire was no more. In the east, emperors continued to rule for a thousand years. Much of Rome's culture, as well as many military institutions, were preserved by the eastern (or Byzantine) Empire. Several of the key events which marked the collapse of the west were military defeats, but it would be a mistake to see the fall of Rome as primarily caused by an inadequate military system. At its best, the late Roman army was considerably more efficient as a fighting force than any of its contemporary opponents. Yet weakening central authority, social and economic problems, and most of all the continuing grind of civil wars eroded the political capacity to maintain the army at this level of effectiveness. A permanent, well-equipped, organized and disciplined professional army was a very expensive institution to support, but also a dangerous one, for no emperor could ever be fully secure when there was the slightest chance of the army backing a usurper. The Byzantine emperors managed to maintain an army which combined a reasonable level of efficiency with a fair record of loyalty, encouraging long periods of political stability which in turn brought the prosperity which permitted them to afford this force. Because of a range of factors, many beyond their control, the last western emperors were unable to achieve this balance, and the army withered along with the central government which in various forms had maintained it for so many centuries.

Glossary

ala: (a) In the Mid Republican period an *ala* of allies was normally attached to support each legion of Roman citizens. It consisted of roughly the same number of infantry, but as many as three times the number of cavalry.
(b) In the professional army, an *ala* was a unit of auxiliary cavalry roughly equivalent in size to an infantry cohort.

aquila: The silver, later gold or gilded eagle which became the most important standard of the legion after Marius, who was elected consul in 107 BC.

aquilifer: The standard-bearer who carried the *aquila* (eagle) standard of the legion.

beneficiarius: Experienced soldier attached to the staff of a provincial governor. They often performed policing functions and were detached as individuals or small groups.

caliga (pl. *caligae*): The hob-nailed military boot worn by soldiers. By the 2nd century AD these were often replaced by enclosed boots.

canabae: The civilian settlement that grew up very quickly around virtually every permanent or semi-permanent base established by the Roman army.

capite censi: The 'head count' (also known as *proletarii*) of citizens who lacked sufficient property to qualify them for military service and so were listed simply as numbers in the census. Marius openly recruited volunteers from this class.

century (*centuria*): Basic administrative unit of the Republican and early imperial army, which ranged in size from 30 to 160 men, depending on period and unit, but on average had a 'paper' strength of 80.

centurion (*centurio*): Officer commanding a century.

cohort (*cohors*): A unit of some 400–800 men, the cohort was the basic tactical unit of the professional army.

cohors equitata: A 'mixed' cohort consisting of both auxiliary infantry and cavalry. Horsemen in these units were not as well paid as the cavalrymen of the *alae*.

comes: Late Roman senior officer in one of the field armies.

comitatenses: The units of the field armies at the immediate disposal of the emperors or their commanders in the 4th and 5th centuries AD.

contubernium: Term applied to the group of eight men who shared a tent and messed together.

cornicularius: Clerk on the staff of a unit officer or provincial governor.

corvus: The 'raven', a type of boarding-bridge fitted to each Roman vessel, devised and used with great success by the Romans during the First Punic War.

cuneus: Title given to some cavalry units in the army of Late Antiquity.

decurion (*decurio*): Cavalry officer originally in command of a group of 10 men. By the Principate a decurion commanded a *turma* or about 30 men.

dictator: At times of extreme military crisis, the Republic appointed a dictator, a single magistrate with supreme power who held office for six months. The appointment of a dictator was extremely rare. However, during the 1st century BC, men like Sulla and Caesar seized power by force and employed the title.

dilectus: The levy by which the Republic recruited its armies. It is unclear how such levies were held from the 1st century BC onwards.

duplicarius: Soldier receiving double pay and probably acting as a junior officer.

dux: Senior officer in the Late Roman army, commanding a region and its garrison of *limitanei*.

equites: The 'Knights' were originally the citizens wealthy enough to equip themselves as cavalrymen in the militia army. The name was adopted by the social class immediately below the senatorial class.

foederati: Initially simply an irregular unit of auxiliaries, in Late Antiquity the term was used to describe allied troops serving under their own leaders.

funditores: Slingers are often mentioned in descriptions of the army, and sling bullets of lead or stone crop up relatively often in the excavation of Roman military sites. However, we know of no unit specifically described as slingers.

gladius: The Latin word for sword has conventionally been associated by modern scholars with the short, thrusting weapon which was the basic sidearm of the Roman legionary for many centuries.

hastati: The front line of heavy infantry in the manipular legion, consisting of the youngest men.

hoplite: A Greek heavy infantryman armed with a spear, 90-cm (3-ft) round shield (or hoplon), and wearing bronze helmet, armour, and greaves. Such men normally fought in a dense block formation, known as a phalanx.

imago: A standard topped by a bust or image of the emperor or a member of his family. The *imagines* were kept with the other standards of the unit as a reminder of their duty to remain loyal to the emperor.

immunis: Soldier exempt from fatigues, often because he possessed a specialist skill or trade.

legatus: Literally a representative, *legati* or legates were the senior subordinates of a Roman general. Virtually without exception, such men were senators. Under the Principate two types of imperial legate were most important:
(a) the *legatus Augusti proparetore* who held command in all imperial provinces (apart from Egypt) containing a legionary garrison, and
(b) the *legatus legionis* who commanded a legion.

legion (*legio*): In the Republican and early imperial army a legion numbered some 4,000–6,000 men and was the largest and most important sub-unit within an army. By the 4th century AD the size of the legion appears to have shrunk to *c.* 1,000–1,200.

librarius: Junior clerk in the headquarters of a unit.

limitanei: In late Antiquity the *limitanei* were the units assigned to garrison a particular region, most often in a frontier area.

Magister Equitum (Master of Horse): The deputy of a Republican *dictator*. Tradition insisted that the *dictator* command the infantry, hence his deputy led the cavalry.

Magister Militum: One of a range of titles given to the most senior officers of Late Roman field armies. Also *Magister Peditum* or *Magister Equitum*.

maniple (*manipulus*): In the Republican army two centuries combined to form a tactical unit known as a maniple. It varied in size from *c.* 60 to 160 men and was commanded by the centurion of the right-hand century.

numerus: Name given to units of irregular auxiliary soldiers under the Principate. Later the title was adopted by some cavalry units.

optio: A centurion's deputy and second-in-command of a century.

paenula: A type of cloak frequently worn by soldiers. These fastened together with toggles, were often hooded, and were worn like a poncho.

palatina: Units named *palatina* were the elite of the field armies in Late Antiquity.

paludamentum: A formal cloak often worn by centurions and other officers. It was common to drape part of the cloak over the left arm.

pilum: The heavy javelin which was the distinctive armament of the Roman legionary from the time of the militia army until at least the end of the Principate.

prefect (*praefectus*): (a) One of three senior officers leading a Republican allied *ala* and effectively equivalent to a tribune in a legion. (b) Governor of an equestrian province, e.g. Judaea until AD 66, and Egypt. (c) Commander of an auxiliary *ala* or cohort under the Principate. (d) Regimental commander in Late Antiquity.

praepositus: Unit commander in the Late Roman army. Apparently virtually synonymous with tribune or prefect.

primi ordines: The centurions of the first cohort of a legion. These men were the most senior in the centurionate, and enjoyed considerable status.

primus pilus: The commander of the first century of the first cohort and the senior centurion of the legion.

principes: The second line of heavy infantrymen in the manipular legion, consisting of men in the prime of life.

probatio: The first stage undergone by potential recruits to the army involving investigation of their legal status and medical condition.

pugio: The short dagger often carried by legionaries.

quaestor: *quaestors* had predominantly financial responsibilities, but as the second in command of a provincial governor under the Republic, they also at times led troops into battle.

quinquereme: The 'five' was the standard oared warship of the Punic Wars. The name refers to the basic team of rowers. The ship may have had two banks of oars or, more probably, three banks.

sacramentum: The oath of loyalty sworn by soldiers on enlistment. Under the Principate this was taken to the emperor.

sagum: A type of cloak frequently worn by soldiers. It was fastened with a brooch, usually on the right shoulder.

schola: Guard cavalry regiment in the later Roman army.

sesquiplicarius: Soldier receiving one-and-a-half times normal pay, and probably holding a specialist post or acting as a junior officer.

signum: The standard of the century, the *signum* usually consisted of a number of disks and other decorations mounted on a pole. Some of these standards were topped by an ornamental spearhead, while others had a sculpted hand, often surrounded by a laurel wreath.

signifer: The junior officer who carried the *signum* standard of a century. In the imperial army he was also responsible for a range of administrative roles within the unit, most notably supervising the soldiers' pay and savings.

singulares: The élite bodyguards of a senior Roman officer, such as a legionary or provincial legate. These men were normally auxiliaries seconded from their units. The *singulares Augusti* were an élite cavalry unit drawn from the entire Empire and attached to the praetorian guard.

spatha: The name conventionally used to describe the longer swords used by Roman cavalrymen and, in Late Antiquity, also many infantrymen.

tesserarius: One of the junior officers within a century, their name was derived from the *tessera* tablet on which was written the watchword for the day.

trecenarius: Junior officer in the Late Roman army.

tribune (*tribunus*): (a) Senior staff officer within a legion. (b) Commander of milliary cohort or *ala* in the *auxilia* of the Principate and of a range of regiments in the Late Roman army.

triarii: The third (rear) line of infantry, recruited from the oldest and most experienced soldiers.

trireme: The 'three' had been the standard warship of most fleets from the 5th to 4th centuries BC. They were still employed in auxiliary roles by the Romans. It had three banks of oars, each oar rowed by a single man.

vexillation (*vexillatio*): (a) A detachment of troops operating away from their parent unit or units. (b) Name given to some cavalry units in the Late Roman army.

vicus: After a period of time the informal settlement or *canabae* surrounding a Roman fort was usually granted the status of *vicus*. Such settlements supplied the bases with many of their needs.

vigiles: These cohorts were instituted by Augustus to be the fire-brigade and night police of Rome. They were organized along paramilitary lines.

Further Reading

Introduction

The texts of virtually all the Greek and Roman authors are available in translation in the Loeb Classical Library series produced by Harvard University Press. Many are also available in other translations, most notably the Penguin Classics series.

Sources for documents associated with the Roman army include:

Bowman, A. K. and B. Thomas, *The Vindolanda Writing-Tablets (Tabulae Vindolandenses ii)* (London, 1994).

Collingwood, R. G. and R. P. Wright (updated by R. S. O. Tomlin), *The Roman Inscriptions of Britain. Vol. 1* (1995).

Dessau, H., *Inscriptiones Latinae Selectae* (Berlin, 1892–1916).

Corpus Inscriptionum Latinarum (Berlin, 1862–)

Fink, R. O., *Roman Military Records on Papyrus* (Cleveland, 1971).

An extremely useful collection of translated sources is provided in B. Campbell, *The Roman Army 31 BC–AD 337: A Sourcebook* (London, 1994).

I The Republican Army

The Origins of the Roman Army

Cornell, T., *The Beginnings of Rome. Italy and Rome from the Bronze Age to the Punic Wars (c. 1000–264 BC)*, (London, 1995). An up-to-date general account of the earliest periods of Roman history.

D'Agustino, B., 'Military Organization and Social Structure in Archaic Etruria', in O. Murray and S. Price (eds.), *The Greek City* (Oxford, 1990), pp. 59–82.

McCarteney, E., 'The Military Indebtedness of Early Rome to Etruria', *Memoirs of the American Academy at Rome* 1 (1917), pp. 122–67.

Nilsson, M. P., 'The introduction of Hoplite Tactics at Rome', *Journal of Roman Studies* 19 (1929), pp. 1–11.

Rawson, E., 'The Literary Sources for the Pre-Marian Roman Army', *Papers of the British School at Rome* 39 (1971), pp. 13–31.

Rawlings, L., 'Condottieri and Clansmen: Early Italian Warfare and the State', in K. Hopwood, *Organized Crime in the Ancient World* (Swansea, 2001).

Snodgrass, A. M., 'The Hoplite Reform and History', *Journal of Hellenic Studies* 85 (1965), pp. 110–22.

The Polybian Legion

Adcock, F., *The Roman Art of War under the Republic* (Cambridge Mass., 1940).

Bell, M., 'Tactical Reform in the Roman Republican Army', *Historia* 14 (1965), pp. 404–22.

Brunt, P., *Italian Manpower, 225 BC–AD 14* (Oxford, 1971).

Connolly, P., *Greece and Rome at War* (London, 1981).

Feugère, M. (ed.), *L' Équipment Militaire et L'Armement de la République. JRMES 8* (1997).

Gabba, E., *The Roman Republic, the Army and the Allies* (Oxford, 1976), trans. P. J. Cuff.

Keppie, L., *The Making of the Roman Army* (London, 1984).

The Roman Navy

Basch, L. and H. Frost, 'Another Punic wreck in Sicily: its ram', *International Journal of Nautical Archaeology* 4 (1976), pp. 201–28.

Casson, L., *Ships and Seafaring in Ancient Times* (London, 1994).

Frost, H., et al, *Lilybaeum (Marsala) – The Punic Ship: Final Excavation Report. Notizie Degli Scavi di Antichita Supplemento al vol. 30, 1976* (Rome, 1981), pp. 267–70.

Frost, H., 'The prefabricated Punic Warship', in H. Deviyner and E. Lipinski, *Studia Phoenica X: Punic Wars* (Leuven, 1989), pp. 127–35.

Morrison, J. S. (and J. F. Coates), *Greek and Roman Oared Warships* (Oxford, 1996).

Rodgers, W., *Greek and Roman Naval Warfare* (Annapolis, 1937).

Shaw, T. (ed.), *The Trireme Project: Operational Experience 1987–90; Lessons Learnt.* Oxbow Monograph 32 (Oxford, 1993).

Thiel, J., *Studies on the History of Roman Sea-Power in Republican Times* (Amsterdam, 1946).

Wallinga, H. T., *The Boarding-Bridge of the Romans* (Gravenhage, 1956).

II The Professional Army

General

Le Bohec, Y., *The Imperial Roman Army* (London and New York, 1994).

Campbell, J., *The Emperor and the Roman Army* (Oxford, 1984).

Cheesman, G., *The Auxilia of the Roman Imperial Army* (Oxford, 1914).

Dixon, K. and P. Southern, *The Roman Cavalry* (London, 1992).

Harmand, J., *L'armée et le soldat à Rome de 107 à 50 avant nôtre ère* (Paris, 1967).

Holder, P., *Studies in the Auxilia of the Roman Army from Caesar to Trajan*, BAR 70 (Oxford, 1980).

Parker, H., *The Roman Legions* (Oxford, 1928).

Saddington, D., *The Development of the Roman Auxiliary Forces from Caesar to Vespasian* (Harare, 1982).

Smith, F., *Service in the Post-Marian Roman Army* (Manchester, 1958).

Speidel, M., *Riding for Caesar* (Cambridge, Mass., 1994).

Starr, C., *The Roman Imperial Navy* (Ithaca, NY, 1941).

Webster, G., *The Roman Imperial Army* (London, 1985: reprint with updated bibliography Oklahoma, 1998).

Unit Organization and Career Structures

Birley, E., *Roman Britain and the Roman Army* (Kendal, 1953).

Birley, E., *The Roman Army* (Amsterdam, 1988).

Breeze, D. and B. Dobson, *Roman Officers and Frontiers* (Stuttgart, 1993).

Dobson, B., *Die Primipilares* (Cologne and Bonn, 1978).

Devijver, H., *The Equestrian Officers of the Roman Army*, 2 vols. (Amsterdam, 1989 and 1992).

von Domaszewski, A., *Die Rangordnung des römischen Heeresgeschichte*, 2nd ed. Ed. B. Dobson (Bohlau and Cologue, 1967).

Gilliam, J., *Roman Army Papers* (Amsterdam, 1986).

Saller, R. P., 'Promotion and patronage in equestrian careers', *Journal of Roman Studies* 70 (1980), 44–63.

Spaul, J., *ALA²* (Andover, 1994).

Spaul, J., *COHORS²*. BAR International Series 841 (Oxford, 2000).

Speidel, M., *Roman Army Studies*, 2 vols (Stuttgart, 1984–1992).

III The Life of a Roman Soldier

Enlistment and Daily Routine

Alston, R., 'Roman Military Pay from Caesar to Diocletian', *Journal of Roman Studies* 84 (1994), pp. 93–104.

Alston, R., *Soldier and Society in Roman Egypt* (London, 1995).

Bidwell, P., *Roman Forts in Britain* (London, 1997).

Brunt, P., 'Pay and superannuation in the Roman Army', *Papers of the British School at Rome* 18 (1950), pp. 50–71.

Campbell, B., 'The marriage of soldiers under the Empire', *Journal of Roman Studies* 68 (1978), 153–66.

Cotton, H. M. and J. Geiger, *Masada II, the Latin and Greek Documents* (Jerusalem, 1989).

Davies, R., *Service in the Roman Army* (Edinburgh, 1989).

Davison, D. P., *The Barracks of the Roman Army from the First to Third centuries AD*, BAR 472 (Oxford, 1989).

Fink, R. O., A. S. Hoey and W. F. Snyder, 'The *Feriale Duranum*', *Yale Classical Studies* 7 (1940), pp. 1–222.

Goldsworthy, A. and I. Haynes (eds.), *The Roman Army as a Community in Peace and War. Journal of Roman Archaeology Supplementary Series* (Ann Arbor, Michigan, 1999).

Helgeland, J., 'Roman Army religion', *Aufstieg und Niedergang der römischen Welt* (Berlin, 1978), pp. 1470–505.

Holder, P., *The Roman Army in Britain* (London, 1982).

Johnson, A., *Roman Forts* (London, 1983).

MacMullen, R., 'The Legion as Society', *Historia* 33 (1984), pp. 440–56.

Mann, J., *Legionary Recruitment and Veteran Settlement during the Principate* (London, 1983).

Maxfield, V., *The Military Decorations of the Roman Army* (London, 1981).

Maxfield, V., *Soldier and Civilian: Life beyond the ramparts. Eighth Annual Caerleon Lecture* (Cardiff, 1995).

Nock, A. D., 'The Roman Army and the Religious Year', *Harvard Theological Review* 45 (1952), 187–252.

Roxan, M. M., *Roman Military Diplomas 1954–1977* (London, 1978).

Roxan, M. M., *Roman Military Diplomas 1978–1984* (London, 1985).

Speidel, M. A., 'Roman Army Pay Scales', *Journal of Roman Studies* 82 (1992), pp. 87–106.

Watson, G., *The Roman Soldier* (London, 1969).

Equipment

Bishop, M. (ed.), *The Production and Distribution of Roman Military Equipment. Proceedings of the Second Roman Military Equipment Conference.* BAR 275 (Oxford, 1985).

Bishop, M. and J. Coulston, *Roman Military Equipment* (London, 1993).

Connolly, P., *Greece and Rome at War* (London, 1981).

Connolly, P. and C. Van Driel-Murray, 'The Roman Cavalry Saddle', *Britannia* 22 (1991), pp. 33–50.

Coulston, J. C. (ed.), *Military Equipment and the Identity of Roman Soldiers. Proceedings of the Fourth Roman Military Equipment Conference.* BAR 394 (Oxford, 1988).

Dawson M. (ed.), *Roman Military Equipment: the Accoutrements of War. Proceedings of the Third Roman Military Equipment Conference.* BAR 336 (Oxford, 1987).

van Driel-Murray, C. (ed.), *Roman Military Equipment: the Sources of Evidence. Proceedings of the Fifth Roman Military Equipment Conference.* BAR 476 (Oxford, 1989).

Gilliver, C. M., 'Hedgehogs, caltrops and palisade stakes', *JRMES* 4 (1993), 49–54.

Hyland, A., *Equus: The Horse in the Roman World* (London, 1990).

Hyland, A., *Training the Roman Cavalry* (Gloucester, 1993).

Junkelmann, M., *Die legionem des Augustus* (Mainz am Rhein, 1991).

Junkelmann, M., *Die Reiter Roms*, 3 vols (Mainz am Rhein, 1990–92).

Junkelmann, M., *Römischen Helme* (Mainz am Rhein, 2000).

Lepper, F. and S. S. Frere, *Trajan's Column* (Gloucester, 1988).

Richmond, I., *Trajan's Army on Trajan's Column* (London, 1982).

Robinson, H. R., *The Armour of Imperial Rome* (London, 1975).

Rossi, L., *Trajan's Column and the Dacian Wars* (London, 1971).

Stephenson, I. P., *Roman Infantry Equipment: the Later Empire* (Stroud, 1999).

Sumner, G., *Roman Army: Wars of Empire* (London, 1997).

The *Journal of Roman Military Equipment Studies* (Oxford, 1990+) is dedicated to papers discussing various aspects of the army's equipment.

Garrisons and Frontiers

Breeze, D. and B. Dobson, *Hadrian's Wall* (London, 1987).

Dyson, S., *The Creation of the Roman Frontier* (Princeton, N. J., 1985).

Ferrill, A., *Roman Imperial Grand Strategy* (New York, 1991).

Freeman, P. and D. Kennedy (eds.), *The Defence of the Roman and Byzantine East*, BAR International Series 297 (Oxford, 1986).

Isaac, B., *The Limits of Empire. The Roman Army in the East* (Oxford, 1992).

Johnson, S., *Hadrian's Wall* (London, 1984).

Kennedy, D., *The Roman Army in the East. Journal of Roman Archaeology Supplementary Series 18* (Ann Arbor, 1996).

Kennedy, D. and D. Riley, *Rome's Desert Frontier from the Air* (London, 1990).

Luttwak, E., *The Grand Strategy of the Roman Empire* (New York, 1976).

Mann, J., 'The Frontiers of the Principate', *ANRW* II. 1 (1974), pp. 508–33.

Mattern, S., *Rome and the Enemy: Imperial Strategy in the Principate* (Berkeley and London, 1999).

Maxfield, V., 'Pre-Flavian Forts and their Garrisons', *Britannia* 17 (1986), pp. 59–72.

Maxfield, V., 'Conquest and Aftermath', in M. Todd, *Research on Roman Britain 1960–1989* (1989), pp. 19–29

Wheeler, E., 'Methodological limits and the mirage of Roman strategy', *The Journal of Military History* 57 (1993), pp. 7–41, 215–40.

Whittaker, C., *Frontiers of the Roman Empire. A Social and Economic Study* (Baltimore, 1994).

IV The Army at War

Austin, N. and B. Rankov, *Exploratio: Military and Political Intelligence in the Roman World from the Second Punic War to the Battle of Adrianople* (London, 1995).

Breeze, D., 'The Logistics of Agricola's Final Campaign', *Talanta* 18–19 (1986–7), pp. 7–28.

Delbrück, H. (trans J. Renfroe), *History of the Art of War within the Framework of Political History*, vols 1–2 (Westport, 1975).

Elton, H., *Warfare in Roman Europe, AD 350–425* (Oxford, 1996).

Erdkamp, P., *Hunger and Sword: Warfare and Food Supply in Roman Republican Wars 264–30 BC* (Amsterdam, 1998).

Gilliver, C. M., *The Roman Art of War* (Gloucester, 2000).

Goldsworthy, A., *The Roman Army at War, 100 BC–AD 200* (Oxford, 1996).

Goldsworthy, A., *Roman Warfare* (London, 2000).

Hawkes, C., 'The Roman Siege of Masada', *Antiquity* 3 (1929), pp. 195–213.

Labisch, A., *Frumentum Commeatusque. Die Nahrungsmittelversongung der Heere Caesars* (Meisenheim am Glan, 1976).

Marsden, E. W., *Greek and Roman Artillery: Historical Development* (Oxford, 1969).

Peddie, J., *The Roman War Machine* (Gloucester, 1994).

Richmond, I. A., 'The Roman Siege Works at Masada, Israel', *Journal of Roman Studies* 52 (1962), pp. 142–55.

Roth, J., *The Logistics of the Roman Army at War, 264 BC–AD 235* (1999).

Warry, J., *Warfare in the Classical World* (London, 1980).

V The Army of Late Antiquity

Austin, N., *Ammianus on Warfare. An Investigation into Ammianus' Military Knowledge.* Collection Latomus 165 (Brussels, 1979).

Barnes, T., *The New Empire of Diocletian and Constantine* (Cambridge, Mass. and London, 1981).

Burns, T., *Barbarians within the Gates of Rome: A Study of Roman Military Policy and the Barbarians, CA. 375–425 AD* (Indiana, 1994).

Coello, T., *Unit Sizes in the Late Roman Army.* BAR S645 (Oxford, 1996).

Crump, G., *Ammianus Marcellinus as a Military Historian*, Historia-Einzelschriften 27 (Wiesbaden, 1975).

Dodgeon, M. and S. Lieu, *The Roman Eastern Frontier and the Persian Wars, 226–363* (London, 1991).

Ferrill, A., *The Fall of the Roman Empire: The Military Explanation* (London and New York, 1986).

Goodburn, R. and P. Bartholomew (eds.), *Aspects of the Notitia Dignitatum.* BAR 15 (Oxford, 1976).

Heather, P., *Goths and Romans, 332–489* (Oxford, 1991).

Johnson, S., *Late Roman Fortifications* (Totowa, NJ, 1983).

Jones, A. H. M., *The Later Roman Empire* (Oxford, 1964).

Lee, A., *Information and Frontiers* (Cambridge, 1993).

Liebeschuetz, J., *Barbarians and Bishops. Army, Church and State in the Age of Arcadius and Chrysostom* (Oxford, 1990).

MacMullen, R., *Soldier and Civilian in the Later Roman Empire* (Cambridge, Mass., 1963).

Nicasie, M., *Twilight of Empire* (Amsterdam, 1998).

Southern, P. and K. Dixon, *The Late Roman Army* (London, 1996).

Tomlin, R. S. O., 'Seniores-Iuniores' in the Late Roman Field Army', *American Journal of Philosophy* 93 (1972), pp. 253–78.

Treadgold, W., *Byzantium and its Army, 281–1081* (Stanford, 1995).

Williams, S., *Diocletian and the Roman Recovery* (London, 1985).

Illustration Credits

Abbreviations
l=left; r=right; c=centre; a=above; b=below

AKG London 37a
AKG London/Andrea Baquzzi 20
AKG London/Peter Connolly 22–23, 35b, 57,
74–75, 85b, 107b, 113a, 178–79
AKG London/Hedda Eid 142a, 142b
AKG London/Museum Kalkriese 12
AKG London/Erich Lessing 1, 135
AKG London/A. Lorenzini 59b, 61, 119, 126–27,
147, 162–63, 168–69, 177r, 180–81, 181
AKG London/Pinazzi 211
Archivi Alinari, Florence 25
Ancient Art & Architecture Collection/Mike
Andrews 39
Ancient Art & Architecture Collection/Ronald
Sheridan 38l, 42b
Centre Belge de Recherches Archéologiques à
Apamée, Apamea 201
The Art Archive/Rheinischeslandesmuseum,
Bonn/Dagli Orti (A) 49
The Art Archive/National Museum,
Bucharest/Dagli Orti 78–79, 116–17
The Art Archive/Musée de la Civilisation Gallo-
Romaine, Lyons/Dagli Orti 198–99
The Art Archive/Archaeological Museum,
Naples/Dagli Orti (A) 18–19, 22b, 24
The Art Archive/Museo Capitolino, Rome/Dagli
Orti 43, 165
The Art Archive/Museo della Città Romana,
Rome/Dagli Orti 72
The Art Archive/Archaeological Museum,
Strasbourg/Dagli Orti 203a
The Art Archive /Archaeological Museum,
Venice/Dagli Orti (A)183b
Bildarchiv Preussischer Kulturbesitz, Berlin 104
Robin Birley 13a
The British Museum, London 21r, 47a, 76, 114,
212b
Richard Burgess 36–37, 40–41, 52–53, 182–83,
190–91, 210–11
Photography by Cambridge University
Collection of Air Photographs 12–13, 93
Giovanni Caselli 10–11, 170, 194a
C.A.T. Medienproduktion 141
Grosvenor Museum, Chester 117a
Collections/Robert Estall 2–3
Römisch-Germanisches Museum der Stadt
Köln/Rheinisches Bildarchiv 115
Michael Duigan 71, 183a
© The Trustees of the National Museums of
Scotland, Edinburgh 128a, 132, 133r, 138l, 138r
English Heritage Photographic Library 110,
205a, 212a
English Heritage Photographic Library/Andrew
Tryner 86–87, 107ar
English Heritage Photographic Library/Skyscan
Balloon Photography 89b, 105
English Heritage Photographic
Library/Jonathan Bailey 92a, 100a, 206–07
English Heritage Photographic Library/Jeremy
Richards 159a
Fototeca Unione 213a
Adrian Goldsworthy 16, 17, 34a, 58, 62, 64, 65,
88b, 92b, 94, 97, 100b, 101, 102a, 106–07, 112–13,
131a, 131b, 139l, 148a, 148b, 151, 172. 178, 184,
185l , 185r, 191, 196
Courtesy Chris Haines 70, 81a, 125, 194–95
© Sonia Halliday photographs 186–87, 207a, 214
Peter Inker 29, 31a, 54, 111, 122, 123, 128b, 130,
133l, 139b, 176–77, 209
Kobal Collection, London 7
Courtauld Institute of Art, University of London
200b
Museum of London 144
ML Design 26, 32b, 46, 82, 83, 89a, 156, 157a
Landesmuseum, Mainz 50, 55, 56, 96, 120, 136r,
139ar, 166, 175, 180
Foto Marburg 197
Senhouse Museum, Maryport 108, 109
Museo Nacional de Arte Romano, Mérida 73
Bayerische Staatsbibliothek, Munich 203b
Museum of Antiquities, Newcastle upon Tyne
136l
After Napoleon III, *Histoire Jules César* 1865–66
9
Sally Nicholls 53, 189bl
Museum Het Valkhof, Nijmegen 137
Musée du Louvre, Paris, photo © RMN 44–45, 211
Graeme Peacock 68, 189a, 205b
Museo della Civiltà Romana, Rome 34
Photo Scala 42a, 195
After Schulten 32a
Society for the Promotion of Roman Studies
173a
South Shields Museum 102b
I Musei Vaticani, Vatican, Rome 77
Roger Wilson 4–5, 6, 8, 28, 30, 31b, 33, 48, 59a, 60,
63l, 66, 67, 69, 81b 84, 85a, 87, 88a, 98, 99, 103,
116a, 118, 121, 134, 140, 150, 152, 153, 155, 157b,
158–59, 160, 164, 167, 173b, 187r, 189r, 193a,
193b, 202, 213b

Acknowledgments

Generations of scholars have devoted
considerable effort to reconstructing the Roman
army. However, many of their discoveries are
little known outside the narrow confines of the
academic community. The aim of this book is to
bring some of this material before a wider
audience. It is then a work of synthesis, and, to a
great extent, of synthesis of the work of others,
so it is only fitting that I acknowledge my debt to
these scholars. The bibliography lists the works
on which I have drawn directly, or where useful
introductory material may be found, but in spite
of its size it represents only a tiny fraction of the
ever-growing literature on the subject. The text
attempts to reflect some of the major debates
concerning aspects of the army's life and
practices, but inevitably it is impossible in a
work of this length to deal with each
controversy in detail. I hope that the balance
helps to give an impression of how the army
developed over time, and reduce the impression
of an unchanging, monolithic institution. The
reader must look elsewhere for narrative
histories of the periods covered. The choice of
what to include, and many of the interpretations
put forward, largely reflect my own views as to
what is most important. Thus, whilst I have
leaned heavily on the work of others, not all will
necessarily agree with all of the interpretations
presented here.

I would like to thank Ian Hughes for reading
so quickly and commenting so usefully on earlier
drafts of the text. A large part of the book was
read by Ian Haynes of Birkbeck College,
University of London – at a time when he was
theoretically on sabbatical and more than busy
with his own research. His comments were
doubly helpful because they gave me a more
archaeological perspective on many issues.
Thanks should also go to Lawrence Keppie and
Duncan Campbell, who both provided detailed
comments on the first draft to reach the
publisher. Their contribution certainly improved
the text, although it should be emphasized that
they do not share all of the opinions expressed
within it. Less specifically, the text also reflects
numerous conversations at conferences and
seminars with others working in the field. They
are too many to name individually, but all have
my thanks.

Page numbers in *italics* refer to illustrations